# KEYSTONE & BEYOND

*Tar Sands and the National Interest in the Era of Climate Change*

John H. Cushman, Jr.

Copyright © 2014 InsideClimate News
All rights reserved.

ISBN: 0692271414
ISBN 13: 9780692271414

Library of Congress Control Number: 2014914499
InsideClimate News, Brookyln, NY

# TABLE OF CONTENTS

| | | |
|---|---|---:|
| Introduction | by David Sassoon and Susan White | vii |
| Chapter One | The No-Brainer | 1 |
| Chapter Two | A New Agenda | 25 |
| Chapter Three | The Social Cost | 55 |
| Chapter Four | The Tipping Point | 80 |

This book was made possible thanks to support from Simon and June Li, the Common Sense Fund and the Ford Foundation.

# INTRODUCTION

A line on a map running from Canada to the Texas Gulf Coast marks the full route of the proposed Keystone XL pipeline. If it is built, it will bisect America right through its heartland.

The Keystone has already divided the nation on the fundamental questions of how we should respond to climate change and what our energy future should look like.

Will we continue with business as usual and open an 830,000 barrel-a-day spigot to help drain Alberta's oil sands?

Or will this be a turning point where the momentum of the world's carbon energy industry is slowed and forced to follow a cleaner course?

Standing at this crossroads is President Obama who must decide whether to approve the project, knowing that the nation and the world cannot retreat from the path he chooses.

How did he—and we—get to this point?

John H. Cushman, Jr. answers this question by constructing a comprehensive and authoritative account of the Keystone saga. Coming off a 27-year career in the Washington, D.C., bureau of The New York Times, he brings an encyclopedic knowledge, analytic precision and deep Beltway experience to the task.

One of the first things we learn from him is that the Keystone pipeline system has its origins in energy policy decisions made by President George W. Bush and Vice President Dick Cheney almost from the moment they took office.

What they did not foresee is that Obama would be the decider on their plan to make Canada's tar sands the linchpin of U.S. energy security, and that, unlike them, he would aim to make climate action an enduring part of his legacy.

The view of the energy landscape from Obama's Oval Office is dramatically different from what his predecessors saw and feared.

Domestic production of oil and gas is not declining, but booming. Demand for fuel at home is not rising, but flat and shrinking. As for climate change, its impacts are no longer uncertain, if they ever were, but are exhibiting their destructive fury even sooner than scientists expected.

Keystone and Beyond shows how these new realities are forcing Obama to reevaluate the question George Bush thought was a no-brainer: Is approving the Keystone XL pipeline in the national interest?

As Obama struggles to answer that question, he is being pressured to grant a presidential permit for the Keystone XL by powerful proponents in the oil industry and in Congress, including some of his bitterest political enemies.

Opponents of the pipeline are a motley horde—farmers and ranchers, hunters and anglers, environmentalists and conservationists—who want Obama to protect their land, their water and their planet and humble the fossil energy Goliath. They have thrust the president into the role of their champion and would-be hero, and it is hard to tell how he will decide to play the part.

Like Michelangelo's statue of David at the moment truth, he stands alone, armed with the power of his pen and naked in the glare of time.

*David Sassoon, Publisher*
*Susan White, Executive Editor*
*InsideClimate News*

# 1

## THE NO-BRAINER

It was lunchtime at the Hyatt in San Diego, and the oil refinery executives were hanging on every word of former President George W. Bush.

The Keystone XL pipeline question, he told members of the American Fuel and Petrochemical Manufacturers, was a "no-brainer." The United States needed more fuel and more jobs, and the Keystone could provide both. It would haul hundreds of thousands of barrels a day of oil from the almost limitless tar sands reserves of Alberta, Canada all the way to refineries on the U.S. Gulf Coast. Approving the pipeline was in the nation's best interest. Slam dunk.

Bush had stood fast on this kind of reasoning through his two terms in office. To this day he repeats the "no-brainer" line to sympathetic crowds like the oilmen he addressed in San Diego in 2012. His view is shared by a steadfast contingent of lawmakers and their industry allies, as well as by many energy analysts: The United States must break its addiction to shaky foreign sources of oil, so it is in the nation's interest to import more of Canada's tar sands bitumen, just as it is in Canada's interest to relentlessly ramp up its production.

The case for piping in Canada's tar sands oil, the industry and its backers argue, is so compelling that resisting it is futile.

No matter that bitumen is costly to pull from the ground, that it sucks up energy as it is prepared for shipment, that it leaves behind toxic waste or that it is all but impossible to clean up when it spills into waterways. No matter that its carbon footprint is higher than that of almost any other fuel. Canada's tar sands production will double, and then double again, because the world wants this fuel—needs it.

But calling the Keystone decision a no-brainer in this day and age assumes that nothing has changed since the turn of the century, when Bush and his vice president, Dick Cheney, believed domestic oil and gas production would be shrinking, demand for fuel would be growing, and climate change was an uncertain and distant threat.

Even as Bush was speaking in San Diego the American energy and climate landscape was changing faster than anyone could have predicted when he took office in 2001.

Thanks to a production technique known as hydraulic fracturing, or fracking, the United States was extracting so much gas and oil that the once-desperate need for oil from a friendly neighbor was vanishing. Meanwhile, another threat—climate change—was arriving faster than expected.

The vast majority of the world's climate scientists agreed, and with ever more certainty, that the earth is warming and sea levels are rising because of the carbon dioxide released by the combustion of fossil fuels. To ward off the worst effects of global warming, climate leaders say most of the fossil fuels already at hand, including Canada's tar sands, must be left in the ground.

A year before Bush's San Diego speech, the National Academy of Sciences issued a report, the product of years of rigorous honing, that recommended that the nation think soberly before building expensive infrastructure projects that lock in decades of emissions of carbon dioxide, the greenhouse gas most responsible for warming the planet.

"Each additional ton of greenhouse gases emitted commits us to further change and greater risk," the report said.

The Keystone XL—a 36-inch pipeline costing billions of dollars to build, and designed to operate for easily 50 years—is just such a project. For reasons both symbolic and practical, it has become a turning point on the nation's path toward the new realities of energy and climate. It confronts President Barack Obama with a decision that will last far past his own time in office.

If Obama approves the pipeline, it will become another building block in the far-reaching oil-sands importing and refining enterprise the Bush team helped to nurture. With the Keystone approved, how could the next project, or the one after that, be denied?

If Obama rejects the Keystone, however, he will signal—in a way no other single order could achieve—that America has changed course and is moving toward an energy future in which fossil fuels no longer hold the only key to the economy. For the first time, the nation's fuel choices would be measured against a new objective: cutting carbon dioxide emissions in order to head off the ever riskier disruption of the world's climate.

This book lays out the energy decisions that brought the nation to this crossroads and form the context for the decision that the president, alone, must make.

A pipeline like the Keystone XL that crosses an international border requires a presidential permit before it can proceed. The secretary of state is delegated by the president to carry out a complex review that involves several agencies, a comprehensive environmental impact assessment and multiple opportunities for the public and interest groups to weigh in. But ultimately, it is the president who decides the fundamental question: Is this project in America's national interest?

The urge to stay the course—to follow business as usual as previous presidents did—is deeply entrenched. A generation of Americans, having lived through the searing experience of fuel shortages during the 1970s, believes that finding ever more reserves of fossil fuels is a manifest destiny. Everywhere we look, at every corner gas station, in every SUV, oil is baked into the American pie. If we go on momentum alone, the Keystone XL pipeline is inevitable.

But too much has changed for the old formulas to be applied as if by rote, memorized in a distant past from some immutable multiplication table. The changing climate is muscling its way into political decisions with ever more force, its arrival heralded by superstorms and megadroughts, by the vanishing Arctic ice cap and glaciers, by the rapid acidification of the oceans and the dangerously higher sea levels. Meanwhile, America's oil consumption is declining while its domestic production and its reserves in the ground are swelling. When so much has changed, is it safe to make tomorrow's decision based on yesterday's circumstances?

When George W. Bush took office in 2001, U.S. oil production was widely thought to have peaked. About 60 percent of the nation's oil was coming from foreign countries, many of them politically unstable or even hostile to the United States. Domestic consumption of petroleum was forecast to rise 25 percent by the year 2020. Where on earth would America get the oil it was going to need?

The United States had made little progress in stabilizing its fuel supply since the 1970s, when Arab oil states embargoed sales to the U.S. in retaliation for supporting Israel in the 1973 Yom Kippur war. Americans faced the economically debilitating shock of rising prices, rationing and gas lines. From the military, from the markets, and from Main Street, conventional wisdom held that America needed to establish its energy independence. One president after another espoused the creed. None achieved the goal.

But other problems were emerging that would complicate forecasts about America's energy future and its relationship with fossil fuels.

In 1962, Rachel Carson's landmark environmental classic, "Silent Spring," helped introduce the general public to the damage that pollution from humans, particularly the pesticide industry, was doing to the environment.

In 1965, President Lyndon Johnson warned that pollution was changing the air not just in a few choked cities, but around the world. "This generation has altered the composition of the atmosphere on a global scale through... a steady increase in carbon dioxide from the burning of fossil fuels," he said in a sweeping message to Congress about the destruction of America's natural beauty.

In 1972, John Stanley Sawyer, a prominent British meteorologist, predicted in the journal Nature (accurately, as it would turn out) that the planet would warm by about 0.6 degrees Celsius by the year 2000, as carbon dioxide concentrations in the atmosphere increased by 25 percent because of fossil-fuel use. The National Research Council reported in 1977 that warming from carbon dioxide emissions was likely—a clear sign that the problem was becoming a significant concern.

During the 1970s energy crisis, President Jimmy Carter installed solar cells on the White House roof, a symbol of frugality, sacrifice and innovation. His successor, Ronald Reagan, tore them down.

In the early 1980s, a young member of the House, Rep. Al Gore of Tennessee, held hearings on the changing climate, a subject he had first encountered as a Harvard undergraduate. But few paid attention until, on a sweltering summer day in 1988, NASA scientist James Hansen appeared at a Senate hearing that Tim Wirth, a Colorado Democrat, had called to grab the public's attention. Hansen announced that he was almost certain that the record setting heat that year came not from natural variations in temperatures, but from a phenomenon that was just gaining name recognition: the "greenhouse effect."

"It's time to stop waffling so much," Hansen told reporters. "The evidence is pretty strong that the greenhouse effect is here."

It has been called a turning point in the public awareness of the problem.

That year, the United Nations chartered an extraordinary assembly of scientists from around the world, the Intergovernmental Panel on Climate Change, or IPCC, to review and assess the growing body of science so governments could figure out what to do.

On the campaign trail that summer, candidate George Herbert Walker Bush promised to take action.

"Those who think we are powerless to do anything about the greenhouse effect forget about the 'White House effect,'" he said. "As President, I intend to do something about it. We will talk about global warming, and we will act."

Those turned out to be empty words.

Dan Becker, the Sierra Club's first official "climate advocate," stumbled upon a copy of talking points the new administration had prepared for its cabinet members. He handed it over to Phil Shabecoff of The New York Times, who latched early onto the budding climate story.

"Not beneficial to discuss whether there is or is not warming," the paper said. "In the eyes of the public we will lose this debate."

"Don't get into an advocacy position of the merits of various policy proposals," it went on. "Don't use specific numbers i.e., degrees, dollars, rates, etc. "

President Bush reacted to the emerging science of the greenhouse effect in much the way his son would later– cautiously, in a way that emphasized uncertainty.

The U.S. posture toward climate change and other international environmental issues would be "aggressive and thoughtful," but maintaining free markets would be the first principle and economic growth would be the foremost goal, he said in a 1990 speech to the IPCC.

The IPCC's first assessment was unambiguous. The climate is warming, mainly due to man-made pollution, it said bluntly. The scientists did not yet have all the details, but they were confident that unless carbon dioxide emissions were reduced, the problem would worsen in the century to come.

Goaded by green Democrats, Bush traveled to Rio de Janeiro for the landmark 1992 Earth Summit. Sen. John Kerry, a Massachusetts Democrat, attended. So did Al Gore, by then a senator and the Democratic candidate for vice president.

The conference was a turning point in the effort to gain worldwide agreement to take action on climate change, and Bush promised the U.S. would lead the way. When it came to confronting the emerging threat of climate change "we are the leaders; we're not the followers," he said.

Gore's book "Earth in the Balance," was published during the 1992 presidential campaign, when he was Bill Clinton's running mate. In it, he declared it was time to make the environmental struggle, especially concerns about the climate, "the central organizing principle of human civilization."

A few months later, Clinton defeated Bush for the presidency. Like Gore he was determined to take on the leadership role Bush had talked about.

The new president's first step was to propose a tax on the heat content of all sources of energy. The "BTU tax" would have raised lots of money and encouraged energy conservation across the board, driving down carbon emissions as a result. But the plan went down in flames, a victim of the lingering Reagan-Bush anti-tax ideology and of determined lobbying by industries whose bottom lines would have been affected.

Meanwhile, international negotiations on climate change inched forward.

The Rio conference had produced the U.N. Framework Convention on Climate Change, which led in 1997 to the Kyoto Protocol, a treaty that attempted to set binding limits on the emissions of advanced industrial countries.

The Kyoto accord asked the United States, and the other developed countries that produced most of the world's greenhouse gases, to cut emissions 7 percent below their 1990 level. This milestone was supposed to be achieved between 2008 and 2012. To make that happen, both Clinton and the second Bush would have had to dramatically reduce emissions dramatically in the 15 years before Barack Obama was elected.

Instead, here is what happened:

In 1990, emissions of carbon dioxide, methane and other heat-trapping gases were the equivalent of 6.2 billion metric tons of CO2. In Bill Clinton's first year in office, they rose to 6.4 billion tons and at the start of his second term to 6.8 billion. George W. Bush's first year saw them at 7 billion. In his second term, they peaked at 7.3 billion in 2007, before the onset of the Great Recession sent them down suddenly as the economy contracted and less fuel was burned.

It was far from the progress Kyoto had sought. But Kyoto, as far as Washington was concerned, was basically a thing of the past.

During the Clinton years, industry groups and their conservative supporters began building a broad political base that opposed taking action against climate change.

In 1998 a leaked memo exposed their strategy: enlist a handful of contrarian experts to undermine the consensus about climate change that was rapidly gaining strength among researchers in the peer-reviewed tradition of mainstream science. The eight-page memo written in the Washington headquarters of the American Petroleum Institute outlined a campaign to "recruit a cadre of scientists who share the industry's views of climate science and to train them in public relations so they can help convince journalists, politicians and the public that the risk of global warming is too uncertain to justify controls on greenhouse gases like carbon dioxide that trap the sun's heat near Earth."

The plan was effective, especially when it came to Congress.

President Clinton never presented the Kyoto treaty to the Senate for ratification, because he knew it wouldn't pass. And when Gore ran for president against George W. Bush in 2000, he studiously avoided the topic of climate change—it was a divisive topic, and the green vote was expected to rally naturally to his side.

During the campaign, the younger Bush hit hard at the Clinton-Gore energy policies.

Bush's views on fossil fuels and carbon dioxide seemed to be visceral, a sentiment as strong as blood. In the 1992 campaign his father lost to Clinton-Gore, the elder Bush had jokingly referred to Gore as "ozone man." Now the younger Bush had the enthusiastic support of fossil fuel industries eager to reverse the Clinton administration's fledgling attempts to bring greenhouse gas emissions under control.

During a campaign speech in Michigan Bush excoriated Gore as one who "believes the consumption of energy is the problem and must be discouraged - by taxes and regulations. It helps explain why he has never made energy production a priority. It is the reason he views American oil producers as adversaries, and the automobile as a threat."

Bush opened that speech with a simple message about oil dependence, a world view that would become his mantra as president:

"Never before has our country been more dependent on foreign supplies," Bush said. "Today, we import 56 percent of our oil. In 20 years, on our current path, that figure could be as high as two-thirds… Let me put it plainly: oil consumption is increasing, our production is dropping, our imports of foreign oil are skyrocketing, and this administration has failed to act."

Still, Bush went on to make an environmental promise—one that, had he carried it out, would have set the nation early onto a course that Barack Obama would later pursue.

"With the help of Congress, environmental groups and industry, we will require all power plants to meet clean air standards in order to reduce emissions of sulfur dioxide, nitrogen oxide, mercury and carbon dioxide within a reasonable period of time," Bush said in the speech. "And we will provide market-based incentives, such as emissions trading, to help industry achieve the required reductions."

If Bush had followed through on his campaign promise, industrial emissions of carbon dioxide would have been regulated as a pollutant under the Clean Air Act a decade ago. And they would have been governed by the same kind of cap-and-trade system his father had worked on with Congress to solve the problem of acid rain caused by sulfur dioxide emissions. Not only had the system achieved that goal, it had done so at lower costs than expected.

By the time the Supreme Court affirmed Bush's disputed election over Gore in 2000, Bush and Cheney had already assembled an energy policy transition team dominated by industry representatives. It was led by Andrew Lundquist, an Alaskan who had worked on Capitol Hill for the state's two influential Republican senators, both strong supporters of oil development.

The group mapped out a plan to spark an energy renaissance by overhauling the rules governing the industry. After the inauguration, Lundquist joined the formal energy policy team that Cheney controlled. Lundquist later became a senior vice president for government affairs with ConocoPhillips, a major tar sands operator.

Almost immediately, there were signs of the changes Bush would bring to energy and environmental policy. In March 2001, after just two months in office, he officially withdrew the United States from the Kyoto agreement, saying he would never settle for any pact that set binding limits on how much carbon dioxide the United States could pour into the atmosphere. With about 5 percent of the world's population, the U.S. was producing a quarter of the world's greenhouse gases at that time, more than any other country. China, however, was gaining fast.

That same month, in a move apparently orchestrated by Cheney, Bush abandoned his campaign promise to use the Clean Air Act to regulate carbon dioxide emissions from coal-fired power plants.

Bush announced his decision in a letter to senators Jesse Helms, Larry E. Craig, Pat Roberts and Chuck Hagel. He declared that carbon dioxide "is not a 'pollutant' under the Clean Air Act" and that, given concerns about energy supplies and prices, "we must be very careful not to take actions that could harm consumers. This is especially true given the incomplete state of scientific knowledge of the causes of, and solutions to global climate change."

Bush told the senators he would seek "other creative ways to address global climate change."

Bush's reversal, described at length in Ron Suskind's memoir "The Price of Loyalty" and in investigative reporting by Rolling Stone, was a direct rebuke to Christine Todd Whitman, the new administrator of the Environmental Protection Agency, who had favored controls. She got the news after returning home from Europe where she had assured U.S. allies that Bush would engage forcefully in the fight against climate change. She later resigned, humiliated.

Cheney, meanwhile, set out to overhaul the entire energy landscape. During the administration's first months in office, the energy task force he led met in secret with dozens of industry officials. An environmental advocacy group, the National Resources Defense Council, later sued for access to the task force papers.

One email the NRDC obtained was from Jim Ford of the American Petroleum Institute to the task force. Dated March 20, 2001, it included 10 attachments on Big Oil's agenda, including one that Ford highlighted: "A suggested executive order to insure that energy implications are considered and acted on in rulemakings and other executive actions."

A couple of months later the White House obliged by issuing Executive Order 13211. The order tracked the API's recommendations closely, and in one key section verbatim, directed government agencies to "expedite reviews of permits as necessary to accelerate the completion of energy production and transmission projects."

In May, the White House issued a sweeping energy policy report calling for 73 actions that could be carried out by presidential fiat and 20 that would need legislation. Increased production, not energy conservation, was the primary target, Cheney said as he described the policy.

"Conservation may be a sign of personal virtue," he said, "but it is not a sufficient basis all by itself for a sound, comprehensive energy policy."

The report contained the first serious commitment by U.S. policymakers to Canada's fledgling tar sands industry, which at the time was producing barely 600,000 barrels a day, about a quarter of today's output.

From its earliest days in office, the Bush team saw Canada's tar sands, which contain an estimated 170 billion barrels of recoverable crude, as the most reliable source of the additional oil the nation was bound to need.

Tar sands, formally known as bituminous crude and called "oil sands" by the industry these days, are a dense, grainy mixture of partially formed petroleum and sand that lies beneath ancient boreal forests and peat bogs.

Unlike the "liquid gold" that produced the famous gushers of the industry's early wildcatting days, it must be extracted by giant digging machines or by injecting steam deep into the earth until the bitumen melts and can be sucked to the surface. To make it suitable for transport, the bitumen is generally mixed with diluents, or solvents, that thin it to a consistency close to that of conventional oil. But when diluted bitumen, or dilbit, spills into waterways, it is much more difficult to clean up. The diluents evaporate, but the tarry bitumen that is left behind sinks out of sight.

Producing a barrel of tar sands oil can dump two or three times more carbon dioxide into the atmosphere as producing a barrel of conventional crude oil. Astonishingly, it can take almost as much energy to produce a barrel of fuel from tar sands as the energy it provides when it's ultimately burned.

(The terms "oil sands" and "tar sands" are used interchangeably, and until fairly recently they carried no particular political connotation. But as the development of Alberta's bituminous deposits became more controversial, environmentalists tended toward "tar" and the industry toward "oil.")

Despite Canada's plentiful oil sands reserves, second only to Saudi Arabia's fabled fields, the rewards of extracting this type of oil didn't justify the high investment costs until the mid-1990s, when a team of oil industry and Canadian government representatives called the National Oil Sands Task Force created a 25-year plan to capitalize on this vast resource.

"The Oil Sands: a New Energy Vision for Canada," envisioned production reaching 800,000 to 1.2 million barrels a day by 2020. In fact, that target would be met far earlier. By 2006, in George W. Bush's second term, production of bitumen would average 1.25 million barrels a day.

Most of the tar sands reserves are in the province of Alberta, whose royalty scheme provided the industry with generous incentives, especially in its early years. America's thirst for Canadian crude, along with a series of technical innovations, made it profitable to extract the oil. With little or no regulatory pressure to restrict greenhouse gas emissions in the United States, there was nothing to hold tar sands crude off the market—nothing except a shortage of transportation capacity. The problem of climate change a hundred years hence seemed a remote issue.

The terrorist attacks of Sept. 11, 2001, and the wars in Afghanistan and Iraq that followed drew attention away from climate concerns and underscored the frailty of the U.S. oil supply. Behind the scenes, Washington redoubled its efforts to build up North American supplies.

The prophecy of Cheney's energy task force, which called "continued development" of the tar sands "a pillar of sustained North American energy and security," seemed to be coming true.

One hint of a problem came when Canada's liberal prime minister, Jean Chrétien, ratified the Kyoto Accord in 2002. The ratification put the tar sands expansion on a collision course with the global aim of bringing carbon dioxide under control.

Opposition leader Stephen Harper quickly declared war on the treaty, calling it "a socialist scheme to suck money out of wealth-producing nations." The ratification also made waves in the tar sands industry.

A subsidiary of Koch Industries, one of Canada's biggest oil exporters, had recently been given approval for a massive tar sands project, known as the Fort Hills project, which would produce 190,000 barrels of oil a day. But after the treaty was ratified Koch—which had been operating in the Alberta oil patch for 40 years—sold its 46,000-acre holding in the project for $125 million.

In industry circles and the trade press, the Koch pullout was seen as the first oil-patch casualty of Kyoto.

The problem with producing one's way out of a petroleum addiction was that any growth in the production, refining and use of fossil fuels, whether at home or abroad, would increase greenhouse gas emissions.

Bush tried from time to time to mollify those who were worried about carbon dioxide emissions. His formula, which he followed throughout his presidency, was to reject any binding limits or reductions in the amount of $CO_2$ the United States would emit. Instead, he emphasized increasing energy efficiency and reducing carbon intensity.

In 2002, Bush proposed an explicit target to make the energy economy more carbon-efficient. The United States would reduce what's known as "emissions intensity"—the ratio of greenhouse gas emissions to economic output—by 18 percent. By improving the overall carbon-emissions efficiency of the economy, less carbon dioxide would be dumped into the air for each dollar's worth of economic activity. The nation could keep growing its fuel production and consumption, while making the expansion seem greener by focusing on the amount of pollution per unit.

But as long as the economy grew faster than energy efficiency increased, the inevitable result was to put ever more greenhouse gases into the atmosphere.

The alternative was either to set strict limits on carbon dioxide emissions, or to put a tax on emissions. Either way, the marketplace could be left to decide how to bring down carbon pollution.

But neither approach could get through Congress.

In 2003 Senators Joseph Lieberman, a Democrat, and John McCain, a Republican, introduced the Climate Stewardship Act, which would have capped industrial emissions at their 2000 levels and driven them successively lower, right down to the 1990 levels--closely tracking the Kyoto accord's targets.

The Bush White House issued a statement opposing the bill, saying it was "inconsistent with the President's comprehensive, long-term strategy to address the challenge of global climate change." The bill's effect, it said, would be to raise energy prices sharply, cost hundreds of thousands of jobs, increase the budget deficit and inhibit economic growth.

"The administration is acting aggressively to address the issue of global climate change, and does not believe further legislation is necessary," the statement declared.

The Lieberman-McCain bill failed in the Senate, and attempts to revive it over the next few years fell short too.

In the 2004 presidential election, Bush faced Massachusetts Sen. John Kerry, a committed environmentalist who called for action on global warming through most of his career in Washington. Kerry's wife, Teresa Heinz Kerry, had founded an environmental think tank and was as dedicated as he to the cause of climate change.

But, like Gore before him, Kerry rarely mentioned the subject during the campaign, which was dominated by the U.S. invasion of Iraq in 2003. The idea of controlling carbon pollution was unpopular not just in oil states like Texas but also in many swing states, including the industrial-belt fossil-fuel strongholds of Ohio, Pennsylvania and West Virginia.

In a televised debate just weeks before the election, Bush scoffed at the Kyoto treaty. It would have cost "a lot of jobs," he said. "It's one of those deals where in order to be popular in the halls of Europe you sign a treaty."

Kerry fired back: "Bush didn't try to fix it, he just declared it dead, ladies and gentlemen. And we walked away from the work of 160 nations over 10 years. You wonder why it is that people don't like us in some parts of the world! You just say, 'Hey, we don't agree with you—goodbye.'"

Beset by many issues, Kerry lost the election by 3 million votes and an Electoral College margin of 35. In December, political validation in hand, the Bush administration repeated its climate stance in Buenos Aires, at the 10th session of the U.N.'s climate negotiations.

Under Secretary of State Paula Dobriansky, a key Bush negotiator at the talks, emphasized that the science was in doubt and that binding targets were to be avoided.

"Science tells us that we cannot say with any certainty what constitutes a dangerous level of warming, and therefore what level must be avoided," Dobriansky declared. It was a do-nothing argument straight out of the oil industry playbook.

That agnostic position on climate change was reflected in the bipartisan Energy Policy Act of 2005, which House and Senate Republicans, backed by the White House, steered through Congress.

The bill's authors saw the problems of energy not through the prism of greenhouse gas emissions, but through the traditional lens of national security and the need to break U.S. reliance on unreliable oil suppliers. The 2003 war had ejected Saddam Hussein from Kuwait but left the oil fields in flames and Saddam in iron-fisted control of Iraq's substantial oil reserves.

The energy bill included expansive tax credits for all kinds of technology—including more efficient cars, electric vehicles, fuel cells, wind, solar and biomass—as well as for the traditional fossil fuels. The largesse was spread broadly, and it attracted broad support.

Some complained that the bill gave too much to fossil fuel companies. And Kerry tried to add a non-binding amendment expressing the "sense of the Senate" that the United States should "address global climate change through comprehensive and cost-effective national measures and through the negotiation of fair and binding international commitments."

But the amendment failed in a close vote, mostly along party lines, and the bill passed overwhelmingly in both the House and the Senate. Both Kerry and then-Sen. Barack Obama voted for its passage.

By throwing money at many different ways to expand energy supplies, Congress showed the political appeal of what later came to be called the "all of the above" energy philosophy—an approach that doubters deride as "business as usual."

Research money was even set aside to mine U.S. tar sands deposits in Utah, Kentucky and elsewhere. Although they are paltry compared to Alberta's reserves, Bush wanted them developed. Funding would go toward "unlocking vast amounts" of "energy now trapped in shale and tar sands," Bush said as he signed the bill in August.

The focus, however, remained on Canada's much larger projects.

At a meeting at Bush's Texas ranch, Prime Minister Paul Martin of Canada and President Vicente Fox of Mexico shook hands with Bush on a "Security and Prosperity Partnership" that called for "greater economic production from oil sands."

That year, crude oil prices crossed above $50 a barrel for the first time; they have never gone below that level since. The rising prices made the mining and upgrading of tar sands profitable, and production took off.

At the 2005 U.N. negotiations in Montreal, Bush again resisted committing the United States to a binding level of emissions. This time, Dobrianski and her lead negotiator, Harlan Watson—a physicist and longtime Republican congressional aide who had been recommended to his post by Exxon Corp.—walked out of an informal session rather than engage in further talks about what kind of arrangement should replace Kyoto after it expired in 2012.

In Bush's 2006 State of the Union speech he never used the words "climate," "warming" or "carbon." The issue remained one of security of supply, not of meeting an emissions target.

"We have a serious problem: America is addicted to oil, which is often imported from unstable parts of the world," he declared. To satisfy that addiction he promised to increase support for alternative energy supplies, whether the new sources were renewable fuels or unconventional fossil fuels. His "great goal," he said, was "to replace more than 75 percent of our oil imports from the Middle East by 2025."

That goal would be within reach if Canada doubled or tripled its annual rate of tar sands production, as the industry was promising.

The public knew very little about tar sands oil back then. Even environmentalists weren't thinking much about it.

Carl Pope, then the executive director of the Sierra Club, had written a book excoriating the Bush administration's policies. But Pope focused on Bush's effort to open public lands to the energy industry and to dismantle federal regulations. "I was not focused at all on the tar sands," said Pope, looking back on that time.

So, flying under the radar, Canada and the United States set about to increase by fivefold the production of one of the dirtiest fossil fuels on the planet—and one of the most abundant.

In January 2006, a group of experts met under U.S. and Canadian government auspices in Houston to discuss the expansion of Canada's oil sands, as "a significant contributor to energy supply and security."

The tar sands flow already exceeded a million barrels a day and was expected to double by 2010 or 2012. The experts predicted Canada's output would eventually reach 5 million barrels a day. That, they realized, would reshape the energy landscape.

To fulfill that dream they needed pipelines.

"The fivefold expansion anticipated for oil sands products in a relatively short time span will represent many challenges for the pipeline industry," said the group's report. "New and expanded pipelines will move more volume into existing and expanding interior U.S. markets."

Visiting Alberta in 2006, Bush's new energy secretary, Samuel Bodman, said Canada's deposits, second only to the fabled reserves of Saudi Arabia, represented America's best shot at weaning itself off OPEC and Middle Eastern supplies. "No single thing can do more to help us reach that goal than realizing the potential of the oil sands," he declared.

Even as the expansion plans were being made, warnings from mainstream scientists about global warming were gaining currency among the general public. After Al Gore lost his presidential bid, he traveled the world promoting the science of global warming. "An Inconvenient Truth," a film that documented his crusade, won an Oscar and reached millions of people. Although climate skeptics disputed and ridiculed Gore's message, he and the IPCC were awarded the 2007 Nobel Peace Prize "for their efforts to build up and disseminate greater knowledge about man-made climate change, and to lay the foundations for the measures that are needed to counteract such change."

As Canadian leaders fell in love with the tar sands, they started to fall out of love with the Kyoto Protocol.

Stephen Harper, the opposition leader who had opposed Canada's ratification of the accord, took office in 2006 as the new Conservative prime minister. He was not to be outdone by Bush in his disdain for the treaty. Harper had long declared that Kyoto would ruin Canada's fossil-fuel industries, and now that he was in office, momentum increased for a grand tar sands expansion.

Inside the Washington bureaucracy the White House political team took aim not just at Kyoto but also at the scientists who were working on the climate problem.

On several occasions, Bush aides intervened to water down reports that might be used to argue for more forceful action against global warming. Their actions came to light at a February 2007 Senate hearing, where Kerry and other Democrats lambasted the administration's tactics.

Their key witness was Rick Piltz, who had worked for years on the government's annual climate reports to Congress. Piltz had recently left that job to work for the Government Accountability Project, a liberal watchdog group.

Piltz told the committee that the reports, which had been submitted to Congress every year since 1990, were done in consultation with 90 career science professionals, "with them clearing every step of the way, to put together the most careful, reviewed language on what was understood, the highlights of recent research, and what the issues were."

When the draft reports arrived at the Clinton White House, where Al Gore wielded oversight on climate matters, nobody stood in their way. But when they arrived at the Bush White House, Piltz said, "political gatekeepers would step in" to soften the edges. Among them was James Connaughton, a former industry lobbyist running Bush's Council on Environmental Quality. Connaughton "clearly had a political agenda," Piltz testified.

"I don't think it was a question of toning down extremes," Piltz said. "I think it was a question of White House misrepresentation of language that had been agreed upon by science professionals."

At the hearing, Kerry accused Bush's team of "willfully, purposefully quashing science from reaching the American people. Willfully stepping in the way of legitimate global climate change conclusions being drawn. Willfully stepping in the way of proactive steps to try to deal with this. In effect, a dodge and a duck, an avoidance of reality."

"Where is the plan for this administration to cut carbon?" Kerry asked William Brennan, Bush's director of climate science.

Brennan said the administration was working to reduce greenhouse gas intensity.

Kerry pushed ahead, and when Brennan responded with vague promises, Kerry declared the Bush administration's tactics "the most serious dereliction of public responsibility that I've ever seen. Ever."

Kerry was so tough on Brennan that Piltz came to Brennan's defense, noting that the White House had refused to send a more senior witness, and that Brennan was left "hanging out here to get beat up."

From Brennan, Kerry wanted specifics—namely, a commitment to restrain emissions to a level that would keep the planet's warming within safe boundaries.

"To reduce carbon to the levels that will hold us to 450 parts per million, which is the scientifically agreed-upon level that we must accept?" he asked Brennan. "Where's the plan?"

Kerry's use of the 450 number was telling, because it showed how closely he was following the scientific debate over climate change.

For decades scientists had watched concentrations of $CO_2$ rising in the atmosphere, using a measurement known as the Keeling curve for the scientist who began tracking the numbers in Hawaii decades ago.

But how high could the number safely rise? Today, many think 350 is the safe limit—that's where the group 350.org, which opposes the Keystone XL pipeline, gets its name. Scientists with the IPCC, recognizing the difficulty of reversing course, thought the number shouldn't exceed 450 parts per million. That would be a challenging target, but it offered a good chance of keeping temperatures from going up more than 2 degrees Celsius.

Because carbon dioxide stays in the atmosphere for so long, the 2 degrees of warming were already all but inevitable. To avoid even more warming, worldwide emissions must peak soon and fall rapidly. Every year of delay would make it more difficult and costly to hit the 450 target.

The number was just beginning to find widespread use in discussions about the risks of climate change. The International Energy Agency, which advises developed countries on sustainable energy paths, included a 450 scenario for the first time in its annual 2007 World Energy Outlook. At the time, the concentration of carbon dioxide was about 384 parts per million, and growing faster than ever.

In December 2007 delegates at the U.N.'s 13th annual negotiations in Bali proposed that the world should accept the 450 parts per million limit.

But Bush again stood firm against setting concrete targets, and the proposal was dropped in favor of two more years of talks. By then, Bush would be out of office.

The next year, European nations tried to persuade the G-8, a group including the United States and seven other leading industrial nations, to endorse the 450 ppm goal at its annual summit. If those eight nations could at least agree to cut their own emissions in half by 2050, they would be making a big down payment on the global objective and set a marker for other countries, including China and other fast-growing nations, to consider. They would also build momentum for replacing Kyoto with an international pact to bring global warming under control.

But Bush scuttled that plan, too.

"We don't think that's a very practical approach," Connaughton, Bush's key environmental aide, told reporters when he was trying to explain the administration's objection to setting emissions targets. "You can't manage the temperature."

Just days before the G-8 meeting, Bush called for the leading nations to begin discussions outside the established U.N. process about individual, voluntary approaches to reducing emissions. Without the support of its biggest power, the G-8 could do little but clear its throat. Bush's idea weakened the U.N. process and left the G-8 leaders without a united plan.

If ever the slogan "mission accomplished" was deserved, it was in Bush and Cheney's success in rebuffing attempts to bind the United States to reductions in the use of fossil fuels.

"Mission accomplished" could also be applied to the nation's tar sands partnership with Canada.

In February 2008, Bush's State Department approved an application filed by TransCanada, a Canadian pipeline operator, to build the first Keystone pipeline, which would carry tar sands oil from Alberta to Cushing, Okla.

Bush's decision was based principally on the same mindset he had held throughout his term in office. U.S. demand for fuel would rise 25 percent in 25 years. American production could not fill the gap. Overseas supplies were shaky, but Canada's were plentiful and nearby. The tar sands would be needed and so would new pipelines. The report said that by 2015, an additional million barrels a day of pipeline capacity would be needed to carry the Canadian oil. The Keystone, which would barely cover half that, was clearly needed.

Nowhere in the discussion did these words appear: "carbon dioxide," "global warming," "climate change" or "greenhouse gases."

When Barack Obama accepted the Democratic nomination for president at the 2008 convention, he listed climate change as a 21st century challenge on a par with terrorism, nuclear proliferation, poverty, genocide and disease.

As for oil, he said, "Now is the time to end this addiction and to understand that drilling is a stop-gap measure, not a long-term solution, not even close," he said.

The Republican nominee, John McCain, also took climate change seriously.

McCain wanted a cap-and-trade bill aimed at reducing greenhouse gas emissions 15 percent below 2005 levels by 2020 and 66 percent by 2050—ambitious targets that would have reversed the history of emissions since Kyoto. In his convention speech, McCain disparaged the energy bill Bush had signed in 2005. "Instead of freeing ourselves from a dangerous dependence on foreign oil, both parties—and Senator Obama—passed another corporate welfare bill for oil companies."

Like Bush, however, both Obama and McCain cast their energy policies in terms of breaking the nation's dependence on foreign oil. They spoke favorably of nuclear power, renewables, cleaner ways to use coal, and natural gas—the "all of the above" approach. They stressed that America needed to replace its risky overseas sources of oil, sounding very much like the president they hoped to replace.

But there were big differences between the two presidential candidates, and between their political audiences, differences that could be seen in their choices of running mates. Obama chose Delaware Sen. Joe Biden, a mainstream Democrat with an 84 percent pro-environment rating from the League of Conservation Voters. McCain chose Sarah Palin, a conservative governor from the oil state of Alaska, who didn't believe in the science of global warming.

Palin's attitude, and that of the Republican Party at large, was captured in a slogan that the delegates to the Republican convention repeated with giddy enthusiasm that summer and throughout the campaign.

"The chant is 'drill, baby, drill,'" she reminded Biden in their vice presidential debate. "And that's what we hear all across this country…"

As the campaign continued, TransCanada quietly applied to build another pipeline in the United States, this one known as the Keystone XL. It would be a bigger pipe than the first Keystone and, if approved, would carry Canada's oil all the way to the Texas Gulf Coast.

# 2

## A NEW AGENDA

Barely a month in office and facing an economy in collapse, President Barack Obama stood before a joint meeting of Congress and proposed an expansive agenda for rebuilding. "It begins with energy," he declared on Feb. 24, 2009.

In some ways the new president sounded a lot like George W. Bush. He cast his energy policy more in terms of independence from dicey foreign oil suppliers and less in terms of carbon pollution from fossil fuels. He wanted more jobs in greener sources of energy—solar and wind—but also in oil and especially natural gas, a somewhat cleaner fuel where production was starting to expand.

"We have known for decades that our survival depends on finding new sources of energy," he said. "Yet we import more oil today than ever before."

But there was a difference between the two presidents. For Obama, subsidizing clean energy and removing tax subsidies for oil wasn't enough. He wanted to do what Bush, stubborn as the Alamo, had resisted: impose binding caps on emissions and put a price on carbon, if not by taxing it, then by setting up a system of trading emissions permits.

His goal, he said, was to move the nation once and for all away from fossil fuels and carbon pollution and commit it instead to tackling the rapidly mounting risks of climate change.

"To truly transform our economy, protect our security, and save our planet from the ravages of climate change, we need to ultimately make clean, renewable energy the profitable kind of energy," he said that day. "So I ask this Congress to send me legislation that places a market-based cap on carbon pollution and drives the production of more renewable energy in America."

If Congress would agree to revolutionize the U.S. energy markets in this way, the impact would be as profound as the health care legislation Obama was also determined to see passed. With carbon pollution priced to reflect its true environmental costs, demand for low-carbon fuels would skyrocket. High-carbon fuels such as tar sands oil would be driven out of the market whenever cleaner alternatives were readily available.

Obama was also contemplating something else that Bush had consistently opposed: reaching a binding global treaty that would put the whole world on a path to lower carbon pollution. To do that, however, the United States had to prove itself at home.

The new president's first budget request, submitted to Congress in March, reflected his ambitions to rein in climate change.

In the budget, Obama vowed to work with Congress on a national plan to reduce greenhouse gas emissions 14 percent below the 2005 levels by the year 2020. By 2050, he wanted even steeper cuts—83 percent, a target that would require extraordinary reductions in the use of fossil fuels. Given the right lever, he could shift the world of energy. His crowbar would be a cap-and-trade law setting limits on $CO_2$ emissions across the economy. Billions of dollars would be raised from fees collected under the law.

The budget also sought tens of billions of dollars in the next few years for climate-related research and investment. Much of the money would come from the emergency stimulus package Congress had just enacted to help dig the nation out of the recession.

Billions would be available for academic and industrial research, billions more for weatherproofing homes, and yet more billions in tax credits for green investments and loans for clean energy startups. The goal was to create jobs and at the same time trigger a boom in renewable energy and fuel efficiency.

With employment plunging to near-Depression levels, Congress was willing to accept this kind of jobs project. But passing a stimulus package and addressing climate change were just two pieces of Obama's ambitious four-part legislative agenda. The president also wanted to overhaul the health care system and impose financial reforms that would protect the country from another speculative boom-and-bust like the housing debt crisis that had so paralyzed the economy.

Not since the Great Society—perhaps not even since the New Deal—had a president entered office with a more ambitious economic agenda. But his ambitions would prove extraordinarily divisive.

Two long-time climate champions, Democrats Henry Waxman of California and Ed Markey of Massachusetts, introduced a cap-and-trade bill in the House of Representatives, where the Democrats held a narrow majority.

Cap-and-trade wasn't exactly a new idea in environmental regulation. Economists of many political persuasions had come to agree that the most efficient way to limit greenhouse gases would be either a direct tax on the carbon dioxide given off by the combustion of fossil fuels, or a cap-and-trade system that allocates emissions permits and lets the marketplace decide how best to control the regulated pollutants. Those who find cheap, efficient ways to cut carbon pollution end up with extra credits, which they can sell to those who can't afford the costs of pollution controls. As the cap is steadily lowered, emissions will shrink across the whole economy.

Republicans had seized on cap-and-trade years ago as an archetypal "market mechanism," and it had worked before. Under the first

President Bush, the Clean Air Act was amended with an innovative cap-and-trade mechanism that sharply cut the corrosive sulfur dioxide emissions that came from burning coal. As polluters installed scrubbers or turned to lower-sulfur coal, the cost turned out to be much lower than expected, and the legislation solved the problem of acid rain that had vexed the United States and Canada for decades.

When the same concept was suggested for the fight against carbon, however, it fell from favor among Republicans and among Democrats from coal country and the oil patch. They argued that using such a scheme to sharply reduce carbon dioxide would cripple the economy by raising industrial costs and cutting deeply into the consumption of coal and other fossil fuels.

The Waxman-Markey bill not only limited carbon emissions, but also set a border tax aimed squarely at high-carbon fuel imports, such as tar sands oil. Heavy, dirty oil imports from anywhere in the world would be reduced as refineries shifted to cleaner, lighter fuels in order to avoid the tax penalty.

To economists, a cap-and-trade bill had the same effect as a carbon tax. Both allowed the government to collect revenues, some of which would be used to subsidize clean sources of energy. The coal industry, for example, would receive tens of billions of dollars for new technology that could capture carbon dioxide emissions and store them permanently under ground.

But the Republican Party denounced the climate change bill as a "massive national energy tax." Conservatives took to calling the idea "cap and tax." The cry was taken up by the Tea Party, an anti-tax, anti-big-government, anti-compromise wing of the Republican Party that was just beginning to flex its muscles in elections around the country.

Obama called the approaching vote "historic."

"I know this is going to be a close vote, in part because of the misinformation that's out there that suggests there's somehow a contradiction between investing in clean energy and our economic growth," he said in a Rose Garden appearance. "But my call to those members of Congress who are still on the fence, as well as to the American people, is this: We cannot be afraid of the future, and we can't be prisoners of the past. We've been talking about this issue for decades, and now is the time to finally act."

The House vote on Waxman-Markey, on June 26, 2009, was a cliffhanger. Dozens of Democrats were wavering, especially those from coal states, swing districts and economically distressed areas. The horse-trading lasted into the wee hours of the morning as the Democrats tried to persuade a handful of Republicans to join their cause. Past midnight, John Boehner of Ohio, the minority leader, tried to stall the action by reading aloud from the bill's text, but to no avail. The bill passed, 219-212.

The legislation's passage was celebrated as a sign of early momentum for Obama's energy policies. Some environmentalists, including NASA climate hawk James Hansen, declared it too weak. But climate campaigner Dan Lashoff of the Natural Resources Defense Council told The Washington Post the compromises were understandable and called the authors "champions."

Both sides expected a much bigger fight in the Senate, which was embroiled in other domestic-policy duels over spending, taxes, finance, immigration and, especially, health care.

Meanwhile, the Great Recession had done what no policy program had ever accomplished—sent carbon dioxide emissions down two years in a row. Once the economy turned around, carbon pollution would likely turn around with it, as fuel consumption resumed. But Obama could begin to claim that his energy policies were working.

As Obama's first year in office sped by, the momentum Bush and Cheney had built up for Canada's bitumen and the pipelines needed to carry it still prevailed.

Construction began on TransCanada's original Keystone line, approved by Bush in 2008. But aside from a devoted core of pipeline opponents, the public wasn't yet paying much attention to TransCanada's pending application for the bigger and longer Keystone XL pipeline.

In August, Obama's State Department approved an application by Canadian-owned Enbridge energy to build another cross-border pipeline, the 327-mile, 36-inch Alberta Clipper. The line would run from Hardisty, Alberta across the border to Superior, Wis. and carry 450,000 barrels a day, with the amount increasing over the years.

A legacy of the Bush administration, the draft environmental impact statement for the Clipper had been published in the Federal Register just 10 days after Obama was sworn in. The pipeline's emissions would be "negligible…relative to refinery emissions, total U.S. emissions, or global emissions," the report said.

In the 30-day public comment period that followed, the State Department received just 900 comments. When the final EIS was released, only four comments were filed and "none contained any new substantial or substantive arguments regarding the proposed project," the State Department said.

The formal declaration that the Clipper was in the national interest was signed not by Obama's secretary of state, Hillary Clinton, but by her deputy, James Steinberg. His reasoning hewed closely to the logic presented by the Bush administration: the need for secure oil supplies trumped environmental concerns.

"The Alberta Clipper project would serve the national interest in a time of considerable political tension in other major oil producing regions and countries by providing additional access to a proximate stable secure supply of crude oil with minimum transportation requirements," Steinberg ruled.

The administration had considered the problem of greenhouse gases, he said, and "considers that on balance they do not outweigh the benefits to the national interests.

"The United States will continue to reduce reliance on oil through conservation and energy efficiency measures … as well as through the pursuit of comprehensive climate legislation and a global agreement on climate change."

Compared to the way greenhouse gas emissions would be considered later in the Obama administration, the Clipper environmental impact statement gave the climate change problem scant attention. It looked at the pipeline in isolation from the broader context of tar sands expansion, examining not the emissions from the oil the pipeline would carry, but at the direct pollution from building and operating the line, a relatively small source of carbon dioxide.

If each new cross-border pipeline were waved through on that basis, the overall oil sands emissions would continue to mount as Canada's production grew.

Environmental groups sought an injunction against the Alberta Clipper, but Enbridge raced ahead with its construction, and a federal judge declined to intervene. The economic harm an injunction would cause the company and its workers outweighed any environmental concerns, the judge ruled.

By 2009, scientists were increasingly certain that the planet should be kept from warming more than 2 degrees Celsius—and that to do that the amount of carbon dioxide in the atmosphere would have to remain below about 450 parts per million.

Although the Kyoto treaty was foundering—the United States and Canada had both withdrawn from its terms—U.N. talks toward a new global emissions treaty continued.

In December 2009 the signatories to the U.N. Framework Convention on Climate Change, the umbrella agreement signed at the 1992 Earth Summit in Rio, were scheduled to meet in Copenhagen for their annual negotiating conference. Many of the participants hoped to reach a binding new treaty then and there, so the world could ratchet down emissions in time to head off the worst effects of global warming.

Those hopes rose when Obama announced he would attend the meeting, something Bush had never done. The roster of attending heads of state surged past 100 names.

To be sure of having an impact, Obama decided to join the talks on his way home from Oslo, where he was to accept the Nobel Peace Prize. That's when other heads of state or their leading ministers would be making the big decisions and negotiations would be most tense.

But Obama had little negotiating leverage.

With the Waxman-Markey climate change bill still tied up in the Senate, the U.S. delegation in Copenhagen was negotiating without knowing what Congress would support. Indeed, some senators wanted to tie the negotiators' hands.

A controversy that came to be known as Climategate had recently erupted, after a hacker leaked emails stolen from computers at the prominent Climate Research Unit (CRU) of the University of East Anglia. Climate skeptics, including Oklahoma Sen. James Inhofe, seized on the messages as proof that IPCC researchers had manipulated the data that provided the scientific underpinning for the Copenhagen negotiations.

A series of investigations later cleared the scientists of any improper behavior. But coming just weeks before Copenhagen. the scandal played into the hands of those who wanted the talks to fail.

"The interesting part of this is it's happening right before Copenhagen. And, so, the timing couldn't be better," Inhofe said. "Whoever is on the ball in Great Britain, their timing was good."

Inhofe later showed up in the pressroom at the Copenhagen conference, telling reporters he wanted to "make sure that nobody is laboring under the misconception that the U.S. Senate is going to do something."

"There's not a chance in the world" that the Senate is going to pass a cap-and-trade bill, he said.

In the end, the best Obama could do was commit the United States to joining other countries that agreed to the nonbinding, skeletal Copenhagen Accord to reduce their emissions at their own pace. The advanced industrial countries would make the steepest cuts and help finance efforts by the less wealthy.

Obama pledged to reduce U.S. emissions 17 percent below the 2005 levels by 2020, a bit more aggressive than his budget had proposed, but still in line with the Waxman-Markey bill.

Obama headed back to Washington before the conference wrapped up, to get home before a record-setting snowstorm shut down the capital. "I want to be very clear that ultimately this issue is going to be dictated by the science," he said before he left, "and the science indicates that we're going to have to take more aggressive steps in the future."

He declared the Copenhagen pact "a meaningful and unprecedented breakthrough."

His critics disagreed.

Climate hawks complained of being betrayed in Copenhagen, saying Obama had compromised too much. Bill McKibben, an environmentalist writer and professor at Middlebury College who was building a new grassroots campaign called 350.org, said Obama had let down his most avid supporters, who wanted nothing less than a binding treaty.

"Obama has taken the mandate that progressives worked their hearts out to give him, and used it to gut the ideas that progressives have held most dear," McKibben said. "The ice caps won't be the only thing we lose with this deal."

John McCain, who had run for president with a climate change bill in his hip pocket, derided Copenhagen's toothless accord as "a nothing burger."

As 2009 drew to a close, the Environmental Protection Agency set in motion the most far-reaching initiative ever exercised by a federal agency over greenhouse gas emissions.

In a ruling known as the endangerment finding, it decreed that carbon dioxide and five other greenhouse gases "taken in combination endanger both the public health and the public welfare of current and future generations." The EPA had relied heavily on the IPCC in reaching its conclusion.

The administration was on firm ground: the ruling was backed up by a two-year-old decision by the Supreme Court.

Some interpreted the EPA's action as an attempt by Obama to blackmail Congress into enacting a broad climate bill. If it refused, he would impose rules unilaterally under the Clean Air Act.

Republicans threatened to pass legislation to overturn the finding and urged the EPA to reverse itself.

The state of Texas, whose governor, Rick Perry, was a prominent presidential contender, filed a petition that challenged the endangerment finding by attacking the objectivity and validity of the IPCC's scientific consensus that greenhouse gases threaten the planet's ecological balance. To bolster its argument, it pointed to the Climategate brouhaha.

No government policy involving climate change, the Texans were saying, should be influenced by the peer-reviewed, consensus-driven science of the IPCC.

The EPA brushed aside the Texas petition, and the endangerment finding has survived all subsequent legal challenges intact.

By early 2010, Obama had succeeded in getting three of his ambitious programs through Congress. The stimulus bill, the banking overhaul and health care reform passed, each with a nearly absolute party-line vote.

But the climate bill was faltering in the Senate, where Republicans were more interested in offering legislation that would undermine environmental protections.

In January, Sen. Lisa Murkowski of Alaska, one of the energy industry's strongest allies in Congress, proposed a bill to overturn the EPA's endangerment finding. It failed by a vote of 47–53.

That was a Pyrrhic victory for environmentalists. They had enough votes to stop egregiously harmful legislation, but not enough to move their agenda forward.

Republicans, for their part, were determined to stop any more legislation favored by the president. With the midterm elections looming, they began digging in their heels on global warming. Some Senate Democrats joined them, especially those from conservative, energy-rich states.

Their efforts were buttressed by well-financed groups—including Americans for Prosperity, funded by the billionaire Koch brothers—that "not only played a major role in confounding public understanding of climate science, but also successfully delayed meaningful government policy actions to address the issue," according to Robert Brulle, a sociologist at Drexel University in Philadelphia.

If they could stave off action on climate change for a few more months, Republican leaders figured, they might gain control of the House or even the Senate. That way they could block Obama's agenda for the remainder of his first term and focus on ousting him in 2012.

"The single most important thing we want to achieve is for President Obama to be a one-term president," declared Senate minority leader Mitch McConnell from the coal state of Kentucky.

Given Obama's on-again off-again attention to climate change, there seemed to be few obstacles in sight for the Keystone XL. But that would soon change.

On April 20, 2010 a BP oilrig exploded in the Gulf of Mexico, killing 11 and sending oil gushing out of the sea floor. For three months, Americans watched live video of a catastrophe no one knew how to control.

The BP disaster was followed in July by an oil pipeline rupture in Michigan. More than a million gallons of Canadian dilbit poured out of an Enbridge pipeline and contaminated more than 30 miles of the

Kalamazoo River. The fact that the spill went undetected for 17 hours made it all the worse.

The difficulty of cleaning up the Kalamazoo—at a cost that would rise over the years to more than $1 billion—made a deep impression on people whose land would be crossed by the Keystone. Small groups of environmentalists and landowners had been protesting the project in Nebraska, but the BP disaster and the Kalamazoo spill began drawing the attention of the larger groups. Suddenly, the Keystone XL, which had once seemed a shoo-in for a State Department permit, was being questioned by powerful advocates.

The Sierra Club released a long list of other recent spills that it said showed that federal pipeline safety regulations were dangerously inadequate.

In January 2010, an Enbridge pipeline had spilled more than 3,000 barrels of crude oil in North Dakota. In late April, another Enbridge pipeline had ruptured and leaked more than 210 gallons of tar sands crude into Minnesota wetlands. In May, a power outage on the Trans-Alaska Pipeline opened relief valves and spilled several thousand barrels of crude oil. In June, a spill from a Chevron oil pipeline was discovered in Salt Lake City, Utah and an abandoned pipeline in Oklahoma spilled more than 250 barrels of oil into a river.

Concerns grew about the Keystone XL, which would cross one of the world's largest aquifers, the Ogallala.

The Ogallala lies fairly shallow below 174,000 square miles across eight states and holds 3 billion acre-feet of water that is vital for irrigation.

What if the Keystone XL ruptured where it crossed the Ogallala or any of the streams that lie at the surface? How long would it take to get emergency equipment to an isolated area? What would happen if oil entered the aquifer?

Under pressure from the public and regulators, TransCanada took steps to beef up the Keystone's spill defenses. But a few small accidents on the first Keystone pipeline, which had recently opened, gave the Keystone XL's opponents more ammunition. At one point the pipeline had to be shut down temporarily, an unusual measure for a new pipeline.

Meanwhile, supporters of the cap-and-trade bill were trying to gain traction in the Senate.

Obama was counting on two senators– his thwarted Republican presidential opponent John McCain, and Democrat Joe Lieberman of Connecticut, who had been Al Gore's running mate. Years earlier, in more bipartisan times, they had co-sponsored a similar bill.

John Kerry of Massachusetts, who had lost to George W. Bush in 2004, also played a leading role, as did up-and-comer Lindsey Graham, a South Carolina Republican.

Kerry, Lieberman and Graham, who came to be called the Three Amigos, worked hard to come up with a compromise bill, while Obama stayed on the sidelines. The Three Amigos offered incentives for nuclear power, offshore drilling, or anything else that might tempt a filibuster-proof 60-vote majority of senators to come aboard.

But nothing could tamp down the fear that the climate bill would cost jobs in fossil fuels, a sector of the economy that, despite the recession, was still going strong. McCain, who was facing a primary challenge from the far right, participated only fitfully in the attempt to find a deal this time. He had begun to rue his record on climate change. Graham, too, began backing down under pressure from conservatives at home.

On July 27 Democrats officially gave up on a broad energy bill and introduced a stripped-down substitute intended to address the BP spill and a few other relatively minor issues. But even that modest proposal went nowhere.

"We've always known from Day One that to pass comprehensive energy reform you've got to have 60 votes," Kerry said. "As we stand here today we don't have one Republican vote."

The nation's major environmental groups had picked a big fight and lost. Some analysts blamed the defeat on Obama, saying he should have worked harder to get the bill through Congress. Others blamed the green groups, who had invested more time and money on Washington lobbying than on grassroots activism.

Theda Skocpol, a Harvard researcher, later offered this critique.

"Neither the first-term Obama nor environmentalists pushing for comprehensive legislation have paid any heed to the president's heritage as a grassroots organizer," she wrote. "Instead, all the focus has been on bargains with polluting corporations and attempts to woo a few votes from congressional Republicans—a strategy that badly failed in the Senate in 2010 when no Republicans were willing to vote for cap and trade, no matter how many concessions were offered.

"The inside game has failed in part because climate reformers have not invested in building an outside game, a nationwide network of groups that reaches into localities and states."

In November, Republicans, capitalizing on the nation's economic angst, seized control of the House. The prospect of doing anything at all about climate change turned distinctly darker. Large numbers of Republicans, both in the new House leadership and among the freshmen newcomers, were outspokenly hostile to the science of climate change. Key committees—Science, Energy & Commerce, Natural Resources—were now under their control.

Even in the Senate, where Democrats held on to their majority, the same trend prevailed. Ron Johnson, a newly elected Republican senator from Wisconsin, told the Milwaukee Journal Sentinel during his campaign that trying to solve global warming was "a fool's errand." The science was "lunacy" and its adherents were "crazy," he said.

"I absolutely do not believe in the science of man-caused climate change," Johnson said. "It's not proven by any stretch of the imagination."

The past decade, 2001 to 2010, had been the warmest ever recorded globally. Like the rest of their generation, Obama's two daughters had never experienced a single month in which the world's temperature was cooler than what had been typical when their parents were growing up. Every month of their lives, weather reports confirmed that global warming had arrived.

Scientists accepted with ever more certainty that a major factor in the planet's warming was emissions of carbon dioxide and other greenhouse gases, mostly from the burning of fossil fuels. Clearly it would be difficult to keep temperatures within 2 degrees Celsius of the pre-industrial average.

A new way of looking at the math of the problem began to gain currency. It was based on a simple question: How much more carbon dioxide could the people of the world add to the atmosphere before a dangerous warming became inevitable? Sometimes it was called the world's carbon diet, sometimes its carbon budget.

The most sophisticated estimate to date came from researchers at the Potsdam Institute. In a 2009 article in the prestigious journal Nature, they calculated how much warming is forced on the planet by a given amount of carbon dioxide in the air and looked at the emissions trends that were driving up the atmospheric concentrations. Then they figured out how much headroom was left and how soon the margin would be used up.

To be reasonably confident of keeping warming below 2 degrees, they found that the world could emit no more than 1 trillion tons of carbon dioxide between the years 2000 and 2050. What was frightening was that a third of that quota had already been used up.

"If we continue burning fossil fuels as we do, we will have exhausted the carbon budget in merely 20 years, and global warming will go well beyond two degrees," said Malte Meinshausen, the study's lead author. "Only a fast switch away from fossil fuels will give us a reasonable chance to avoid considerable warming."

That finding led to a stunning conclusion: Less than a quarter of the world's proven fossil fuel reserves—coal, natural gas and oil—could be burned and their carbon dioxide released in the next several decades. Otherwise, the climate would almost certainly warm by four degrees, six degrees or even more, depending on how quickly the rate of emissions expanded.

The blunt message—leave most of the world's fuel in the ground, or face disaster—would come to be embraced by institutions as diverse as the World Bank, the International Energy Agency and the U.S. National Academy of Sciences. Ultimately, the U.N.'s Intergovernmental Panel on Climate Change, representing the consensus of the world's climate experts, would sign on. The argument would also underpin the fast-spreading fossil fuel divestment movement at universities.

In effect, the world would either have to find a way to capture carbon dioxide emissions and lock them up—or it would have to abandon fossil fuels altogether.

Where the Bush administration had emphasized the uncertainty and the need for more climate research, Obama embraced the new information that was pouring in and used it to support a rush to action.

The military bought into the new way of thinking about oil. The top brass and the nation's intelligence agencies warned that climate change—with its attendant drought, famine, disease, migration and potential armed conflict over resources—posed at least as much of a strategic threat to American interests as did the need to protect U.S. access to distant oil deposits or to build up oil production near home.

"While climate change alone does not cause conflict, it may act as an accelerant," said the Pentagon's 2010 Quadrennial Defense Review.

The financial markets and the energy industry were pondering the question, too. If three-quarters of the world's known reserves of fossil fuels were left in the ground, what did that mean for the value of energy companies? Their assets were the oil reserves they owned. Left in the ground, they would be worthless—stranded assets.

Following the new math to its logical conclusion, Canada's tar sands, among the dirtiest forms of fossil fuels, had another strike against them, one that a Canadian think tank articulated.

Canada's fossil fuel reserves are equivalent to one-eighth of the world's carbon budget, said the Canadian Centre for Policy Alternatives. "Putting this carbon into the atmosphere would represent a climate catastrophe."

Although Obama's influence over Congress had largely evaporated, the president had a ready tool at his disposal. He could control carbon dioxide under the existing authority of the Clean Air Act.

The EPA began by setting stricter standards for the fuel efficiency of automobiles. It would be the single biggest control on carbon dioxide emissions ever imposed—and it would save consumers huge amounts of money and offer major health benefits at the same time.

In a 2010 court settlement with environmental groups and state officials, the EPA also promised to control carbon dioxide emissions from electric power plants—and, eventually, from factories and refineries. To do this, the agency turned to a section of the Clean Air Act that had been in the law for decades but that no president had ever invoked. Jaded environmentalists had come to refer to the unused statute as the "40-year-old virgin."

Tax credits and other subsidies, extended by Congress in a deal over broader tax policies, began flowing to wind, solar and other green energy sources. So did some spending on research aimed at capturing carbon dioxide from industrial smokestacks and locking it deep underground, the costly and elusive enterprise known as carbon capture and sequestration. Energy-efficiency standards were set for a wide range of consumer and industrial products.

All these actions were based on the administration's all-encompassing belief that federal policy should discourage the continuing investment of capital in fossil fuel infrastructure—whether in the form of cars, power plants, oil refineries, factories or pipelines—that would pour ever more unregulated carbon dioxide into the atmosphere for decades to come.

The Keystone XL pipeline, however, seemed to be treated as a separate case.

In 2010 and 2011 the State Department made its first halting attempt to assess the likely environmental impact of the Keystone project.

The administration was still struggling with the way big energy infrastructure problems should be addressed under the National Environmental Policy Act, or NEPA, which since 1970 had guided the writing of environmental impact statements for major federal decisions—such as whether to approve a pipeline.

In February 2010, the White House's Council on Environmental Quality (CEQ) for the first time published draft guidelines explaining how agencies should consider greenhouse gas emissions, or GHGs, when writing a NEPA review. It warned that even though a single project's emissions might look small compared to the whole world's carbon dioxide problem, they still had to be considered carefully. The goal was not to focus on incremental changes, but on cumulative effects.

"Because climate change is a global problem that results from global GHG emissions, there are no dominating sources and fewer sources that would even be close to dominating total GHG emissions," it said. "The global climate change problem is much more the result of numerous and varied sources, each of which might seem to make a relatively small addition to global atmospheric GHG concentrations. CEQ proposes to recommend that environmental documents reflect this global context and be realistic in focusing on ensuring that useful information is provided to decision makers."

The State Department had relatively little expertise in handling such a comprehensive NEPA assessment and seemingly little interest in fully examining the project's implications for climate change.

Its first draft environmental impact statement (DEIS) on the Keystone project, issued in April 2010, reached this basic conclusion: the "incremental impact of the project on GHG emissions would be minor."

Waxman, whose cap-and-trade bill was on its deathbed in the Senate by this time, wrote scathing letters to Clinton and her underlings, accusing them of almost completely ignoring global warming, which he called "the most significant environmental problem associated with the project."

The EPA, charged with judging the adequacy of all other agencies' environmental reviews, gave this one a failing grade.

It "does not provide the scope or detail of analysis necessary to fully inform decision makers," wrote Cynthia Giles, E.P.A.'s enforcement chief. She called for complete estimates of "emissions associated with long-term importation of large quantities of oil sands crude."

"Based on our review, there is a reasonably close causal relationship between issuing a cross-border permit for the Keystone XL project and increased extraction of oil sands crude in Canada intended to supply that pipeline," she declared.

The State Department announced that it would go back to the drawing board and prepare a new draft EIS. But Secretary of State Clinton seemed comfortable with the business-as-usual approach that had guided the Bush administration – more focused on secure energy supplies than on global warming. Even as the review process foundered, she seemed not to be taking heed of rising opposition to the pipeline.

In a speech at the Commonwealth Club in San Francisco in October she lamented the failure of the Waxman-Markey bill but said she was "inclined" to approve the Keystone XL.

"We're either going to be dependent on dirty oil from the Gulf or dependent on dirty oil from Canada," she said. "And until we can get our act together as a country and figure out that clean, renewable energy is in both our economic interests and the interests of our planet, I mean, I don't think it will come as a surprise to anyone how deeply disappointed the president and I are about our inability to get the kind of legislation through the Senate that the United States was seeking."

The State Department's second draft environmental impact statement for the Keystone supported Clinton's inclination to approve the pipeline.

Issued on April 15, 2011, the report conceded that the fuel to be carried via the Keystone would have a higher carbon footprint than comparable fuels. But it said the emissions were small compared to overall U.S. greenhouse gas emissions, and that if the Keystone weren't built, Canada would simply export its fuel elsewhere, and American refineries would import dirty fuel from some other country.

In the public comment period that followed, the EPA responded with another tough critique, calling the new EIS "insufficient" in part because it didn't adequately discuss climate change.

Environmentalists also challenged the process.

The review "makes a good start in acknowledging that tar sands oil has higher lifecycle greenhouse emissions than conventional oil," four major environmental groups said in comments to the State Department. "But it then incorrectly finds that these additional emissions do not need to be considered."

Friends of the Earth said the report was slanted in favor of the industry and accused the State Department of tolerating conflicts of interest. Clinton's former campaign chief, Paul Elliot, had been hired to lobby for TransCanada. The Los Angeles Times later reported that a department official had coached TransCanada on ways to improve its message. Cardno Entrix, the contractor brought in to help prepare the review, had deep ties to the oil industry and to tar sands players, the environmentalists said.

Democrats in Congress challenged the fairness of the process and ordered a review by the State Department's inspector general.

The IG shrugged off the claims of conflict and said the department hadn't compromised its review by selecting Cardno Entrix. But the IG also found that the department's "limited technical resources, expertise and experience" had hamstrung its assessment.

Federal and industry officials told the IG that the State Department shuffled career foreign service officers in and out of its NEPA office, and that some of the neophytes "had little or no prior NEPA experience and had to seek training and learn quickly on the job."

A prominent Canadian lawyer, Jocelyn Stacey, looking on from abroad, saw it all as a signal that the NEPA process was flawed.

"Keystone XL shows that, perversely, it can be easier to use environmental assessment to hide and deny the problem of climate change then it is to confront and meaningfully assess it," she said on a legal blog. "Rather than an information-forcing tool, environmental assessment becomes an information-obscuring tool that stifles debate and perpetuates denial of climate change impacts."

The State Department had accepted what was supposed to be its final environmental impact statement in August 2011, giving the pipeline a green light. Now it had 90 days to consider whether the pipeline was in the national interest. The agency promised to issue a verdict on the Keystone XL by the end of 2011, and it seemed on track to do that.

The Keystone's opponents made it clear to Obama that he would pay a political price if he approved the project. For two weeks in August they held sit-ins and nonviolent civil disobedience outside the White House. More than 1,200 people were arrested as they chanted and sang, undeterred by a minor earthquake that damaged the nearby Washington Monument, or by the bluster of Hurricane Irene, which swept up the coast, sideswiped New York City, and ravaged Vermont and neighboring states with extraordinary flash flooding.

Bill McKibben of 350.org, whose catalyzing leadership had energized the civil disobedience and the Keystone fight, spent two days in jail near the start of the protests. NASA's greenhouse-effect icon James Hansen was arrested as the demonstrations wound down. He was booked, fined $150 and released.

TransCanada and its industry partners pressed their case hard, too. They emphasized two economic claims: that the pipeline would create tens of thousands of jobs—even hundreds of thousands—and that it would lower the price American consumers paid for gasoline.

Glenn Kessler, the fact-checking columnist at The Washington Post, gave the jobs claims "two Pinocchios," meaning significant exaggeration.

He was especially critical of TransCanada's assertion, based on a study the company commissioned, that the Keystone would create 118,000 spin-off jobs through increased business for local restaurants, hotels and suppliers. The study suggested that the number of permanent jobs would top 250,000.

"Caveat emptor," wrote Kessler. "The company building the pipeline is obviously going to offer the rosiest scenario possible. One should especially view with a large grain of salt any study for which it paid good money."

The State Department's employment estimates have been far more modest. Actually building the pipeline would employ only a few thousand temporary workers for less than six months each summer. Once in service, the pipeline would need only 35 full-time workers to keep it running.

Figuring out where Obama stood in the debate was impossible.

In an interview with an Omaha television station, the president said that "my general attitude is: What is best for the American people? What's best for our economy both short term and long term? But also: What's best for the health of the American people?"

"Folks in Nebraska, like folks all across the country, aren't going to say to themselves, 'We're going to take a few thousand jobs if it means our kids are potentially drinking water that would damage their health,'" Obama said. "We need to make sure that we have energy security and aren't just relying on Middle East sources, but there's a way of doing that and still making sure that the health and safety of the American people and folks in Nebraska are protected."

With the next presidential election just a year away, Obama supporters and anti-pipeline activists began showing up at his campaign offices with a simple message: We're not going to work for you or contribute to your campaign if you say yes to the Keystone XL.

In October, about 1,000 people—including Susie Tompkins Buell, a co-founder of the Esprit clothing company and one of the Democratic party's most important donors—gathered outside the exclusive W Hotel in San Francisco, where an Obama fundraiser was being held. Tompkins Buell, who normally would have been one of the high-rolling guests inside, was among the protestors outside. The San Francisco Chronicle later quoted Tompkins Buell as saying, Obama "needs to be a leader" on this project.

The pipeline's opponents scheduled a high-profile march for Nov. 6 where they would join hands around the White House.

McKibben described the event as "a kind of ring-around-Obama" designed to remind him that he had deep support for blocking the project. The event was also a warning, however. If Obama didn't come through, he could lose that support in his reelection bid. Many of his donors were wealthy liberals, the green of their environmental ardor matching the color of their money.

The ring "will look either like a big O-shaped hug for a guy who's had a hard time from Congress and now with this pipeline decision can finally do the right thing all by himself—or like a kind of symbolic house arrest for the guy who's already opened the Arctic to oil drilling and is now poised to bust the carbon ceiling wide open with tar sands oil," McKibben said. "For most of us, torn between hope and fear, it's probably a little bit of both."

The Saturday night before the march, some 500 people packed a church hall in nearby Columbia Heights, laying plans, giving each other pep talks and painting signs.

The next day, an estimated 12,000 people formed a boisterous conga line around the White House, exceeding their own expectations with a human chain several people deep around the long, fenced-off perimeter. It was a diverse crowd, with farmers, ranchers, Native Americans, clergy, scientists, students and eco-activists joining in.

"We need to remind him he is the leader who we elected," said Courtney Hight, who had worked on Obama's campaign and at the White House before becoming executive director of the Energy Action Coalition. Hight urged the president to "give back some of the hope he gave us three years ago."

Nebraska Gov. Dave Heineman supported the pipeline but sensed rising opposition in his state, especially among people concerned about the pipeline's route through the Sandhills, a region where the water lay just a few feet from the surface. To see if a deal could be struck—perhaps one with a less worrisome route—Heineman called a special legislative session to write bills that would give the state more leverage over the siting of the Keystone and future pipeline routes.

The lawmakers were still hammering out that legislation on November 10, when the State Department upped the pressure by announcing it was delaying the national interest review for the project until Nebraska settled on the route.

The legislature voted to set up a strict new review process under the state's independent utilities commission. But it also offered TransCanada a short cut: Because the company already had an application under way in Washington, the Keystone would be vetted instead by the Nebraska Department of Environmental Quality (NDEQ), which was controlled by the governor.

The Nebraska route was still in limbo when the Keystone's impatient friends in Congress put their thumbs on the scale by writing legislation that gave Obama 60 days to make a final decision on the Keystone. To get it through both the House and the Senate, they attached the legislation to a bill the president desperately wanted, extending a popular payroll tax cut.

It was a time-honored maneuver known as a budget rider, in which an unwelcomed piece of policy is attached to a piece of must-pass legislation, breezing through the capital like a hobo riding the express freight train. But this time the tactic backfired.

Obama signed the bill. Then a few weeks later, on January 18, he rejected the Keystone permit.

He had no choice, he said, because he didn't have enough information to make the decision so quickly. He blamed the "rushed and arbitrary deadline insisted on by Congressional Republicans."

After so many setbacks—cap and trade, Copenhagen—the pipeline's opponents were euphoric.

The victory over corporate lobbyists, proclaimed Erich Pica, president of Friends of the Earth, belongs to "the indigenous communities who first sounded the alarm on the dangers of tar sands extraction, to the Nebraskan farmers and Texan ranchers who withstood TransCanada's bullying in the name of their land and livelihoods, to the activists from across the country who were arrested on the president's doorstep, and to all of us fighting for a safe climate and justice-fueled future."

But Obama had signaled only a subtle change of course on the Keystone, not a 180-degree about face or a permanent decision.

"This announcement is not a judgment on the merits of the pipeline," he said. "I'm disappointed that Republicans in Congress forced this decision, but it does not change my Administration's commitment to American-made energy that creates jobs and reduces our dependence on oil. Under my Administration, domestic oil and natural gas production is up, while imports of foreign oil are down."

Now it was TransCanada that was left in the lurch. Without an application pending in Washington, the company had lost the loophole the Nebraska legislature had so carefully provided.

The day after Obama's rejection, Nebraska State Sen. Jim Smith stepped in to help with another pro-Keystone bill. LB 1161 circumvented what he called "the actions that occurred at the federal level that now jeopardize the agreement we reached last fall." It allowed TransCanada to get its project vetted by the Department of Environmental Quality, even if it no longer had a permit pending in Washington.

TransCanada immediately submitted documents for a slightly different route through Nebraska.

But the change in the route meant that the State Department's "final" environmental impact statement was now moot. A new, supplemental draft environmental impact statement would have to be done, and the whole rationale for the Keystone XL argued all over again.

This time, the examination of climate questions would have to be much deeper, if only to mollify the EPA. And that could take almost a year.

By slipping the legislative trap, Obama had succeeded in delaying the Keystone XL decision until after the 2012 presidential election.

TransCanada reacted by breaking the project into two segments. The southern segment, from Cushing, Okla. to the Gulf, didn't cross an international boundary, so it didn't need a presidential permit. TransCanada said it would file a new application with the State Department for the northern segment.

The 2012 campaign found the nation in a troubled mood over jobs and the economy. There was also a growing partisan divide over the role of federal regulations, which the Republicans said were the main thing holding down employment. In the Republican primaries, one candidate or another blasted the White House's environmental priorities, even pledging to abolish the EPA or the Energy Department. In a famous campaign blunder, Texas Gov. Rick Perry had a hard time remembering which one he wanted to do away with.

The environment played second fiddle to jobs. And climate change, it seemed, wasn't even in the concert house.

Obama argued that his environmental record and his all-of-the-above energy policies were creating, not destroying jobs. He said he supported TransCanada's plan to carve off the southern half of the Keystone XL project as a stand-alone enterprise.

In March, Obama traveled to Cushing and posed for a carefully orchestrated photo in front of a pile of pipes that TransCanada would be using to build the southern leg. He used the occasion to announce an executive order that would speed up permit approvals for domestic pipelines.

"Today, we're making this new pipeline from Cushing to the Gulf a priority," he said. "But the fact is that my administration has approved dozens of new oil and gas pipelines over the last three years, including one from Canada. And as long as I'm president, we're going to keep on encouraging oil development and infrastructure, and we're going to do it in a way that protects the health and safety of the American people."

Obama's itinerary that week showcased what had long since become his favorite slogan about energy and the environment: "all of the above." He said he wouldn't rule out any form of energy that would help give the country an adequate supply of affordable fuel. But he also promised to protect the environment and keep the United States on a path to meet the 17 percent reduction in greenhouse gas emissions he had pledged in Copenhagen.

Environmentalists were deeply suspicious of the all-of-the-above plan. They didn't want more money invested in infrastructure projects that encouraged fossil-fuel production.

"In expediting the southern portion of Keystone XL, President Obama is trying to have it both ways," Kim Huynh of Friends of the Earth, a campaigner against dirty fuels, told The Hill's E2-Wire blog. "The administration cannot purport to protect the climate while simultaneously bending over backward to allow a pipeline to the continent's biggest carbon bomb."

At one point on his energy tour Obama stood before an array of solar electric panels in sun-drenched Nevada and promised never to "walk away from the promise of clean energy." Then he pivoted to New Mexico's oil and gas fields, where dozens of rigs were pumping fossil fuels.

In May, TransCanada applied to the State Department for a permit to build the northern leg of the Keystone XL.

Republicans were furious at the seemingly endless delays the company had faced since it submitted its application in 2008. The Keystone's completion, should the work ever begin, was slipping into 2015 and beyond.

As TransCanada moved fast to build the southern section, as landowners dug in their heels against the Nebraska route, as TransCanada moved fast to build the southern section of the project, as Republicans tried again and again to ram a permit for the northern section through Congress, as Obama ducked and weaved around the issue, Sen. John Kerry had something else on his mind: the frustrating lack of progress toward a binding and comprehensive international climate treaty.

On June 19, on the eve of the Rio Earth Summit's 20th anniversary, he poured out his vexation in a long soliloquy on the Senate floor.

"Believe me – we've had our chances to act," he said, the despair unmistakable in his voice. "But every time we get close to achieving something big for our country, small-minded appeals to the politics of the moment block the way."

The pattern was "staggering for its irresponsibility," he said. Delay would only make it more difficult, more costly and, in the end, less likely to stave off the worst effects of climate change.

"We need people marching up the steps of the Capitol, pounding on the doors of Congress, demanding a solution to our climate crisis," he said. "We Americans need to face up to the climate change challenge—not just as individuals or separate interests, but as a nation with a national purpose."

Kerry was preaching to the choir, or at best to a C-SPAN audience. As is customary at such moments, only a few Senators stood by to listen to his harangue.

The subject of climate change wasn't raised by any moderators of the autumn presidential debates between Obama and his Republican opponent, Mitt Romney. And neither candidate made any effort to steer the debates in that direction.

Writing in The New York Times, John Broder commented, "Throughout the campaign, Mr. Obama and Mr. Romney have seemed most intent on trying to outdo each other as lovers of coal, oil and natural gas—the very fuels most responsible for rising levels of carbon dioxide in the atmosphere."

It took an act of nature to bring climate change to the political forefront that year.

On the evening of Oct. 29, Superstorm Sandy slammed into the Atlantic seaboard, flooding downtown Manhattan and the Jersey Shore and wreaking immense damage across the heavily populated states of the mid-Atlantic, New England and even deep into the Midwest.

The situation was so dire that New Jersey Gov. Chris Christie, a rising star in the Republican party, stood side by side with the president his party so hated.

"I've got 2.4 million people out of power," said Christie, praising Obama's leadership repeatedly after the two men toured a ruined beach community. "I've got devastation on the shore. I've got floods in the northern part of my state. If you think right now I give a damn about presidential politics then you don't know me."

The Nov. 1 cover of Bloomberg BusinessWeek screamed what many people were thinking: "It's global warming, stupid!"

That same day, the magazine's billionaire publisher, New York City Mayor Michael Bloomberg, an independent, endorsed Obama, calling him better suited than Romney to address the ever more evident problem of climate change.

"The devastation that Hurricane Sandy brought to New York City and much of the Northeast—in lost lives, lost homes and lost business—brought the stakes of Tuesday's presidential election into sharp relief," the mayor said in a Bloomberg View editorial.

"Our climate is changing. And while the increase in extreme weather we have experienced in New York City and around the world may or may not be the result of it, the risk that it might be—given this week's devastation—should compel all elected leaders to take immediate action."

Sandy's winds helped fill Obama's sails and its waves helped drown out Romney's voice. Obama won by a solid margin—5 million ballots and 126 Electoral College votes. His vindication would empower him to revive his climate agenda.

# 3

## THE SOCIAL COST

A week after his re-election, Obama stood at the podium in the White House pressroom and again spoke about climate change, this time with the chastened demeanor of a man who recognized his uncomfortable new status as a lame duck.

"I am a firm believer that climate change is real, that it is impacted by human behavior and carbon emissions," Obama said when a reporter asked about the lessons of Hurricane Sandy.

But he also said he was "pretty certain" there was no stomach in Washington for the "tough political choices" needed to deal urgently with the problem.

"Understandably, I think the American people right now have been so focused and will continue to be focused on our economy and jobs and growth that, you know, if the message is somehow we're going to ignore jobs and growth simply to address climate change, I don't think anybody's going to go for that," he said. "I won't go for that."

As Obama began his final four years in office, the question was whether he would persist in his tentative and ambiguous commitment to rein in global warming or launch a crusade against the obstructionists in Congress who had thwarted his every move.

He signaled his intentions in his Second Inaugural Address, when he elevated the climate problem from the realm of political horse-trading to the status of a moral imperative.

"We will respond to the threat of climate change, knowing that the failure to do so would betray our children and future generations," he said. "Some may still deny the overwhelming judgment of science, but none can avoid the devastating impact of raging fires and crippling drought and more powerful storms.

"The path towards sustainable energy sources will be long and sometimes difficult," he went on. "But America cannot resist this transition, we must lead it. We cannot cede to other nations the technology that will power new jobs and new industries, we must claim its promise. That's how we will maintain our economic vitality and our national treasure—our forests and waterways, our croplands and snow-capped peaks. That is how we will preserve our planet, commanded to our care by God."

In his State of the Union address a few weeks later, Obama brought that revival-tent inspirational tone back down to the world of brass-knuckle politics.

"I will work with anyone in this chamber," he told the assembled senators and representatives, "but I intend to fight obstruction with action."

Those fighting words included the struggle over climate change.

"If Congress won't act soon to protect future generations, I will," he declared. "I will direct my cabinet to come up with executive actions we can take, now and in the future, to reduce pollution, prepare our communities for the consequences of climate change, and speed the transition to more sustainable sources of energy."

Obama didn't stray from the all-of-the-above approach that favored fossil fuels alongside green energy. He said he would open up more public land for renewable energy, but also more offshore oil and gas reserves for drilling.

Still, climate activists were encouraged. Under a 2010 court settlement Obama was already obliged to regulate the uncontrolled burning of coal in electrical power plants, so they activists expected him, finally, to take that major step.

Beyond that, it was hard to know what to expect, particularly when it came to the Keystone XL. It was one thing to make promises about regulations that would take years to put into force, or to launch new research initiatives that might or might not pan out, and that Congress might or might not agree to pay for. It was quite another to unilaterally flex his executive-power muscles to kill the Keystone.

"We applaud his vow to prioritize innovative climate solutions—these are critical steps forward in the fight against climate disruption," Michael Brune, the executive director of the Sierra Club, said after the speech. "But that progress would be rolled back by more destructive oil drilling and gas fracking, and the burning of toxic tar sands."

The Sierra Club was so committed to stopping the Keystone that it had decided to join the campaign of civil disobedience against the pipeline, a tactic the 120-year-old organization had never before officially embraced. Brune said his group would push Obama "every step of the way."

Sen. Marco Rubio, an up-and-coming Republican from Florida, gave his party's response to Obama's address. It was a conservative manifesto that emphasized the virtue of fossil-fuel production and belittled the mounting evidence of climate change and the calls to do something about it.

"Let's open up more federal lands for safe and responsible exploration," Rubio said. "And let's reform our energy regulations so that they're reasonable and based on common sense. If we can grow our energy industry, it will make us energy independent, it will create middle class jobs and it will help bring manufacturing back from places like China.

"No matter how many job-killing laws we pass," he added, "our government can't control the weather."

Obama's recognition that the need to act on climate was more pressing than ever may have been controversial in Congress, but it was squarely in the mainstream of the world's established multilateral institutions.

One of the most measured voices on energy economics, the International Energy Agency, warned that long-lasting fossil fuel projects already on the drawing board would commit the world to a calamitous path. "The door is closing," said its chief economist. "I am very worried."

The World Bank had predicted that a 2-degree safe climate target was receding beyond reach and that a 4-degree warming would bring "unprecedented heat waves, severe droughts, and major floods."

The World Meteorological Office confirmed that the century's first decade had been the warmest in the global record book, fully half a degree warmer than the average of the 1960s, '70s and '80s. The year 2012 had been the warmest ever recorded in the United States.

"Unless we take action on climate change, future generations will be roasted, toasted, fried and grilled," said Christine Lagarde, managing director of the International Monetary Fund.

If anyone was impatient and frustrated with the decades of inaction on climate change, it was Sen. John Kerry, who was angling to succeed Hillary Clinton as secretary of state in Obama's second term.

It had been plain for years that Kerry wanted the job. He had been passed over at the start of the administration, when Obama gave Sen. Clinton the cabinet post as a way of unifying the Democratic Party. Now Kerry had a second chance.

But as Clinton prepared to leave office, it looked as if Kerry would lose out again. Susan Rice, the United Nations ambassador and an Obama confidante, was widely considered to be the front-runner.

Rice's impending ascension worried Keystone opponents. She didn't have Kerry's environmental credentials. In fact, she and her husband owned stock in TransCanada, the pipeline builder. She was expected to be in the same camp as Clinton, a presumed supporter of the pipeline who had Obama's ear every day.

But Rice's candidacy faltered when conservative Republicans mercilessly attacked her for parroting White House talking points about the deadly attack on an American diplomatic compound in Benghazi, Libya. In December 2012 she withdrew her name from consideration. Kerry immediately emerged as a candidate who could survive the scrutiny of the foreign relations committee, which he chaired, and the Senate as a whole.

Just days before Kerry's confirmation hearing, a majority of the Senate, including some Democrats, signed a letter urging Obama to approve the Keystone project swiftly. But the pipeline was mentioned only briefly when Kerry appeared before the committee, and he refused to be pinned down on any timetable for a decision, allowing only that the review should proceed apace.

Kerry didn't tip his hand even after he took over his palatial new office at Foggy Bottom at the end of January, with its ornate reception rooms resplendent in their antique décor. If he decided to shift the agency's posture on the Keystone, it would be a more delicate operation than moving a few pieces of colonial-era furniture.

Protests against the Keystone XL grew as the winter of 2013 turned the corner toward spring.

On Feb. 13, the Sierra Club's Brune made good on his promise to engage in civil disobedience. Along with several dozens of others he was arrested at a Keystone protest outside the White House.

Soon after, on the three-day Presidents Day weekend, busloads of protesters poured into the capital, and a crowd of more than 35,000 took over the National Mall. Obama wasn't there to see them, however. He was golfing in Florida with Tiger Woods and two Texas energy executives who were regular donors to Democratic campaigns.

Deep down, was the administration still in the thrall of the all-of-the-above, business-as-usual energy policy? For a clearer signal, environmentalists waited nervously for the State Department to release its next review of the Keystone's environmental implications, the 2013 Draft Supplemental Environmental Impact Statement, or DSEIS.

The National Environmental Policy Act, or NEPA, required the government to prepare a detailed statement of the environmental impacts that would result from any major federal action. The Obama administration had made it clear that those statements must now consider climate change along with traditional factors such as public health and wildlife habitat.

Recent court decisions had affirmed that this would mean more than simply looking at the carbon dioxide emitted during the building and operating of the pipeline. In one NEPA case, a court told the government to tally the greenhouse gas emissions from Mexican power plants before granting a permit for electric transmission lines that crossed the border. In another case, involving a railroad that was seeking government approval, a court asked for an accounting of the emissions produced by burning the coal the train would carry.

Despite this legal trend, other pipelines from Canada had been approved with scarcely a glance at this question. The Bush administration had ignored the question entirely in approving the first Keystone pipeline, and the Obama administration had sidestepped it in the case of the Alberta Clipper, saying the best way to control emissions was through cap-and-trade legislation or a global climate treaty. But now it was clear that Congress would not pass a broad climate law, and an international climate treaty seemed unlikely in the near future.

For years, the EPA, which by law supervises all federal NEPA studies, had been prodding the State Department to make a fuller accounting of how the global climate would be affected when all that Canadian tar sands crude, so heavily laden with carbon, was produced and burned. The latest environmental statement was expected to be the most exhaustive look to date at the overall carbon footprint of a pipeline that would carry more than half a trillion gallons of one of the planet's dirtiest fossil fuels to world markets over the next 50 years.

The long-awaited draft was released on a Friday afternoon. Instead of focusing on how much carbon dioxide would be added to the atmosphere if Keystone were approved, the State Department's analysts peered at the problem from the other end of the telescope. They asked what environmental gain would be accomplished if the Keystone XL were rejected.

After spending hundreds of pages gnawing on this counterintuitive bone, the State Department came up with basically the same answer it had reached in the 2011 impact statement: It wouldn't make much difference to the climate whether the Keystone XL was—or wasn't—built.

Even without the pipeline, tar sands production would proceed in the next decade or two as it had in the past, doubling or even tripling Alberta's output, the assessment said. Other pipelines would be built, east to the Atlantic, west to the Pacific, perhaps even north to the Arctic. The oil could be shipped to the United States by rail rather than pipe. It could go down river on barges. Somehow, as if drawn by gravity, Canada's bitumen would find its way to market.

In short, the planet's atmosphere would be no cleaner if the Keystone were denied.

John Kerry didn't comment publicly on the report, which had been in the works for almost a year before he joined the cabinet. He left Kerri-Ann Jones, an assistant secretary of state, to brief reporters.

"This paper does not come out one way or the other and make a decision about what should happen with this project," Jones said. "We want to make sure we serve the best interests of our country and so we are really taking a very thorough look and we're waiting for everyone to comment and to give us their feedback."

The pipeline's advocates were delighted with the State Department's findings. They had always shrugged off the project's importance to climate change, and now they had a document that said they were right. The Keystone was just one pipeline among many, they argued. Its 830,000 barrels a day of crude oil represented just a fraction of the U.S. oil market—barely one percent of the whole world's output.

"In terms of affecting climate change, [the Keystone] would truly be a drop in the bucket," said Dan Simmons, director of regulatory affairs at the Institute for Energy Research, which favors the pipeline and the increased development of fossil fuels generally. "Is the Keystone XL pipeline in the national interest? The environmental impact statement presents no information about why it isn't."

This was only a draft, subject to revision in the year to come, but Congressional Republicans welcomed it as if the jury had issued a final verdict.

The State Department's findings "confirm what we already knew—this pipeline is safe and in the best interest of the American people," said two powerful House Republican committee chairmen, Fred Upton of Michigan and Ed Whitfield of Kentucky. "There are no legitimate reasons not to move forward on the landmark jobs project."

Environmentalists disagreed.

The findings were "not in keeping with the letter or spirit of NEPA," said Pat Parenteau, an environmental law professor at the Vermont Law School. "It stands the whole concept of examining your actions on its head, it really does."

"The fundamental question for State should have been, will this pipeline lead to an increase in greenhouse gas emissions?" said Danielle Droitsch, director of the Canada project at the Natural Resources Defense Council. "We don't have to go through this circular, roundabout argument. It's just a really, really nice way to escape doing that analysis."

The State Department gave the public 45 days to file comments, up until April 22—Earth Day, as it happened. By law, those comments, along with insights provided by the EPA and other federal agencies, would have to be considered before the final impact statement could be produced. After that, the State Department would begin anew the national interest determination that it had suspended in the fall of 2011.

Environmental groups said they needed more time to prepare their rebuttals. They hadn't even received copies of all the materials the agency had relied upon, they complained. But the State Department refused.

A coalition of green groups began cranking out hundreds of pages of detailed criticisms of the report. Grassroots organizers circulated petitions and set up widgets on their websites to make it easy for members to send individual comments.

John Kerry steered clear of the work his department was doing on the Keystone line. Asked about it during an April appearance before the House Foreign Affairs Committee, he said, "I am staying as far away from that as I can now."

"It's not ripe," he added.

But Kerry continued to talk about the mounting evidence of climate change, described in one study after another and manifested by one extreme after another.

"The science is screaming at all of us and demands action," he said in an Earth Day message.

The effects of global warming were being felt in ever more spectacular ways: accelerating sea rise, disappearing glaciers and ice caps, drought, storm, flood, infestation and fire.

As spring arrived, an early fire season brought deadly conflagrations across the western states.

By September, the Yosemite region was ablaze in the third biggest fire California had ever seen. Forestry experts said there could be no doubt that these conflagrations were due in large part to climate change, because persistently warmer weather patterns were extending the fire season and producing steadily drier conditions. Models predicted that the fire problem would only worsen in the most vulnerable parts of the country.

That summer Arctic ice again melted at a near-record pace, if not as extreme as 2012. Scientists predicted the Northwest Passage would be open to summertime transit in just a few years.

Especially troubling was the milestone surpassed at Hawaii's Mauna Loa Observatory; for the first time, atmospheric concentrations of carbon dioxide rose above the 400 mark. It seemed to be going up about 2 units a year. At the current pace, the fateful mark of 450 parts per million was only two or three decades away.

"We have failed miserably," one of the Mauna Loa scientists told the Associated Press.

Something else was increasingly evident in the spring and summer of 2013—America's domestic energy supplies were growing faster than ever.

In January, deep within the bureaucratic machinery that was preparing the new environmental report on Keystone, Adam Sieminski, administrator of the U.S. Energy Information Administration (EIA), had given the State Department a memorandum about an early draft of the agency's annual energy report.

The EIA, the statistical and forecasting branch of the Energy Department, is sometimes criticized for its business-as-usual stance, but it calls the statistical shots as it sees them and stays clear of making policy judgments.

Sieminski's memo noted drily that the agency's new projection "reflects some important updates."

The supply of domestic crude oil was expected to rise from 5.7 million barrels a day in 2011 to 7.5 million barrels a day in 2019. That was 12 percent more than the agency's estimate a year earlier. After 2019, the EIA predicted output would drift back down as the drilling bonanzas played out.

For Sieminski, the encouraging data didn't change the agency's basic view that the U.S. would continue to need imported crude oil, or that Canadian oil sands production would continue to grow.

But oil and gas production was accelerating so fast that the EIA could scarcely keep up.

Just seven weeks later, Sieminski presented fresher numbers, from the agency's February short-term outlook, to a meeting of the Consumer Energy Alliance. On one slide, he showed a striking new graph. Drawn above the numbers he had shared with the State Department just the month before was a new dotted line predicting that U.S. oil production was going to explode even faster.

The monthly estimates that followed showed more astonishing gains.

In April, the United States Geological Service doubled its official estimate of the Bakken's recoverable reserves and nearby deposits, suggesting that domestic crude production might not tail off as soon as Sieminski had assumed.

In May, the EIA said it now expected domestic crude oil production to surge 20 percent from the start of 2013 to the end of 2014. An additional 1.4 million barrels of U.S.-produced oil would be available every day—twice as much as the Keystone line could carry from Canada.

"With this outlook, why would the United States need the controversial Keystone XL pipeline?" asked Earle Gray, the former editor of Oilweek magazine and author of several books about Canadian oil, in the Toronto Star.

"We do not really need the oil," said an editorial entitled "Pipeline to Nowhere," by Jerald L. Schnoor, editor-in-chief of Environmental Science and Technology, published by the American Chemical Society.

Ian Goodman, an economist working with the environmental groups as they prepared their comments on the Keystone review, said the new data should be factored into the State Department's calculations.

This "matters for evaluating KXL, since the emerging market realities are considerably less favorable for tar sands expansion," said Goodman, who has decades of experience analyzing oil markets.

EIA analysts even suggested that the refineries in the Gulf, custom-built for the kind of dirty oil that would flow through the Keystone system, might consider revamping their machinery to take advantage of the abundant crudes from Texas and North Dakota. Using the lighter U.S. oil would also significantly reduce the refineries' carbon footprint.

Throughout the next year, the startling new numbers continued to escalate, casting more doubt on the need for tar sands imports.

"The rate of increase in domestic production continues to surpass even the most optimistic forecasts," Sieminski testified before Congress in July.

Public comments on the draft EIS poured into the State Department by the millions.

At first, the agency said it wouldn't make them public. But after InsideClimate News filed a Freedom of Information Act request, the agency reversed course. It began publishing them in batches on regulations.gov, a public-access Web site the government maintains for such purposes.

In an age of electronic democracy anybody could have their say.

No sooner was the 3,000-page draft published on-line than this terse ricochet came back: "Please say no to the transcanada pipeline !! Joan Krueger Sent from my iPhone ; - ) ?"

Jennifer Sutton, of Phelps, N.Y., reminded Kerry that she had walked door to door for him when he ran for president in 2004. "The main reason I drove 16 hours north to a town I'd never visited and then spent 4 days knocking on doors (with my four year old son) was because you had shown your commitment to positive action on environmental issues," she wrote.

Many people cited climate change as their reason for opposing the project. In the nation's heartland, however, the possibility of a spill dominated the list of concerns.

"The Ogallala Aquifer is right at the surface where I grew up, exposed to the sky, fed by the creeks and lakes and rainwater of that region," wrote Christopher Gotschall, who lived in the Sandhills of Nebraska as a child. "The KXL export pipeline threatens the livelihood of my family in north-central Nebraska, threatens their neighbors, threatens the wildlife and livestock, the farms and ranches, threatens all that make the Sandhills their home."

As if to punctuate Gotschall's concerns, an ExxonMobil pipeline ruptured on March 29, 2013 and sent Canadian dilbit into the streets of a neighborhood of neat brick homes in Mayflower, Ark. Dozens of residents were forced from their homes.

One Keystone commenter sent the State Department a picture of a heavily oiled wood duck, a victim of the Mayflower spill.

The oil industry and Canadian politicians weighed in on the other side.

The premier of Alberta, Alison Redford, described her province as "North America's most responsible energy provider," and boasted of its "proud track record in developing some of the world's most progressive environmental initiatives."

The American Petroleum Institute and 13 other advocacy groups urged Kerry to accept the findings and move toward granting the permit.

"After more than four years of an unprecedentedly thorough review, it is time to move forward beyond the findings of this review and determine that this project is in our nation's interest," they said. "The environmental assessment is but one factor in making this determination. After spending over four years on the environment impact statement, it's certainly time to consider the other key factors in making the national interest determination, including energy security, foreign policy and economic impacts."

The groups said that the project would create tens of thousands of jobs across the economy, and add hundreds of billions of dollars to the U.S. economy over 25 years. (The number, large as it sounds, would add up to less than one-thousandth of the nation's Gross Domestic Product.)

To hear the industry tell it, the pipeline would make a significant contribution to jobs, economic growth, government tax revenues and international trade. The only exception to the rule: It would have no material effect on greenhouse gas emissions.

"U.S. demand for petroleum consumption will be the same whether we get that supply from Canada or less friendly sources," the trade groups argued.

Lawyers and other experts for a coalition of 13 environmental groups burned the midnight oil pulling together their opposition brief, complaining all the while that the State Department hadn't released some of the key studies underlying its analysis, in violation of federal regulations. They filed their brief at the last moment, on Earth Day.

The 200-page comment picked the draft apart in excruciating detail. It concluded that the State Department had violated NEPA because it hadn't conducted "a full assessment of the project's direct, indirect and cumulative impacts including its climate impacts."

"Perhaps the most glaring error," the groups said, "is the State Department's assertion that the tar sands will be developed at the same rate regardless of whether Keystone XL is built ... This assumption is flawed and unsupported, [and] is directly contradicted by nearly all sectors including the oil industry itself."

Ian Goodman, the group's economic consultant, concluded that the State Department's use of older data, along with other errors, rendered it "deeply flawed and not a sound basis for decision-making."

Goodman examined emerging crude oil markets, factors driving tar sands expansion, availability and costs of pipeline and rail transportation, and tar sands break-even costs. He found that the State Department analysis overstated the inexorable expansion of Canada's oil sands production, exaggerated the likelihood that the crude would be shipped by rail if the pipeline permit were refused, and wrongly concluded that the Keystone would have little or no effect on the future of Canada's oil sands.

"In reality, this large expansion is no longer so inevitable or even likely," his report said.

"...Building KXL will help to shore up the deteriorating profitability and prospects for tar sands expansion, so that more projects go ahead despite an otherwise increasingly challenging context," Goodman concluded. "Not building KXL will accelerate the shifts away from tar sands expansion by discouraging near-term project development and giving more time to emerging market realities (and other factors) to constrain future tar sands expansion."

The most anticipated comment, from the EPA, also came in at the last minute.

The EPA had criticized the State Department's earlier reviews for shortcutting the climate problem and questions regarding oil spills. This time, too, it rebuked the agency—if not quite flunking the report, issuing a verdict that it was still incomplete.

The EPA challenged several of the review's key assumptions, including its conclusion that dilbit could be easily moved by rail in the absence of pipelines.

The EPA also objected to the way the report addressed spills. Citing the lessons learned from the 2010 Michigan dilbit disaster, the EPA said the final EIS should "more clearly acknowledge that in the event of a spill to water, it is possible that large portions of dilbit will sink and that submerged oil significantly changes spill response and impacts."

One of the report's biggest omissions was that it had again, despite repeated requests, failed to put a dollar figure on the costs future generations would have to pay for global warming. If those costs were calculated, the EPA said, people could understand how much the supposed benefits of the pipeline today would be offset by costs imposed on future generations.

Over the pipeline's expected 50-year lifespan, the EPA said, the unusually dirty fuel that surged through it would release nearly a billion tons of carbon dioxide. The State Department, reasoning that the oil was going to be shipped with or without the pipeline, had glossed over the importance of these emissions.

"It is this difference in greenhouse gas intensity—between oil sands and other crudes—that is a major focus of the public debate about the climate impacts of oil sands crude," the EPA said.

TransCanada dismissed the EPA's criticism of the report.

"EPA's comments are somewhat surprising because EPA has been a cooperating agency throughout the four-plus year NEPA review of the Project," said Shawn Howard, a company spokesman. "As a result, the EPA—as well as almost two dozen local, state and federal agencies—have been intimately involved in the details of this review and are well aware of the four federal environmental impact statements that have already been published by the Department of State on this project. There are no 'new issues' identified in their letter."

In a letter to the State Department, TransCanada disputed the EPA's calculations of how much dirtier tar sands are than other sources of oil. The company also dismissed the EPA's recommendation that the review include an estimate of the costs society would ultimately have to pay for damages from global warming due to the extra emissions from the Keystone line—a calculation known to bureaucrats and economists as the "social cost of carbon."

"Any attempt at estimation of a social cost of carbon (SCC) must recognize the significant uncertainties and limitations related to that exercise," wrote Kristine Delkus, a company vice president. "Given its inherent uncertainties and limitations, a SCC analysis cannot be a determinative factor in agency decision making at this time."

As TransCanada saw it, the pipeline should not be judged according to the costs it might impose on future generations.

Pipeline supporters in Congress had run out of patience.

In May 2013, House Republicans pushed through a bill to force federal approval of the Keystone XL pipeline without further review, a tactic they had tried several times before. The bill waived several environmental laws and blocked potential court challenges to the project.

But the Republicans had over-reached this time. The bill passed, 241 to 175, but only 19 Democrats voted with the majority, compared to 69 who had joined a pro-Keystone vote a year earlier.

What might have changed the minds of so many Democrats?

Anna Aurelio, director of the Washington office of Environment America, a federation of state-based advocacy groups, said her group had tried hard to educate Congressional newcomers about the Keystone. Freshmen Democrats in the House overwhelmingly opposed the pipeline.

Also, some new points had been introduced in the debate. One was that the Canadian producers of the diluted bitumen the Keystone would carry aren't subjected to a crude oil tax that helps finance cleanup costs from spills. It was also pointed out that the refineries that would handle the Canadian crude are located in free trade zones and could export the products tax-free.

The Democrats might simply have been rallying to Obama's defense. "This bill is about seizing power from the president of the United States," said Rep. Bobby Rush, a Chicago Democrat.

Or they may have been swayed by the persistent, growing protests against the controversial pipeline.

"It's finally occurring to official Washington that Keystone is the No. 1 priority for the environmental movement, and we are beginning to see just who is willing to fight for the climate," Bill McKibben of 350.org, the environmental group that was leading the protests, told Reuters.

Rep. Nick Rahall of West Virginia, a Democrat who had voted with Republicans on other pro-Keystone legislation, said the bill was simply too extreme—"the right wing hijacked the bill."

"What right do the promoters of this bill have to jeopardize this pipeline with such a frivolous proposal?" Rahall demanded during the debate. "This is a bumper sticker bill. Ideology driven. Born of fancy, not fact. Jobs hang in the balance. An important supply of energy held hostage. This bill is a mockery. It boils down to this: right-wing politics trumping what is right, what is correct, and what is just for this pipeline to proceed through the permitting process. To be built. To put people to work.

"So let's get serious," he continued. "Let's dispense with the kindergarten tactics. Too much is on the line here. While the promoters of this bill play politics, I can assure them that this is no laughing matter in the heartland of America."

Democrats had tried to soften some of the bill's provisions, but Republicans argued against any revisions. They wanted an ironclad mandate that would cut red tape and force the president to approve the pipeline.

Rep. Pete Olson, a Texas Republican, said it would be possible to walk the entire length of the 1,702-mile pipeline 53 times in less time than the State Department had been reviewing TransCanada's application. "At least walking would be some sort of action," he said.

Like so many pieces of ideologically driven legislation, the bill was not taken up in the Senate.

※

As the State Department began to consider the arguments, the Energy Department quietly issued an obscure regulation that would help force the social cost of carbon into the Keystone debate.

The regulation, issued on May 31, 2013, involved microwave ovens.

Starting in 2016, microwave ovens would have to use between 50 and 75 percent less power—not when they were nuking someone's food, but when they were just standing by, plugged in, their digital displays glowing as they counted the hours to the next bag of popcorn or bowl of ramen.

The change might add a few dollars to the cost of each oven, the Energy Department conceded. But the energy savings over the lifetimes of millions of modern microwaves would save consumers the equivalent of $3.4 billion in today's money.

The energy-efficient appliances would also prevent emissions of 38 million tons of carbon dioxide from electric power plants. The agency said that would be like taking 12 million cars off the road for a year. It would also be like stopping the flow of tar sands oil through a Keystone-sized pipe for two years.

"The net benefit of emissions reductions will be about $1.2 billion," the department asserted.

To come up with this estimate, the Administration had used the "social cost of carbon" formula it had developed in 2010 to measure the future price society must pay for flooding, drought, wildfire or other damages that are expected to occur as a result of current emissions of carbon dioxide.

If the social cost of carbon "is a big number, then we ought to make great efforts to reduce greenhouse gas emissions," explained a white paper from the Stockholm Institute. "If it's a small number, then the case for reduction is weaker, and only easy or inexpensive changes seem warranted."

The formula had been used dozens of times before, for regulations involving automobile fuel efficiency, fossil fuel power plants, and other rules with implications for greenhouse gas emissions. But buried in the fine print of the microwave rule was a price tag for the social cost of carbon.

Until now, the price for a single extra ton of carbon dioxide emitted in 2020 was set at $26. But the figure used in the microwave rule was $43, a two-thirds increase.

Nobody can say for certain what a ton of carbon dioxide released this year will contribute to the bill that humankind will have to pay for damages from global warming 100 years or more into the future. The calculations depend on so many assumptions that valid estimates can vary by an order of magnitude, or even more.

The larger number was the result of new evidence cranked into the climate forecasting models in peer-reviewed literature, including additional climate change damages expected in the years ahead. It was in line with figures used by other countries and by corporations, including oil giants like Exxon and BP, to judge the costs associated with their own carbon footprints.

Several highly regarded experts in the field of environmental economics suggested that the administration's estimates were, if anything, far too low. They said the administration's economists were using too high a discount rate when translating future losses from global-warming disasters back into today's dollars—that, in effect, they were writing down the enormous future costs to just pennies on the dollar.

If the social cost of carbon was properly calculated, they said in Science magazine, it might well be double or triple the amount currently assumed by the Obama administration.

Energy economists and industry groups instantly recognized that the new number would make a big difference in all kinds of government decisions—possibly including the administration's calculation of the costs and benefits of the Keystone pipeline.

According to the EPA, the extra carbon dioxide emissions attributed to the pipeline could amount to 19 million tons a year for the 50 years of its estimated lifetime. That would put the ultimate cost of all that pollution at tens of billons of dollars—perhaps hundreds of billions.

Although the complex notion of the social cost of carbon barely registered with the public, it was impressive to see how quickly industry allies leapt into action against the administration's use of the calculation.

House Republicans called hearings and drafted legislation to block its use. Industry groups filed petitions and threatened litigation to reverse the administration's decisions. A conservative group, the Landmark Legal Foundation, petitioned the Energy Department to withdraw the microwave rule.

At a Congressional hearing, Republicans argued that the social-cost calculations had come out of a bureaucratic "black box." The uncertainties were far too great, they said, to justify expensive new greenhouse-gas regulations.

"The social cost of carbon will affect the cost of electricity, every home and business, the cost of our cars and trucks, the cost to heat our homes, the cost of food, the cost of every product that is manufactured and transported in America," Rep. James Lankford of Oklahoma said at a July 18 hearing. "This is no simple rule change with little effect; this has especially serious consequences for everyone on a fixed income and anyone with limited resources."

Howard Shelanski, a White House official from the Office of Management and Budget, testified that the social-cost-of-carbon calculation was a mainstream idea developed through careful, peer-reviewed research.

Without it, he said, government officials considering policies involving greenhouse gas emissions and climate change "would be saying, we don't care what the costs are for our grandchildren. We are going to impose those costs on future generations and not worry."

Rep. Tim Murphy of Pennsylvania introduced an amendment to limit the use of the social-cost formula in any EPA rule changes.

Rep. Shelley Moore Capito of West Virginia called the formula "nothing more than a gimmick used to circumvent Congress so that job-killing regulations and an anti-domestic-energy agenda can move forward."

On Aug. 1, every Republican voted for Murphy's amendment, while almost every Democrat voted against it.

Henry Waxman of California called the amendment "science denial at its worst. We are telling the EPA the cost of carbon pollution is zero. It's like waving a magic wand."

The amendment passed, but it went nowhere in the Senate, where Democrats held the majority.

The pipeline's opponents, many of them natural allies of Obama and Kerry, continued to pressure the administration in every way they could.

Dozens of prominent scientists issued a statement in May opposing the Keystone. Sixteen of them had won the prestigious Heinz Award in the Environment—a prize created by Teresa Heinz, Kerry's wife, to honor her first husband, the late Sen. John Heinz.

"Stopping the pipeline is necessary to ensure that the problem remains solvable—that we don't become irrevocably committed to emission trajectories that guarantee failure before we mobilize for success," the scientists said.

"There is a strain of fatalism among some opinion leaders regarding Keystone (characteristic of prevailing attitudes toward climate generally): 'Canada will develop the tar sands no matter what we do.' 'We'll get the oil from somewhere, so it might as well be North America.' 'They'll just find another route.'

"These objections are neither analytically defensible nor morally responsible. We can't do everything to address climate disruption, but as the world's biggest economy and the largest historic emitter, we can and should do a great deal. As a nation with unparalleled capacities for innovation and entrepreneurship, we can do even more. Facilitating accelerated investment in fossil fuel infrastructure is flatly inconsistent with this responsibility, and with the diplomatic effort to build our standing as an international leader and facilitator of global cooperation to tackle the climate challenge."

The scientists echoed the EPA's concerns about leaks along the Keystone's route.

"The pipeline will cross 1,073 surface bodies of water, numerous aquifers, wetlands and flood plains," they said. "... the EIS fails to justify why potential spills of tar sands crude are a 'small risk' and ignores the ongoing damage and extraordinary high cost of clean up of the 2010 spill in the Kalamazoo River in Michigan."

In another tactic, environmental groups asked for a moratorium on all new pipelines until safety rules could be overhauled. They urged the State Department to delay the Keystone decision until the investigation of the Pegasus rupture in Arkansas had been completed.

"The recent tar sands oil spill in Mayflower, Arkansas coupled with the fact that the July 2010 tar sands spill into the Kalamazoo River in Michigan is still not cleaned up almost three years later highlight the dangers of tar sands pipelines running through our communities and the lack of sufficient oversight and spill response capabilities," the environmentalists said.

The pipeline's supporters mounted their own campaign.

Alison Redford, the premier of the tar sands province of Alberta, led a lobbying effort that included federal cabinet members and Prime Minister Stephen Harper. They visited Washington frequently, launched an advertising campaign, and kept up a steady drumbeat for the pipeline project.

For years, Harper and Redford had defended the tar sands expansion by claiming that emissions per barrel of tar sands oil had been coming down. That was a key point in their lobbying campaign for the Keystone, meant to assuage any worry that the oil industry wanted to ship south via the Keystone would significantly increase Canada's carbon dioxide emissions. Washington bureaucrats commuting by Metrorail to Foggy Bottom or Capitol Hill could read the claim on advertisements posted in subway cars.

"The truth is that Alberta is home to some of the most environmentally friendly, progressive legislation in the world," Redford declared in an appearance at the Brookings Institution in April. "You wouldn't know that from the clamor of the debate."

Indeed, she said, "we're bringing our emissions down as far and as quickly as possible."

But the reality was not so simple. It was true that emissions per barrel of tar sands oil had declined during the industry's infancy. But since 2005, there had been little or no progress. If production doubled, per-barrel emissions would have to be cut in half for total emissions even to stay flat. Nothing of the kind was happening.

And Redford made another thing clear: Canada was intent on selling more and more tar sands crude.

"We don't see any reason why that is going to slow down," she said. "We see continuing global demand for the product. So we don't foresee any drop in production," with or without Keystone.

In the months that followed, liberal donors and former Obama campaign staff members and volunteers produced one letter after another imploring the administration to oppose tar sands expansion by rejecting the pipeline.

In May, 150 major Democratic donors sent a letter to Obama, urging him to reject the Keystone. The signatories included business leaders, philanthropists and celebrities—including clean-energy entrepreneurs Vinod Khosla, Jigar Shah and Steve Kirsch, long-time Obama bundler Wendy Abrams and actress Blythe Danner.

Evoking Abraham Lincoln's decision to fight for the 13th Amendment to abolish slavery, they called the Keystone XL Obama's "Lincoln moment."

"This decision more than any other will signal your direction, your commitment, your resolve. It is the biggest, most explicit statement you will make in this historic moment."

In June, about 150 of Obama's former campaign workers signed a letter orchestrated by billionaire Tom Steyer, a leading liberal campaign contributor who had made climate change his main cause.

"You can help cement your legacy as a climate champion by rejecting this pipeline," the letter said. "You already know all the reasons we can't afford this pipeline—that it will lock in gigatons of carbon pollution over the next four decades and that it could spill into our nation's most valuable water sources—we're just asking you to think of us when you make up your mind."

Waxman and Sen. Sheldon Whitehouse of Rhode Island, another climate hawk, sent a firmly worded letter to the administration in July.

"We are not just bystanders evaluating likelihoods over which we have no influence," they said. "We should not be investing in infrastructure and locking in higher emissions for decades to come."

# 4

## THE TIPPING POINT

On a steamy sunny day in June 2013, President Barack Obama stood in shirtsleeves before a throng of environmentalists, students and political leaders at Georgetown University to explain how he planned to seize the tiller of climate change policy.

The occasion had been advertised as the most comprehensive expression to date of Obama's climate policies—and the down payment on his promise to act alone if Congress did not.

"We don't have time for a meeting of the Flat Earth Society," Obama declared, his voice dripping with scorn and his brow with sweat as the mercury climbed to 94.

The White House had let it be known in advance that Obama would spell out the executive actions he intended to take unilaterally. At the top of the list were regulations to control carbon dioxide emissions from power plants. He was also prepared to encourage investments in solar and wind power, clamp down on methane emissions from natural gas production, invigorate research, mobilize foreign governments, phase out the powerful fluorocarbon class of pollutants, restrict international loans for coal projects, wean the military from fossil fuels, and set in motion one low-carbon project after another, large and small.

Nobody in the friendly crowd of invited guests expected any mention of the controversial Keystone XL pipeline. Some of them had been briefed in advance to that effect by White House aides. The 100 or so demonstrators that activist groups had deployed nearby had even scissored away the "No KXL" slogan from the bottom of the blue signs they carried whenever they shadowed the president at public events.

Obama opened by invoking the inspirational "Earthrise" view of the blue planet against the barren moonscape that the Apollo 8 astronauts had captured 25 years earlier. The evidence for climate change, he reminded his audience, has become as certain as the orbits of the spheres. The facts are there to see, and what lies ahead is increasingly predictable.

The president began laying out his new climate action plan, just as the crowd had been promised he would. But about a third of the way into the 50-minute presentation, he deviated from his prepared text and veered into forbidden territory—the Keystone XL.

"I put forward in the past an all-of-the-above energy strategy, but our energy strategy must be about more than just producing more oil," he said. "And, by the way, it's certainly got to be about more than just building one pipeline.

"Now, I know there's been, for example, a lot of controversy surrounding the proposal to build a pipeline, the Keystone pipeline, that would carry oil from Canadian tar sands down to refineries in the Gulf. And the State Department is going through the final stages of evaluating the proposal. That's how it's always been done.

"But I do want to be clear: Allowing the Keystone pipeline to be built requires a finding that doing so would be in our nation's interest. And our national interest will be served only if this project does not significantly exacerbate the problem of carbon pollution. The net effects of the pipeline's impact on our climate will be absolutely critical to determining whether this project is allowed to go forward. It's relevant."

It was a pivotal moment in the Keystone XL debate. For the first time, the president had publicly linked the decision about a major fossil-fuel infrastructure project with the threat of global warming. No such thing had happened in the Bush administration, and until now the Obama administration had also avoided making that connection.

People in the audience, and those tuning in remotely, reacted swiftly to the statement. One tweet from the crowd captured the mood: "I feel like we had 12 years of Bush, and we're finally starting the Obama administration."

But Obama's words were ambiguous. Was the president conceding that the tar sands were, as opponents liked to put it, an unacceptable carbon bomb? Or was he slyly endorsing the conclusion the State Department had drawn in its draft environmental impact statement—that a decision on a single pipeline couldn't make much of a dent in greenhouse gas emissions?

Nobody was sure.

The Toronto Star said "it sounded, note for note, like the death knell for Canada's Keystone XL pipeline."

Forbes magazine, on the other hand, said "any rational parsing" of the speech "can only suggest that the pipeline will be approved after all."

As Obama was speaking, a record-breaking flood 2,000 miles away was inundating the most populous city in Alberta, Canada's tar sands province. Fed by unusually rapid melting of the region's heavy upland snowpack, rivers in and around Calgary burst their banks and sent their waters coursing through commercial and residential neighborhoods.

Immediate damages ran into the billions of dollars, quickly establishing the flood as the most costly natural disaster in Canadian history. For days, the downtown headquarters of some of Canada's biggest oil and gas companies were shut down. Traders couldn't buy or sell western Canadian crude oil, including tar sands bitumen.

Prime Minister Harper and other conservative politicians glossed over any link to climate change as they toured their devastated constituencies.

"The stuff that I've read and commentary from scientists say that there is not a connection between weather events of this nature and broader climate issues," Jason Kenney, a cabinet member from Calgary, told the Canadian Broadcasting Corporation.

Canada's ruling Conservatives clearly didn't embrace Obama's thinking on the subject, which accepted the warnings of scientists linking extreme weather with man-made climate disruption. Harper, like Bush, had deep roots in the oil patch. His home province of Alberta was in many ways the Canadian analogue to Texas, and his approach to climate issues mirrored the Bush-Cheney agenda: undermine the science, defer meaningful actions to rein in carbon dioxide emissions, and accelerate oil-and-gas development as quickly as possible.

But others in Canada were growing alarmed.

In August, an internal government report stamped "secret" was delivered to one of Harper's top advisers. It said that Canada, like the United States, was already feeling the effects of climate change. The Arctic sea ice was disappearing, the permafrost was thawing and the same seasonal changes that had brought wildfires to the United States had spread insect infestations across Canada's western timberlands.

"It is likely that these conditions will be exacerbated as the climate continues to change in the future," said the document, which Postmedia News obtained using Canada's access-to-information laws. "These impacts pose increasing risks to infrastructure, water quality and quantity, coastal communities, natural resource industries, food security, human health and safety, and wildlife."

The challenges would grow in the coming years, the report said, so "planning ahead for climate impacts would be responsible risk management."

The report noted another nagging concern: Canada was straying from its emissions control targets for greenhouse gases. Another federal agency, Environment Canada, predicted annual emissions would rise to 734 million tons in 2020, far above Canada's Copenhagen pledge of 612 million tons.

The agency's reports didn't link the tar sands emissions problem to the Keystone XL. But if the extra CO2 from the dirtier fuel the pipeline carried amounted to roughly 20 million barrels a year, as the U.S. Environmental Protection Agency had estimated, the Keystone alone would account for one-sixth of the amount by which Canada would miss its Copenhagen pledge.

Throughout 2013, Harper and his industry allies lobbied hard to make their case for the pipeline. But Canada's overtures didn't seem to sway Obama.

"I meant what I said," he told two New York Times reporters a few weeks after his Georgetown speech. "I'm going to evaluate this based on whether or not this is going to significantly contribute to carbon in our atmosphere. And there is no doubt that Canada, at the sources in those tar sands, could potentially be doing more to mitigate carbon release."

If Canada took such steps, one of the reporters asked, could that offset concerns about the pipeline?

"We haven't seen specific ideas or plans," Obama said. "But all of that will go into the mix in terms of John Kerry's decision or recommendation on this issue."

Washington had sent signals before regarding Canada's tar sands emissions, and the Harper government had promised to pass new regulations. Now, again, there were hints that some kind of grand bargain might be in the works, perhaps as a quid pro quo for approving the Keystone.

Harper suggested as much in a letter to Obama that the CBC revealed in September. The full letter has never been released, but it apparently hinted that Canada would soon unveil new rules limiting emissions from gas, oil and tar sands projects. Reports circulated that Canada was considering a 40/40 proposal. Companies would have to cut emissions intensity by 40 percent or a pay a fee of $40 for each excess ton.

But the 40/40 formula fell woefully short of what was needed to make a real difference, according to the Pembina Institute, an environmental think tank with offices in Alberta.

Companies operating in Alberta had been paying such a fee for years, a maximum of $15 per ton on a fraction—typically 12 percent or less—of their annual emissions. But Pembina found that the fee adds just 10 cents to the cost of a barrel of tar sands oil, not nearly enough to discourage pollution. To do that, the government would have to impose a carbon tax on the order of $100 a ton, Pembina said.

Industry lobbyists resisted the 40/40 formula. In an internal memo written during negotiations with the government, they argued that the fee wouldn't make their business more palatable to environmentalists.

"The objection to the oil sands is ideological; not a concern that Alberta's current framework is not stringent enough," the memo said. "Put another way, if the 40/40 guidelines were enacted, oil sands opponents would claim that they too were insufficient."

Meanwhile, the Harper government's relations with environmental advocates and scientists were becoming strained. Canadian environmental groups were becoming louder and bolder. Working in concert with their American counterparts, they were putting unwelcome pressure on the oil patch regarding not only the Keystone, but also a pipeline being proposed in Canada, the Northern Gateway. It would run from Alberta to Canada's Pacific coast.

The Harper government denounced the groups as extremists.

His Conservative Party also began a deliberate and systematic unraveling of environmental and climate research budgets, defending its actions as a move to cut fiscal deficits. The party eliminated a quasi-official advisory panel, the National Round Table on the Environment and the Economy. It eliminated financing for research stations in the Arctic and monitoring networks that tracked power plant emissions. It closed the climate adaption group within the federal environmental agency. Climate research grants were slashed across the board. Thousands of students and faculty scientists marched through the streets in protest.

The Canadian Revenue Agency launched an audit of Canada's charities, focusing first on those concerned about tar sands development. If the CRA determines they violated restrictions on political advocacy, they could lose their charitable tax status, forcing them to pay taxes and potentially driving away donors.

The relationship between Obama and Harper, too, became strained as the Keystone review dragged on. Harper declared that he wouldn't take "no for an answer." At a joint news conference in Mexico in early 2014, however, Obama refused to say yes.

"I said previously that how Keystone impacted greenhouse gas emissions would affect our decision, but, frankly, it has to affect all of our decisions at this stage, because the science is irrefutable," the president said. "We're already seeing severe weather patterns increase. That has consequences for our businesses, for our jobs, for our families, for safety and security. It has the potential of displacing people in ways that we cannot currently fully anticipate, and will be extraordinarily costly."

While the United States deliberated over the Keystone, the Intergovernmental Panel on Climate Change issued the first in a trio of reports that would guide world leaders as they worked on a new treaty to be signed in Paris in 2015.

The IPCC now asserted with 95 percent certainty that greenhouse gases from human activities were behind the warming recorded in the 20th century. Each of the past three decades had been the hottest ever recorded. Significant warming was already locked into place because of past and ongoing emissions, and it was expected to continue for centuries to come.

The IPCC's most striking departure from past reports was its endorsement of a planetary carbon budget that established how much carbon dioxide the world could afford to emit.

Half of this carbon budget had already been used up, it said. Unless the use of fossil fuels was abruptly reined in, the other half would be consumed in the next two or three decades. After that, the world would have to figure out a zero-carbon energy future. Unless effective technology could be developed to capture carbon dioxide fumes and lock them away, vast amounts of fossil fuels would have to be left in the ground.

In a forceful lecture in November 2013, Angel Gurría, secretary general of the Organization for Cooperation and Development, cited the damages from Superstorm Sandy as an example of "how costly extreme events can be." Then he exhorted the group's members—which include the United States and Canada—to move toward "zero emissions" of carbon dioxide from burning fossil fuels.

"Whatever policy mix we cook up, it has to be one that leads to the complete elimination of emissions to the atmosphere from the combustion of fossil fuels in the second half of the century," he declared.

The world was "nowhere near" any such trajectory, he admitted. "Our dependence on fossil fuels appears to be unshaken."

The Royal Society, in a special issue of its magazine devoted to the world's oil supply and demand, concluded that if world leaders committed their countries to limiting warming to 2 degrees, tar sands oil could be the first fuel squeezed out of the global economy.

"Avoiding dangerous climate change requires the bulk of these resources to remain in the ground," the editors of the special issue wrote.

The world's most authoritative multilateral agencies, armed with the most up-to-date energy data, reached similar conclusions.

The World Bank, the International Monetary Fund, the Organization for Economic Cooperation and Development and its advisory International Energy Agency (IEA) made the same point. One economic model after another—by the IEA, by the Massachusetts Institute of Technology's climate project and others—showed that Canada couldn't possibly reduce its emissions enough to meet international obligations while at the same time developing the tar sands without restriction.

In its November 2013 annual World Energy Outlook, the IEA connected the Keystone and other new pipelines to the Canadians' conundrum. Growth in the oil sands industry depends on the construction of major new pipelines, including the disputed Keystone XL, the institute declared. The faster new pipelines are approved, the more rapid the increase in tar sands production will be over the next two decades, the IEA said.

Achieving the expansion the Canadian industry sought—the 5-million barrel-a-day goal first set in the days of the Bush administration—"is contingent on the construction of major new pipelines to enable the crude to be exported to Asia and the United States," the IEA said.

By linking the Keystone XL directly to increased oil sands production, the IEA handed fresh ammunition to the pipeline's critics.

Anthony Swift, an attorney in the international program of the Natural Resources Defense Council, said the IEA's conclusion contradicted the State Department's reasoning in its draft assessment of the Keystone, that the tar sands pipeline would have no material impact on the industry's expansion plans.

By the end of 2013, pipeline advocates had built a compelling rebuttal to many of the assumptions the State Department had relied on in its draft environmental study. It was a complicated case to articulate, though, involving complex analysis of market forces, a debunking of the argument that railroads could easily carry the Keystone oil if the pipeline were denied, and a sophisticated understanding of climate science and economics.

Two influential groups were honing the message. One, NextGen Climate, was the brainchild of Tom Steyer, a wealthy businessman who wanted to fight the pipeline politically. The other, the Center for American Progress, was run by Democratic insider John Podesta, a close Obama confidant.

Podesta and Steyer had published an op-ed article against the pipeline in 2012 and had been working in tandem ever since. Podesta considered the tar sands "polluting, destructive, expensive, and energy intensive."

In December, Steyer and Podesta sponsored a conference on the Georgetown University campus that was, in effect, a teach-in for activists striving to get the message across. It addressed one question: Could the pipeline pass the climate test? For a full day, experts hammered home the answer in detailed presentations.

The next week, the White House announced that Podesta would be brought into the West Wing as a special adviser, with climate change one of his main responsibilities.

Podesta wouldn't weigh in on the Keystone decision, the White House said, because the process was so far along and Podesta's views on the project were already known.

On January 31, 2014, the State Department issued its final supplemental environmental impact statement on the Keystone project. Assistant Secretary of State Kerri-Ann Jones emphasized that Kerry hadn't reviewed it.

"The secretary has not been briefed on this or read this, and I can't speculate for how he would read it," she told reporters. "I know that he is anxious to delve into it and he's going to look at it from all different perspectives."

The report's central conclusion, succinctly spelled out in the middle of thousands of pages of dense analysis, didn't reflect the spreading consensus among world institutions that most fossil fuels, and especially the dirtiest reserves, needed to be left in the ground.

Instead, it continued to view the Keystone in isolation from the big picture.

"Approval or denial of any one crude oil transport project, including the proposed project, is unlikely to significantly impact the rate of extraction in the oil sands or the continued demand for heavy crude oil at refineries in the United States," the report said, sounding much like a sound bite from the earlier reviews.

TransCanada called the report a major milestone toward the project's approval.

"We do know that our opponents will continue to oppose and make all kinds of claims," said Russ Girling, the company's president and chief executive. "But no matter how much noise they make, or how much misinformation they spread, the facts do support this project."

Environmental groups were outraged. In the outpouring of criticism, they made two points that laid the groundwork for possible litigation.

This report, like the others, had erred by looking at the Keystone XL in isolation, they pointed out. Shouldn't the State Department have at least considered the combined effect of the Keystone and the Alberta Clipper, which Enbridge was seeking to expand?

The first Keystone pipeline and the Alberta Clipper had been approved when federal climate legislation was moving through Congress, on the assumption that the nation would be reducing emissions through an overarching national policy. But with no such law on the horizon, the environmentalists said it was now time to start looking at the combined effects of the various pipeline projects.

The Sierra Club and other groups had made that point in a petition they filed just before the EIS was released.

"The Department cannot plausibly argue that other infrastructure projects are inevitable, and that it is powerless to affect the rate of tar sands development in Alberta, when it is simultaneously deciding whether to approve the second-largest cross-border tar sands pipeline proposal," said the petition, which asked for a broader review that would examine cumulative effects, as NEPA requires.

Pipeline opponents also questioned the report's underlying assumption that the world would fail to address climate change—that there would be no new treaty, no expanded commitment to reduce emissions even more in the years ahead.

Instead, the State Department had assumed a business-as-usual future—one in which no actions would be taken to control emissions and U.S. oil consumption would grow to as much as 19 million barrels a day.

That assumption was very different from the scenario the International Energy Agency had used to calculate what U.S. oil consumption would look like if the nation honored its climate commitments.

Oil consumption would have to drop from 17 million barrels a day in 2011 to just 10 million barrels a day in 2035, the IEA said. In other words, demand would have to be reduced by as much as the Keystone could carry—nine times over.

The next step in the permitting process was a 90-day comment period, where the public and all the interested agencies of the Obama executive branch could weigh in on whether the Keystone was in the national interest. Then the decision would go to Obama, via the State Department.

But once again, events in Nebraska threw a wrench into the works, provoked by a tiny local outfit called Bold Nebraska. The non-profit had long made common cause with ranchers and farmers directly affected by the project, and they had helped challenge the siting of the Keystone XL through their state.

In February State Judge Stephanie Stacy ruled in their favor.

The law that had expedited the project's revised route was unconstitutional, Stacy ruled, because it exempted TransCanada from review by Nebraska's independent regulator of public utilities.

The state's approval of the pipeline was nullified.

Unless the legislature passed yet another pro-Keystone law, or the state Supreme Court reversed Stacy's decision, or the utilities regulator approved the route, the Keystone no longer had a legally approved path through the state where stubborn local opposition had once before stopped the pipeline.

The IPCC's second and third reports, issued in the spring of 2014 were just as comprehensive and compelling as the first one, each alarm ringing more insistently than the last.

The second report looked at more than 10,000 peer-reviewed studies and said with more certainty than ever what NASA's James Hansen had been saying for a quarter of a century. Climate change has arrived, and all of the world's population will feel the effects. There is no longer any point in trying to decide whether one storm or another last year, one drought or another this year, can be tied directly to climate change. Superstorm Sandy and the Calgary floods, the Yosemite fires and the beetle infestations of the Canadian Rockies, are all part of a pattern that can no longer be denied.

The third report outlined what nations need to do to avoid the climate calamities described in the first two reports.

To keep warming within safe boundaries, worldwide carbon dioxide emissions would have to be 40 to 70 percent lower in the year 2050 than they were in 2010. Eventually, they must drop to zero.

The longer countries delay, the report warned, the more difficult—and more costly—it will be to reach the target.

The good news, the IPCC said, was that it is still possible for the world to change course and achieve its safe-climate objective. The process would be expensive and wouldn't avoid all the problems of climate change. But with a thorough transformation of the world's energy practices, it could still happen.

The prescription was tersely summarized by Ottmar Edenhofer, co-chair of IPCC.

"There is a clear message from science: To avoid dangerous interference with the climate system, we need to move away from business as usual."

Secretary of State Kerry issued a statement on the day the report was released.

"Read this report and you can't deny the reality: Unless we act dramatically and quickly, science tells us our climate and our way of life are literally in jeopardy," Kerry said.

"Denial of the science is malpractice. We need to match the urgency of our response with the scale of the science. The clock is ticking. The more we delay, the greater the threat. Let's make our political system wake up and let's make the world respond."

The question now was how Kerry's personal convictions might affect Obama's Keystone decision.

Ever since January 2014, when the final State Department report put the question of the Keystone's national interest officially on the front burner, speculation had run rampant about the president's decision and its timing.

Would the verdict come abruptly, after the 90-day internal review period—say, in the first week of May? Was the long saga at last at an end?

Then came yet another anticlimax, like so many that had come before.

On April 18, 2014, as Good Friday services were being held at Washington's National Cathedral and cars were jamming the highways out of town for the Easter weekend, the State Department announced another delay in the Keystone project.

Because the pipeline's route through Nebraska was still being reviewed by the state's Supreme Court, the State Department said it wouldn't be possible for all the federal agencies involved in the national-interest review to comment by May.

The delay meant the Keystone decision would likely be postponed until after the November mid-term elections. Construction would be delayed even further. There was no way TransCanada could get its first summer of work out of the way in 2014.

The delay meant something more subtle, as well.

The energy marketplace is changing so fast that even a six-month delay could bring more evidence that the United States doesn't need additional imports from Canada, at least not any time soon. Measured in barrels per day, the increase in U.S. oil output during 2013 and 2014 is already substantially more than the amount of oil Keystone can carry. Proven reserves of oil in the ground are gaining 15 percent a year.

Climate diplomacy, too, is barreling ahead at the speed of the train à grande vitesse bound for Paris.

There, in December 2015, the world's leaders are supposed to approve the final draft of a new climate treaty, one that will commit them all to reversing carbon pollution in the decades ahead. The present path, the IPCC scientists have told them, will soon push the world past the moment when dangerous levels of global warming cannot be escaped.

The timetable for the treaty is brisk, the deadline short. In September, Obama and other heads of state will meet at the United Nations to muster their willpower. In December, in Peru, negotiators will hammer out a first draft. Early in 2015, each nation must declare precisely what it's willing to accomplish on its own.

Scientists pondering the most serious risks of climate change sometimes talk about "tipping points," moments when the carbon dioxide building up in the atmosphere might cause extraordinarily swift disruption of the climate system. A melting permafrost belching out methane, the ocean's thermal layers inverting, the collapse of an entire coral reef ecosystem from acidification—however speculative these may seem in advance, or however slow in arriving, none are beyond possibility.

As hard as they are to predict, these scientific tipping points can be just as hard to recognize, even when such big changes are upon us. Even today there are those who pretend that the vanishing of the Arctic's summertime ice, or the onslaught of a historic drought, aren't yet well enough understood to be accepted as signals that the climate is already changing and that no part of the world will be untouched.

In politics and in policy-making, too, there are tipping points. Something changes, and an immovable object is overturned by an irresistible force. The income tax, women's suffrage, voting rights, marriage equality—the times simply changed.

Whoever wins the Keystone debate, the very fact that it has become so intensely charged suggests some kind of tipping point on climate change policy has arrived, with the Keystone its fulcrum.

If Obama rejects the Keystone, he will be opposing a powerful industry that has deep pockets and many allies, including most members of the U.S. Senate.

In early April, 2014, 11 Democrats wrote Obama urging him to approve it right away. Their letter was orchestrated by Sen. Mary Landrieu of Louisiana, chair of the Senate Energy Committee and one of several Democrats facing stiff challenges in the upcoming mid-term elections.

Landrieu and John Hoeven, a North Dakota Republican, had the support of 56 co-sponsors for a binding law that would ram the pipeline through. Four more Democrats would give pipeline advocates the 60 votes they need to move forward under Senate rules.

As this book was being published, it was not yet clear when—or if—the legislation might come to a vote. Its supporters were trying to attach it to a much less controversial bill, a bipartisan energy conservation measure popular with Republicans and Democrats and supported by environmentalists, business groups and the White House.

Senate Republicans weren't limiting their power play to the Keystone, though. They also wanted legislation to overturn the EPA's endangerment finding that put carbon dioxide under Clean Air Act regulations, reject the agency's proposed rules on coal fired power plants, and spurn other central elements of Obama's climate agenda.

In the House, Republicans are simultaneously working on legislation that would entirely eliminate the executive branch's power over the Keystone and similar projects. In some ways, this effort isn't just about climate change or energy policy. It is about Obama.

As the battle over climate action wears on, a new warning emerged via the latest National Climate Assessment, a broad, peer-reviewed, authoritative consensus of federal agencies and their scientific advisors. Published on May 6, its message was blunt and clear: Climate change can no longer be viewed as a distant threat. It has arrived. And so has the time to do something about it.

If Obama approves the Keystone, he will face the wrath of a reinvigorated environmental movement, including wealthy liberal donors and increasingly confrontational grassroots groups.

Close to 100,000 people have gone so far as to sign a "pledge of resistance" declaring themselves willing to risk arrest if Obama approves the Keystone. Mobilized by Credo Action, the political arm of the progressive phone company, they have been trained in nonviolent techniques of direct action and civil disobedience. "It was a huge effort to put behind an action we hope we never have to take," said Elijah Zarlin, one of the organizers.

On Earth Day 2014 and in the week that followed, a colorful group known as the Cowboy Indian Alliance encamped near the White House and demonstrated in full western regalia on the nearby National Mall.

Wizipan Little Elk, of the Rosewood Sioux, and Art Tanderup, a Nebraska farmer, waded into the Reflecting Pool, where a generation ago throngs had listened to Martin Luther King speak of his dream.

Thigh deep, they unfurled a banner of resistance.

"Standing in the water could get me arrested," it said. "TransCanada pollutes drinking water and nothing happens."

Obama's Keystone decision is about whether to break from the past in action and not just in rhetoric.

Almost 15 years ago, Bush and Cheney set forth on the path that leads to Keystone XL on the rationale that America's oil supplies were declining and its oil demand was increasing. They called the science of climate change uncertain. The idea of leaving most of the world's fossil fuel untouched was unthinkable.

Today, America's oil supplies are ample, its innovation unlimited, and its thirst for oil is being quenched. At the same time, the scientific understanding of dangerous, manmade climate change is irrefutable, making the need to reduce emissions of carbon dioxide from the combustion of fossil fuels inescapable.

For Obama to endorse Bush's "no-brainer" mentality now, based on these new facts and instincts, would be like reviewing the post-war evidence of Saddam Hussein's mythical weapons of mass destruction, counting up the trillion-dollar cost of the war in Iraq, looking at what has resulted and deciding to march on Baghdad all over again.

Just as that war defined Bush's legacy, the Keystone decision is central to Obama's.

He has John Kerry to advise him on the science and diplomacy, and John Podesta to weigh in on the politics and the fine print. Both are experts in the issue; both have made their personal commitments clear.

But they cannot make up his mind for him. They cannot turn the decision into a no-brainer. They cannot shield him from blame or share in any credit.

The permit is Obama's to sign, or not. And the pen he uses, or lays aside, will be a souvenir his children will inherit.

# ABOUT THE AUTHOR

John H. Cushman, Jr. has been a writer and editor in Washington, D.C. since 1978, principally with the Washington bureau of The New York Times. He has written extensively about energy, the environment, industry and military affairs, and has edited articles across the full spectrum of national and international policy. Mr. Cushman served on the Board of Governors of the National Press Club and was its president in 2000. He retired from The Times in 2013 after 27 years, and joined the staff of InsideClimate News, where he now writes the Carbon Copy blog.

To write this book, he conducted an exhaustive re-examination of the historical record, as documented in an enormous volume of complex documents. Mr. Cushman took a fresh look at these in the light of emerging science and economics of energy production, and also included a substantive discussion of the global carbon budget and continuing negotiations for a global climate treaty.

*InsideClimate News* is a Pulitzer Prize-winning, non-profit, non-partisan news organization that covers clean energy, carbon energy, nuclear energy and environmental science – plus the territory in between where law, policy and public opinion are shaped. Visit us at www.insideclimatenews.org and to make a fully tax-deductible donation, visit https://donatenow.networkforgood.org/1439575

An interactive version of this book, with photos, video, timelines and documents is available on our app, ICN Books.

Printed in Great Britain
by Amazon.co.uk, Ltd.,
Marston Gate.

could hear the others laughing on the shore at some joke or other, and I saw someone flip a cigarette-end high into the sky like a red star that curved over and extinguished itself at the rim of the sea. I was feeling more and more uncomfortable, and I was just about to call for assistance when, some twenty feet away from me, the sea seemed to part with a gentle swish and gurgle, a gleaming back appeared, gave a deep, satisfied sigh, and sank below the surface again. I had hardly time to recognize it as a porpoise before I found I was right in the midst of them. They rose all around me, sighing luxuriously, their black backs shining as they humped in the moonlight. There must have been about eight of them, and one rose so close that I could have swum forward three strokes and touched his ebony head. Heaving and sighing heavily, they played across the bay, and I swam with them, watching fascinated as they rose to the surface, crumpling the water, breathed deeply, and then dived beneath the surface again, leaving only an expanding hoop of foam to mark the spot. Presently, as if obeying a signal, they turned and headed out of the bay towards the distant coast of Albania, and I trod water and watched them go, swimming up the white chain of moonlight, backs agleam as they rose and plunged with heavy ecstasy in the water as warm as fresh milk. Behind them they left a trail of great bubbles that rocked and shone briefly like miniature moons before vanishing under the ripples.

(*My Family and Other Animals*, Gerald Durrell)

## 4 Section A. Factual Content

Read the extract and the questions carefully.
- Give exact answers.
- Write in short sentences.
- Use quotation marks when asked to quote.
- Watch for any special instructions.
- Read the sentence containing a word if you are asked to give its meaning in context.

In question 4, you are asked to find evidence. This will not be given directly. You will be looking for an activity only a strong swimmer would attempt.

1. Where were the other members of the writer's family when he first sighted the porpoises?
2. How many people were in the swimming party?
3. How did the writer's feelings change during his time in the water?
4. Quote from the extract evidence that he was a strong swimmer.
5. From the context of each of these words (underlined in the passage), choose its correct meaning.
   (a) languidly
      (i) without much energy
      (ii) fast
      (iii) clumsily
      (iv) angrily
   (b) pulsing
      (i) sparkling
      (ii) brilliant
      (iii) recurring in a rhythm
      (iv) heartbeat
   (c) extinguished
      (i) noteworthy
      (ii) distributed
      (iii) shone
      (iv) put out
   (d) ecstasy
      (i) delirium
      (ii) screaming
      (iii) extreme enjoyment
      (iv) annoyance

6. Decide whether each of the following statements is true or false.
   (a) The writer was the only person able to swim.
   (b) It was just dusk.
   (c) The porpoises were afraid of him.
   (d) The porpoises remained absolutely silent.
   (e) He swam along with the porpoises.
   (f) The sea cow was swimming beneath him.
   (g) The porpoises were swimming around him.
   (h) He had had an argument with the rest of his family.

7. What do you imagine the writer feared before he realised there were porpoises nearby?

8. Draw any scene the writer has described vividly.


### Word Meanings from Context

Very few words we use were learnt from looking them up in dictionaries. We heard them, guessed their meaning, heard them again, perhaps modified our guessed meaning, until they became part of our word use. In other words, we arrived at our understanding of them by learning them in the context of other words, by seeing how they fitted in with the words around them. By all means, use dictionaries as often as you can, but try also to work out from its context the possible meaning of each new word as you meet it.

9. Guess the meaning of the words underlined in the sentences below. Read each sentence carefully, then cover the underlined word with a finger, and read the sentence without it. Guess its probable or possible meaning, then look up the word in the dictionary. Don't expect 100 per cent success — but use the exercise to build your confidence in 'over-riding' (temporarily) words which might frighten you into believing a piece of writing is too difficult even to attempt.
   (a) The taxation investigator was expert in finding deliberate misstatements and other fraudulent methods of avoiding payment.

(b) At the injustice of the prison sentence, knowing her brother to be innocent, Ann leapt to her feet and shouted at the judge until she became <u>incoherent</u> with tears and anger.
(c) The old man suffered continual <u>harassment</u> from his snobbish neighbours who did not like his untidy house and garden.
(d) During war time many people disappeared from the records and their whereabouts remained <u>unresolved</u> for years.
(e) Although it was a brilliant invention, its use was limited to astronomers so that its manufacture for sale was not considered economically <u>viable</u>.
(f) <u>Horticulturists</u> aim at improving strains of fruit and vegetables so that the new varieties are more <u>prolific</u>.
(g) Bitterly he introduced his <u>successor</u> to the assembled shareholders.
(h) Large heavy luxury cars with high fuel consumption are becoming <u>obsolete</u>.
(i) Some naturally occurring plants that produce drugs appear <u>innocuous</u> in their natural environment.
(j) Prices for Saturday screenings seem <u>exorbitant</u> when compared to weekday prices.

10. After reading the passage, find words in it to correspond to each of the meanings listed below.

Man inhabits two worlds. One is the natural world of plants and animals, of soils and airs and waters which preceded him by billions of years and of which he is a part. The other is the world of social institutions and artefacts he builds for himself, using his tools and engines, his science and his dreams to fashion an environment obedient to human purpose and direction.

The search for a better-managed human society is as old as man himself. It is rooted in the nature of human experience. Men believe they can be happy. They experience comfort, security, joyful participation, mental vigour, intellectual discovery, poetic insights, peace of soul, bodily rest. They seek to embody them in their human environment.

But the actual life of most of mankind has been cramped with back-breaking labour, exposed to deadly or debilitating disease, prey to wars and famines, haunted by the loss of children, filled with fear and the ignorance that breeds more fear. At the end, for everyone, stands dreaded unknown death. To long for joy, support and comfort, to react violently against fear and anguish is quite simply the human condition.

To some extent, these reactions can be found in other animals. Birds weaving nests, beavers building dams, animals hunting in packs, are altering, 'improving' and safeguarding their lives and their environments in a purposeful way. Man shares with his animal forebears many of the responses required for dealing successfully with a natural world that is at once beneficial and destructive. The original brain was an efficient receiver of sensation and director of appropriate emotional and sensory responses in the rest of the body — running from fire, cowering from attacking beasts, embracing and love-making.

It is with the final stage in the brain's development that man, as man, begins to draw away from his ancestors. At some point, probably about a hundred thousand years ago, the forebrain became enormously larger and more complex. The skull of 'modern' man is three times larger than the so-called Australopithecine hominid who is generally thought to be man's immediate predecessor. This change in size and structure of man's brain increases his ability both to receive sensations and to engage in abstraction, reflection, forethought and the rational choice of goals. To serve abstract thought alone, we are told, the brain contains ten thousand times more components than the present generation of most complex computers. And the computer is yet to be invented that also smells, tastes, sees and touches, thus adding to its capacity for abstract thinking all the emotional richness and complexity of a total human response.

(*Only One Earth*, Barbara Ward and Rene Dubois)

(a) Complicated structure
(b) Relating to the senses
(c) Causing advantage to
(d) Withdrawing an idea from concrete evidence
(e) Causing weakness or illness
(f) Understanding
(g) Ancestors
(h) Strength
(i) Manmade objects
(j) Planning ahead

8  Section A. Factual Content

11. Sometimes a statement is difficult to understand because words are used that are not commonly known. Using a dictionary, restate the meaning of the following in simpler terms.
    (a) Alan facilitated his immediate incarceration by expedient prevarication.
    (b) A plenitude of lachrymose siblings proffered notification of Barbara's misdemeanors.

12. Sometimes people attempt to make what they are saying sound impressive by using long words, but using them wrongly. A famous character called Mrs Malaprop did this and mistakes like those she made are called *malapropisms*. Replace the underlined malapropisms with the correct words. (Use a dictionary if you need to.)
    (a) Most <u>hitchhikers</u> are desperate and carry hand grenades.
    (b) The best remedy for an <u>historical</u> person is to slap him over the face.
    (c) His pillow was stained with excess <u>guillotine</u>.
    (d) He practised for hours until he could perform a double somersault on his <u>tambourine</u>.
    (e) Before he could loosen the bolts, he needed to apply force to the steel <u>wench</u>.

# Unit 2. Surfing

We finally arrived at Honolulu. It was far more sophisticated than we had imagined with masses of hotels and roads and motor cars. We arrived in the early morning, got into our rooms at the hotel, and straight away, seeing out of the window the people surfing on the beach, we rushed down, hired our surf-boards, and plunged into the sea. We were, of course, complete innocents. It was a bad day for surfing — one of the days when only the experts go in — but we, who had surfed in South Africa, thought we knew all about it. It is very different in Honolulu. Your board, for instance, is a great slab of wood, almost too heavy to lift. You lie on it, and slowly paddle yourself out towards the reef, which is or seemed to me — about a mile away. Then, when you have finally got there, you arrange yourself in position and wait for the proper kind of wave to come and shoot you through the sea to the shore. This is not so easy as it looks. First you have to recognise the proper wave when it comes, and secondly, even more important, you have to know the *wrong* wave when it comes, because if *that* catches you and forces you down to the bottom, Heaven help you!

    I was not as powerful a swimmer as Archie, so it took me longer to get out to the reef. I arranged myself on my board and waited for a wave. The wave came. It was the wrong wave. In next to no time I and my board were flung asunder. First of all the wave, having taken me in a violent downward dip, jolted me badly in the middle. When I arrived on the surface of the water again, gasping for breath, having swallowed quarts of salt water, I saw my board floating about half a mile away from me, going into shore. I myself had a laborious swim after it. It was retrieved for me by a young American, who greeted me with the words: 'Say, sister, if I were you I wouldn't come out surfing today. You take this board and get right into shore now.' I followed his advice.

    Before long Archie rejoined me. He too had been parted from his board. Being a stronger swimmer, though, he had got hold of it

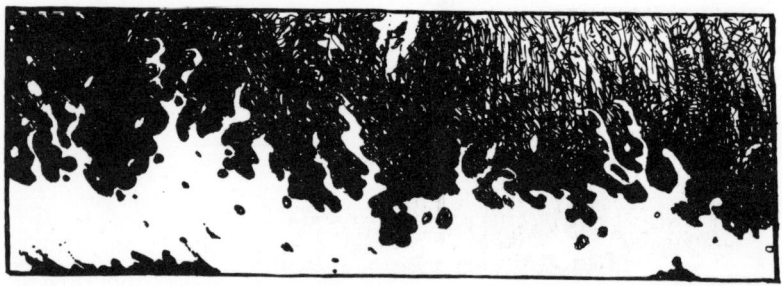

rather more quickly. He made one or two more trials, and succeeded in getting one good run. By that time we were bruised, scratched and completely exhausted. We returned our surf-boards, crawled up the beach, went up to our rooms, and fell exhausted on our beds. I said doubtfully to Archie: 'I *suppose* there is a great deal of pleasure in surfing?'

The second time I took the water, a catastrophe occurred. My handsome silk bathing-dress, covering me from shoulder to ankle, was more or less torn from me by the force of the waves. Almost nude, I made for my beach wrap. I had immediately to visit the hotel shop and provide myself with a wonderful, skimpy, emerald green wool bathing-dress.

All our days were spent on the beach and surfing, and little by little we learned to become expert, or at any rate expert from the European point of view. We cut our feet to ribbons on the coral until we bought ourselves soft leather boots to lace round our ankles.

I can't say that we enjoyed our first four or five days of surfing — it was far too painful — but there were, now and then, moments of utter joy. We soon learned, too, to do it the easy way. Most people had a Hawaiian boy who towed you out as you lay on your board, holding the board by the grip of his big toe, and swimming vigorously. You then stayed, waiting to push off on your board, until your boy gave you the word of instruction. 'No, not this, not this, Missus. No, no, wait — *now*!' At the word 'now' off you went, and oh, it was heaven! Nothing like it. Nothing like that rushing through the water at what seems to you a speed of about two hundred miles an hour; all the way in from the far distant raft, until you arrived, gently slowing down, on the beach, and foundered among the soft flowing waves. It is one of the most perfect physical pleasures that I have known.

(*Autobiography*, Agatha Christie)

Unit 2. Surfing    11

Answer in the shortest possible sentences. Include only what is needed to answer. Leave out everything else. Don't quote from the passage unless asked, and then use the exact words with quotation marks. The writer is Agatha Christie — use her name, not 'I', in your answers.

1. What was surprising about Honolulu to Agatha and Archie Christie?
2. Had they ever been surfing before?
3. What is likely to happen if a surfer tries to catch the wrong wave?
4. What three discomforts did they both suffer during their first morning's surfing? (Give details, but be brief.)
5. Quote the words that show Agatha had doubts about surfing. (Remember, quote only what is needed.)
6. What extra precaution was necessary in Honolulu to avoid being badly cut while in the water?
7. What helped make surfing less exhausting for tourists?
8. How did the Hawaiian boy get the board out into deep water?
9. Quote a sentence which shows that Agatha ultimately became quite expert and enjoyed surfing.
10. What two pieces of evidence suggest these events happened rather a long time ago?

The next two questions ask for your opinion, *not* answers to be found in the passage.

11. What makes people enjoy surfing?
12. List all the sporting activities you know in which speed is a factor.

## Unit 3. Red Indian Heritage

How can you buy or sell the sky? The idea is strange to us. If we do not own the freshness of the air and the sparkle of the water, how can you buy them? Every part of this earth is sacred to my people. Every shining pine needle, every sandy shore, every mist in the dark woods, every clearing and humming insect is holy in the memory and experience of my people. The sap which courses through the trees carries the memories of the red man.

The white man's dead forget the country of their birth when they go to walk among the stars. Our dead never forget this beautiful earth, for it is the mother of the red man. We are part of the earth and it is part of us. The perfumed flowers are our sisters; the deer, the horse, the great eagle, these are our brothers, the rocky crests, the juices in the meadows, the body heat of the pony, and man — all belong to the same family.

So, when the Great Chief in Washington sends word that he wishes to buy our land, he asks much of us. The Great Chief sends word he will reserve us a place so that we can live comfortably to ourselves. He will be our father and we will be his children. So we will consider your offer to buy our land. But it will not be easy. For this land is sacred to us.

The shining water that moves in the streams and rivers is not just water but the blood of our ancestors.

If we sell you land, you must remember that it is sacred, and you must teach your children that it is sacred and that each ghostly reflection in the clear water of the lakes tells of events and memories in the life of my people. The water's murmur is the voice of my father's father. The rivers are our brothers, they quench our thirst. The rivers carry our canoes and feed our children.

If we sell you our land, you must remember and teach your children that the rivers are our brothers and yours, and you must henceforth give the rivers the kindness you would give any brother. We know that the white man does not understand our ways. One portion of land is the same to him as the next, for he is a stranger who comes in the night and takes from the land whatever he needs. The earth is not his brother, but his enemy, and when he has conquered it, he moves on. He leaves his fathers' graves behind and he does not care. He kidnaps the earth from his children, and he does not care. His father's grave and his children's birthright are forgotten. He treats his mother, the earth, and his brother, the sky, as things to be bought, plundered, sold like sheep or bright beads. His appetite will devour the earth and leave behind only a desert.

I do not know. Our ways are different from your ways. The sight of your cities pains the eyes of the red man. But perhaps it is because the red man is a savage and does not understand.

There is no quiet place in the white man's cities. No place to hear the unfurling of leaves in spring, or the rustle of an insect's wings. But perhaps it is because I am a savage and do not understand. The clatter only seems to insult the ears.

And what is there to life if a man cannot hear the lonely cry of the whippoorwill or the arguments of the frogs around a pond at night? I am a red man and do not understand.

The Indian prefers the soft sound of the wind darting over the face of a pond and the smell of the wind itself cleansed by a mid-day rain, or scented with the piñon pine. The air is precious to the red man, for all things share the same breath. The white man does not seem to notice the air he breathes. Like a man dying for many days, he is numb to the stench.

But if we sell you our land, you must remember that the air is precious to us, that the air shares its spirit with all the life it supports. The wind that gave our grandfather his first breath also receives his last sigh. And if we sell you our land, you must keep it apart and sacred, as a place where even the white man can go to taste the wind that is sweetened by the meadow's flowers.

So we will consider your offer to buy our land. If we decide to accept, I will make one condition: the white man must treat the beasts of this land as his brothers. I am a savage and I do not understand any other way.

I have seen a thousand rotting buffaloes on the prairie, left by the white man who shot them from a passing train.

I am a savage and I do not understand how the smoking iron horse can be more important than the buffalo that we kill only to stay alive.

What is man without the beasts? If all the beasts were gone, man would die from a great loneliness of spirit. For whatever happens to the beasts soon happens to man. All things are connected. You must teach your children that the ground beneath their feet is the ashes of our grandfathers. So that they will respect the land, tell your children that the earth is rich with the leaves of our kin. Teach your children what we have taught our children, that the earth is our mother. Whatever befalls the earth befalls the sons of the earth. If men spit upon the ground, they spit upon themselves.

This we know: the earth does not belong to man: man belongs to the earth. This we know. All things are connected like the blood that unites one family. All things are connected.

Whatever befalls the earth befalls the sons of the earth. Man did not weave the web of life: he is merely a strand in it. Whatever he does to the web, he does to himself.

Even the white man, whose God walks and talks to him as friend to friend, cannot be exempt from the common destiny. We may be brothers after all. We shall see. One thing we know which the white man may one day discover — our God is the same God. You may think now that you own him as you wish to own the land; but you cannot. He is the God of man and his compassion is equal for the red man and the white. The earth is precious to him, and to harm the earth is to heap contempt on its creator. The whites too shall pass: perhaps sooner than all other tribes.

Contaminate your bed, and you will one night suffocate in your own waste. But in your perishing you will shine brightly fired by the strength of the God who brought you to this land and for some special purpose gave you dominion over this land and over the red man.

That destiny is a mystery to us, for we do not understand when the buffalo are all slaughtered, the wild horses are tamed, the secret corners of the forest heavy with the scent of many men, and the view of the ripe hills blotted by talking wires. Where is the thicket? Gone. Where is the eagle? Gone. The end of living and the beginning of survival.

(Chief Seattle's Speech)

When asked to quote another person, you should give exactly the words used, enclosing them in quotation marks. You should never quote only a fragment of what was said, as this may be misleading. At the same time, quote only as much as is needed.

Unit 3. Red Indian Heritage 15

1. Read the passage carefully several times, then quote words which:
   (a) indicate the Indians' puzzlement over the ways of white men,
   (b) show the Indians' disapproval of the whites' treatment of land,
   (c) words that show the importance to the Indians of their ancestors' graves.
2. You may be asked the author's ideas without using his words. In your own words:
   (a) How does the Indian see the idea of selling and buying land?
   (b) What condition does the chief set upon selling his land?
   (c) How does the Indian regard all living things?
3. Sometimes a writer is misquoted in one of the following ways:
   (i) it may be claimed that he said or meant more than he actually did say or mean, or

16  Section A. Factual Content

   (ii) his words, taken out of the context of the rest of the passage, may be made to sound foolish or take on a different meaning from that which he intended.

   Explain how each of the following quotes or comments is misleading.
   (a) The Indian is mainly interested in little things like 'every shining pine needle' and 'humming insect'.
   (b) The Indian was silly enough to think a train was a 'smoking iron horse'.
   (c) The Indian's hearing was acute enough to hear sounds such as 'the unfurling of leaves in Spring'.

4. When choosing how much of a passage to quote, be sure that you do not distort what the writer said.

   Quote from the extract evidence for each of the following:
   (a) That a suggestion had been made in Washington to create Indian reserves.
   (b) That the Indians do not understand the white man's killing of animals just for pleasure.
   (c) That the Indians believe God had a purpose in sending the white men to take over their land.

5. Often, leaving out a word or two changes the meaning of a sentence quite crucially. Which of the following is misquoted?
   (a) 'This shining water that moves in the streams and rivers is not water but the blood of our ancestors.'
   (b) 'The wind that gave our grandfather his first breath also receives his last sigh.'
   (c) 'The whites too shall pass: perhaps no sooner than all other tribes.'

6. Sometimes the tone of a sentence contains sarcasm or may be suggesting subtly something quite different from the words. Read each of the sentences below and comment on what the chief intended his reader to understand.
   (a) 'He will be our father and we will be his children.'
   (b) 'But perhaps it is because the red man is a savage and does not understand'.
   (c) 'We may be brothers after all. We shall see.'

Note. For a very long quotation, give the first few words, then indicate the middle section by a row of dots and write the last few words to end the quotation. Don't forget the last inverted commas.

## Unit 4. Tidal Waves

The term *tidal wave* has had an ominous sound in Hawaii since April 1, 1946. My own experience on that day may serve to introduce the discussion of tidal waves, or *tsunamis*. At that time my wife and I were living in a rented cottage at Kawela Bay on northern Oahu. On the previous day, a Sunday, the beaches and reefs were swarming with people and the cottages alive with activity. Fortunately, almost everybody left to go back to Honolulu that night. Early the next morning we were sleeping peacefully when we were awakened by a loud hissing sound, which sounded for all the world as if dozens of locomotives were blowing off steam directly outside our house. Puzzled, we jumped up and rushed to the front window. Where there had been a beach previously, we saw nothing but boiling water, which was sweeping over the ten-foot top of the beach ridge and coming directly at the house. I rushed and grabbed my camera, forgetting such incidentals as clothes, glasses, watch, and pocketbook. As I opened the door I noticed with some regret that the water was not advancing any further but, instead, was retreating rapidly down the slope.

By that time I was conscious of the fact that we might be experiencing a tsunami. My suspicions became confirmed as the water moved swiftly seaward, and the sea level dropped a score of feet, leaving the coral reefs in front of the house exposed to view. Fish were flapping and jumping up and down where they had been stranded by the retreating waves. Quickly taking a couple of photographs, in my confusion I accidentally made a double exposure of the bare reef. Trying to show my erudition, I said to my wife, 'There will be another wave, but it won't be as exciting as the one that awakened us. Too bad I couldn't get a photograph of the first one.'

Was I mistaken? In a few minutes as I stood at the edge of the beach ridge in front of the house, I could see the water beginning to rise and swell up around the outer edges of the exposed reef; it built higher and higher and then came racing forward with amazing velocity. 'Now,' I said, 'here is a good chance for a picture.' I took one, but my hand was rather unsteady that time. As the water continued to advance I shot another one, fortunately a little better. As it piled up in front of me, I began to wonder whether this wave was really going to be smaller than the preceding one. I called to my wife to run to the back of the house for protection, but she had already started, and I followed her just in time. As I looked back I saw the water surging over the spot where I had been standing a moment before. Suddenly we heard the terrible smashing of glass at the front of the house. The refrigerator passed us on the left side moving upright out into the cane field. On the right came a wall of water sweeping toward us down the road that was our escape route from the area. We were also startled to see that there was nothing but kindling wood left of what had been the nearby house to the east. Finally, the water stopped coming on and we were left on a small island, protected by the undamaged portion of the house, which, thanks to its good construction and to the protecting ironwood trees, still withstood the blows. The water had rushed on into the cane field and spent its fury.

Unit 4. Tidal Waves 19

My confidence about the waves getting smaller was rapidly vanishing. Having noted that there was a fair interval before the second invasion (actually fifteen minutes as we found out later), we started running along the emerging beach ridge in the only direction in which we could get to the slightly elevated main road. As we ran, we found some very wet and frightened Hawaiian women standing wringing their hands and wondering what to do. With difficulty we persuaded them to come with us along the ridge to a place where there was a break in the cane field. As we hurried through this break, another huge wave came rolling in over the reef and broke with shuddering force against the small escarpment at the top of the beach. Then, rising as a monstrous wall of water, it swept on after us, flattening the cane field with a terrifying sound. We reached the comparative safety of the elevated road just ahead of the wave.

There, in a motley array of costumes, various other refugees were gathered. One couple had been cooking their breakfast when all of a sudden the first wave came in, lifted their house right off its foundation, and carried it several hundred feet into the cane field where it set it down so gently that their breakfast just kept right on

cooking. Needless to say, they did not stay to enjoy the meal. Another couple had escaped with difficulty from their collapsing house.

We walked along the road until we could see nearby Kawela Bay, and from there we watched several more waves roar onto the shore. They came with a steep front like the tidal bore that I had seen move up the Bay of Fundy at Moncton, New Brunswick, and up the channels on the tide flat at Mont-Saint-Michel in Normandy. We could see various ruined houses, some of them completely demolished. One house had been thrown into a pond right on top of another. Another was still floating out in the bay.

Finally, after about six waves had moved in, each one apparently getting progressively weaker, I decided I had better go back and see what I could rescue from what was left of the house where we had been living. After all, we were in scanty attire and required clothes. I had just reached the door when I became conscious that a very powerful mass of water was bearing down on the place. This time there simply was no island in back of the house during the height of the wave. I rushed to a nearby tree and climbed it as fast as possible and then hung on for dear life as I swayed back and forth under the impact of the wave. Like the others, this wave soon subsided, and the series of waves that followed were all minor in comparison.

After the excitement was over, we found half of the house still standing and began picking up our belongings. I chased all over the cane fields trying to find books and notes that had been strewn there by the angry waves. We did, finally, discover our glasses undamaged, buried deep in the sand and debris covering the floor. My waterproof wristwatch was found under the house by the owner a week later.

'Well,' I thought, 'you're a pretty poor oceanographer not to know that tsunamis increase in size with each new wave.' As soon as possible I began to look over the literature, and I felt a little better when I could not find any information to the effect that successive waves increase in size, and yet what could be a more important point to remember? You can be sure that since then those of us who have investigated these waves in the Hawaiian Islands have stressed this danger, and I was most happy to find recently at a local island store a tidal-wave warning that emphasized the crescendo to be anticipated in future disasters. Nowadays, also, there are tidal-wave warning alarms that send out alerts either when reports of earthquakes under the ocean indicate dangerous possibilities, or when early waves arrive

## Unit 4. Tidal Waves 21

at other islands along the general route, or when the tide begins to fluctuate in an abnormal fashion. The importance of these warnings can be seen when it is noted that most of the 159 people who were lost during the 1946 *tsunami* could have saved their lives by running from the scene to higher ground when the waves first began. The Hawaiians are early risers, and being always attuned to the varying moods of the ocean, almost everyone was conscious of a sudden diminution of the noise of the breakers when the sea withdrew. Most people ran to see the strange sight of the reefs being laid bare, and many went out on the reefs to pick up the stranded fish. The 1957 *tsunami* was almost as destructive to property in Hawaii as that of 1946, but thanks to the warning system no lives were lost. I was shocked to learn that another house in which I had vacationed was destroyed by the 1957 waves.

(*The Earth Beneath the Sea*, F.P. Shephard)


Identify which one or more of the following re-states facts given in the extract.

1. The first indication of the coming tidal wave was:
   (a) the deserted beaches,
   (b) the unusual sound made by the water,
   (c) water rapidly approaching,
   (d) an exposed reef on which the locals were collecting stranded fish.

2. (a) Between 1946 and 1957 there had been many tidal waves in Hawaii.
   (b) Since 1946 Hawaiians have restricted shoreline building to safe areas.
   (c) Since 1957 nothing has been done to ensure no lives are lost in future tidal waves.
   (d) Since 1957 warning systems for tidal waves have been greatly improved.

3. (a) The writer drowned.
   (b) The writer's wife drowned.
   (c) The wave killed all the fish in the water.
   (d) Many people drowned.

4. (a) The writer did not immediately realise the danger.
   (b) The writer and his wife had experienced tidal waves before.
   (c) The writer knew the next wave would be worse.
   (d) The writer's wife was caught by the water.

5. (a) The writer wanted to photograph the waves.
   (b) The writer went to warn others.
   (c) The writer immediately realised the danger.
   (d) The writer wrecked his camera trying to take a photograph of the wave.

6. (a) The best safety measure is to seek higher ground.
   (b) There is at least an hour between waves so that organised evacuation is possible.
   (c) There is only a minute between waves so there is little chance of escape.
   (d) The local Hawaiians knew what to expect and how to reach safety.

7. (a) The waves do not recede but merely take the water higher.
   (b) Each wave is successively stronger than the last without any break in the pattern.
   (c) Each tidal wave is followed by a significant drop in the level of the water.
   (d) There are smaller waves between the larger tidal waves.

8. (a) Their house floated out into the bay.
   (b) The author escaped the second wave only by climbing a tree, surrounded by water.
   (c) Their house was the only one undamaged by the waves.
   (d) Some of their possessions were left unharmed and undisturbed.

9. (a) The tidal wave struck on a Sunday.
   (b) The tidal wave of 1946 occurred at night.
   (c) The tidal wave of 1946 occurred on April Fools' Day.
   (d) The tidal wave had been predicted for some time.

10. (a) Tidal waves can be turned back by most buildings.
    (b) Tidal waves are much slower than normal waves.
    (c) Tidal waves sometimes reach a height of 800 feet.
    (d) Tidal waves contain many tonnes of water.

## Re-Statement

11. Communication is a two-way process. Before you accept or reject what any writer is claiming, check that *he* has presented his statement clearly and that *you* have grasped his meaning. Only then can you judge the value of what he is saying.

    Clearly re-state the following in your own words, without changing the meaning. Try to use no more words than the original.
    (a) With few exceptions, throughout Australia, all traffic must proceed on the left-hand side of the road.
    (b) The continent of Australia is now surrounded by water, although once this was not so.
    (c) When cats are let loose in country areas, they must kill for food and consequently some native animals are declining in numbers.
    (d) It is becoming increasingly difficult for school-leavers to choose careers that are unlikely to change drastically within their working lives.
    (e) Because the days of the week occur in a fixed pattern, it is possible to calculate what day of the week any future date will be.
    (f) Growing orchids is an exciting pastime which everybody can experience and enjoy.
    (g) John Jones is not really a very nice person.
    (h) The great Australian pastime of watching sport is a waste of effort.
    Which statement did you find difficult? Discuss the reason why.

12. Re-statement becomes more difficult whenever you want to disagree! However, a reasonable person needs first to understand exactly what another writer is saying, even if he wishes to oppose his point of view.

    Re-state the following without changing the meaning.
    (a) Old people have better manners than young people. (D. Crepit)
    (b) Classical music is far more exciting to listen to than the Top Ten. (Beethoven)
    (c) Everybody should be made to learn at least two languages other than his native tongue. (Dick Tator)

(d) If there were no doctors and no hospitals, there would be very few sick people. (Health Crank)
(e) If I count the dog's kennel and the shed where I keep my guinea pigs, our house has more rooms than yours. (Sue Perior)

13. Choose one of the statements above. Beginning with the words, 'I disagree with ...', comment upon why you disagree. First answer by arguing against what was originally stated, then add your own comments, if any, on the matter.

# Unit 5. Whaling

The settlers turned to fishing to eke out their dwindling food supply, and they fished with reasonable success in the teeming waters of Sydney Harbour. John Palmer, purser of the *Sirius*, noted in June 1789 that 10,476 pounds of fish had been eaten in ten weeks. The Commissary issued a ration of six pounds of fish as a substitute for one pound of salt pork.

The food situation was so serious that even the civil and military officers took turns in going out for the night in the fishing boats. The problem was that the nets and fishing tackle they had brought with them soon began to decrease from normal wastage and wear and tear. Fishing brought them into regular contact with the Aborigines, who also fished in the harbour, and a convict ropemaker was instructed to spin fishing line from the bark of trees used by the Aborigines for that purpose and also to make a seine or net in the Aboriginal style. By such improvisations they managed to keep going.

The settlers' first contact with whales came in July 1790, and it was disastrous. A midshipman and three marines, fishing from a flat-bottomed boat off Bradley's Head, were pursued by a huge whale. They attempted to distract it by throwing their hats, food bags, and fish out of the boat, but it chased them relentlessly and at last dived under the boat and threw it into the air. The boat broke up and all the men except one marine were drowned.

Two months later a party visited Manly Cove, where 'at least 200 Indians' were cutting up a dead whale and cooking its flesh on fires lit around the carcass. They cut up the whale with shells fixed to the end of their throwing sticks, and asked the white men for hatchets to make the work easier.

The colonial whaling industry began in 1791 when the whaling ships *Britannia*, *William and Ann*, *Mary Ann*, *Salamander*, and *Matilda* arrived in Sydney Harbour. They were bound for the whaling grounds off South America, and had been chartered to carry convicts and stores to Sydney on their way. They saw many whales on the approaches to Sydney and set off in pursuit of them as soon as they had landed their cargoes, but with indifferent success.

Whalers did not return to Sydney until 1799, mainly because the East India Company claimed a monopoly over all British trade in the Pacific and Indian oceans. The British Government opened Australian waters for whale fishing in 1801, but Ebor Bunker, who had commanded one of the first five whalers, came back to Sydney in 1799 and made a successful cruise in nearby waters.

After 1801 there was a regular traffic of whalers from Britain to Australia. They carried stores to sell in the colony and when that part of their trading was finished they set off on whaling cruises. Whales were plentiful and most ships returned home with holds full of casks of whale oil. Whaling has been described as Australia's first industry.

Whale hunting was a dangerous trade. When a whale was sighted the 'mother ship' lowered two or three of the long narrow boats known as whalers or whaleboats, crewed by five or seven oarsmen, a steersman who steered with a long oar, and the harpooner. The crews rowed them at backbreaking pace in pursuit of the whales, with the harpooner standing in the bows of each boat ready to throw his lance. This had a wooden shaft tipped with a long steel point, forged into a razor-sharp barb at the end. The end of the shaft was attached to about 100 metres of thin line, neatly coiled into a tub. The whaleboat had to row very close to the whale before the harpooner could 'sink' his lance, and as soon as the whale felt the stabbing impact of the barb it look off at tremendous speed. Sometimes it would tow the boat for miles, or sound deeply and then leap out of the water, while the boat's crew hung on grimly. At last, when the whale tired and lay motionless on the water, they could approach again so that the harpooner could give it a finishing stroke with another 'iron.' Occasionally a skilful harpooner would kill a whale with the first blow of his lance. The amount of fight that a whale put up depended very much upon how deeply it was wounded to begin with.

When the whale lay dead on the water the boatmen faced the long task of towing it back to the ship, and then they had to cut it up with sharp-edged flensing spades. Whaling was gruesome work and its principal object was to strip the whale of its blubber: the insulating fat lying beneath the thin skin. When the blubber from a single whale was 'tried,' i.e. boiled down, it supplied up to 100 casks of whale oil. In the days before the discovery of petroleum, whale oil was a valuable cargo because it was the most favoured lamp oil as well as

Unit 5. Whaling 27

being useful as a lubricant and for medicines.

Apart from deepsea whaling, there was a vigorous trade in bay whaling. This was the earliest type of whale hunting, practised centuries ago in the northern hemisphere. Various types of whales often cruise close inshore and even into rivers or estuaries, and the bay whalers kept a keen lookout for approaching schools. As soon as they were sighted the lookout passed the word to boats' crews waiting on the beach, who launched their boats and set off in pursuit of the whales. When they had made their kill they towed the whales ashore and cut them up on the beach, where the blubber was melted down in huge iron kettles.

Bay whaling was practised all around the Australian coasts from

## Section A. Factual Content

Sydney to Hobart and from South Australia to Fremantle. Among the most famous whaling entrepreneurs was Benjamin Boyd, who set up an elaborate whaling station at Twofold Bay and ran it as one of his numerous business enterprises. By 1841 there were thirty-five bay whaling stations in Tasmania, employing about 1,000 men, and a large number of whales were killed and landed at Portland in Victoria and Victor Harbor in South Australia. Contemporary accounts refer to the Aborigines who besieged the landed carcasses, slashing off chunks of juicy whalemeat exposed when the blubber was stripped off. The greater part of the huge animals went to waste. In those days of tightly corseted ladies there was a substantial market for the light, springy bone, which was cut into strips to 'bone' the corsets, but a great part of the bone and most of the whalemeat was burnt or thrown back into the sea. The proximity of a whaling station showed Australia's earliest examples of air pollution, with great clouds of greasy smoke drifting across the bush from the try-fires under the pots and the atmosphere reeking with melting blubber and burning or rotting flesh.

(*Early Australian Crafts and Tools*, Lorna Ollif)

1. Below is a series of statements. From the information given in the passage, decide whether each statement is true or false. Write 'can't tell' if the passage doesn't give enough information.

    Don't give your own view on the matter unless you are asked for it. (Unless the writer gives enough evidence for his conclusions, don't answer 'true' on the basis of other information you happen to have.)

    (a) Whaling required courage and skill.
    (b) The Aborigines also hunted whales in boats.
    (c) The English settlers first called the Aborigines by another name.
    (d) Whaling became a continuous industry from 1791.
    (e) Only the whale oil was used.
    (f) Whales were only attacked when they were surrounded by boats.
    (g) Food was scarce in the early days of the colony.
    (h) Whaling stations would be unpleasant places to work in.
    (i) Whaling was an important industry in early New South Wales.

Unit 5. Whaling 29

(j) Whales can attack boats.
(k) The harpoon was fired from the main-deck of the largest ship.
(l) Most whales were killed instantly.
(m) The early settlers never copied any crafts of the Aborigines.
(n) Only British ships came to trade.
(o) Even in the early days, people were concerned at the lessening numbers of whales.
(p) Arthur Phillip was the first governor of New South Wales.
(q) Ship owners earned their profits in more ways than one in the early colonial days.
(r) Whale oil was considered cheaper than petrol in 1841.
(s) People were concerned about pollution from the earliest days in the colony.
(t) The second incident involving sailors and whales ended in success for the sailors.

2. Answer each of the following questions in about six lines.
   (a) What is your opinion of hunting whales today?
   (b) How is today's situation different from the days written about in the extract?

3. It isn't always easy to decide if a statement is true or false. We need all the evidence before we can decide. With only some of the facts, use 'possibly' or 'probably' true or false, or 'can't tell' if there is insufficient evidence.
   Choose, from the range below, conclusions for these statements:

   False ... Possibly false ... Probably false ... Can't tell ... Possibly true ... Probably True ... True.

(a) All bells have a pleasant sound.
(b) No animal can survive for a year without food or water.
(c) My aunt has long whiskers.
(d) Today is my birthday.
(e) I have two left feet.
(f) $2 + 2 + 2 + 2 + 2 + 2 + 2 + 2 + 2 = 18.$
(g) Lions are born small and grow larger.
(h) I know a horse that can sing.
(i) Widows always live longer than their husbands.
(j) Twins always look exactly the same.
(k) There is a tribe in Africa that hasn't been discovered yet.

## Unit 6.  Railroading

I ran out into the yards, jumping dark rails, heavy switches, and darting among the blind cars. A string of black ones were moving backwards in the wrong direction. I mounted the side and went over the top, and down the other side, and took a risk on scrambling between another string at the hitch. I could just barely see, it was so dark. The cars were so blended into the night. But, all at once, I looked up within about a foot of my face, and saw a blur, and a light, and a blur, and a light, and I knew that here was one going my way. I watched the light come along between the cars, and finally spotted an open top car, which was easier to see; and grabbed the ladder, and jumped over into a load of heavy cast-iron machinery. I lay down in the end of the car, and rested.

The train pulled along slow for a while. I ducked as close up behind the head end of the car as I could to break the wind. Pretty soon the old string got the kinks jerked out of her, and whistled through a lot of little towns. Then we hit a good fifty for about an hour, and started up some pretty tough grade. It got colder higher up. The fog turned into a drizzle, and the drizzle into a slow rain.

I imagined a million things bouncing along in the dark. A quick tap of the air brakes to slow the train down, and the hundred tons of heavy machinery would shift its weight all over me. I felt so soft and little. I had felt so tough and big just a few minutes ago.

The lonesome whip of the wind sounded even more lonesome when the big engine joined in on the whistling. The wheels hummed a song, and the weather got colder. We started gaining altitude almost like an airplane. I pulled myself up into a little ball and shook till my bones ached all over. The weather didn't pay any more attention to my clothes than if I didn't have them on. My muscles drew up into hard, leathery strings that hurt. I kept a little warmer by remembering people I'd known, how they looked, faces and all, and all about the warm desert, and cactus and sunshine growing everywhere; picturing in my mind something friendly and free, something to sort of blot out the wind and the freezing train.

On a big slope, that went direct into Bakersfield, we stopped on a siding to let the mail go by. I got off and walked ten or fifteen cars down the track, creaking like an eighty-year-old rocking chair. I had to walk slow along the steep cinder bank, gradually getting the use of myself back again.

I was past the train when the engineer turned the brakes loose, give her the gun, and started off.

I'd never seen a train start up this fast before. Most trains take a little time chugging, getting the load swung into motion. But, setting on this long straight slope, she just lit out. Running along the side, I just barely managed to catch it. I had to take a different car as mine was somewhere down the line. In a few minutes the train was making forty miles an hour, then fifty, then sixty, down across the strip of country where the mountains meet the desert south of Bakersfield. The wind blew and the morning was frosty and cold. Between the two cars, it was freezing. I managed to mount to the top, and pull a reefer lid open. I looked in, and saw the hole was filled with fine chips of new ice.

I held on with all of my strength, and crawled over and opened up another lid. It was packed with chipped ice, too. I was too near froze to try the jump from one car to the next, so I crawled down the ladder between two cars — sort of a wind-break — and held on.

My hands froze stiff around the handle of the ladder, but they were getting too cold and weak to hold on much longer. I listened below to five or six hundred railroad wheels, clipping the rails through the morning frost, and felt the windy ice from the refrigerator car that I was hanging onto. The fingers of one hand slipped from around the handle. I spent twenty minutes or so trying to fish an old rag out of my pocket. Finally I got it wound around my hands and, by blowing my breath inside the cloth for a few minutes, seemed to be getting them a little warmer.

The weather gained on me, though, and my breath turned into thick frosty ice all over my handkerchief, and my hands started freezing worse than ever. My finger slid loose again, and I remembered the tales of the railroaders, people found along the tracks, no way of telling who they were.

If I missed my hold here, one thing was sure, I'd never know what hit me, and I'd never slide my feet under that good eating table full of hot square meals at the big marble house of my rich aunt.

The sun looked warmer as it came up, but the desert is cold when it is clear early in the morning, and the train fanned such a breeze that the sun didn't make much difference.

That was the closest to the 6 x 3 that I've ever been. My mind ran back to millions of things — my whole life was brought up to date, and all of the people I knew, and all that they meant to me.

(*Bound for Glory*, Woody Guthrie)

1. What were the dangers and disadvantages of the first carriage Woody Guthrie chose? Of the second?
2. How did he try to take his mind off his discomfort?
3. What evidence indicates that it was a very dark night?
4. What physical stress did he suffer?
5. Colloquialisms are expressions commonly used by a group of people or in a particular location. Find three examples and give their Australian equivalents.
6. In your own words, what is meant by:
   (a) good eating table,
   (b) some pretty tough grade,
   (c) give her the gun,
   (d) a string of black ones,
   (e) the closest to the 6 x 3?
7. Which of the following are implied in the account?
   (a) The author had committed some crime.
   (b) He had very little money.
   (c) He was a coward.
   (d) What he was doing was illegal.
   (e) Others were in the same difficulties.
   (f) He had a poor education.
8. Quote two examples of the author's ability to make his experience clearer by using comparisons.
9. Quote an example of his tendency to exaggerate. Does it spoil his writing in your opinion?

## Generalisations

10. Whenever we make a statement that applies the same comment to a number of individual cases, we generalise. In conversation we often say 'always' when we mean 'most times', or 'all' when we mean 'most' or 'some'. Try to be exact in how general you make your statements. Use words like 'probably', 'some', 'might', 'perhaps' whenever you want to state a conclusion about a number of cases where there might be some exceptions.
    Which of the words best applies in each of the following?

    all    most    some    a few    none    no

    (a) .... roses have thorns.
    (b) .... dogs bark.

(c) .... flowers have strong perfume.
(d) .... public libraries contain many books.
(e) .... crimes deserve hanging.
(f) .... schools should have compulsory attendance.
(g) .... registered doctors are uneducated.
(h) .... belief is worth giving up your life for it.
(i) .... pilots are women.
(j) .... cars use fuel.

11. Re-write the following, changing words that are too extreme.
    (a) Everybody loves Australian Rules football.
    (b) Nobody could ever beat the champion.
    (c) None of the people moved a muscle; they were petrified.
    (d) The man was a success with everybody he met.
    (e) It is impossible to remember all the history we've had this term.
    (f) You always eat too much.
    (g) All your relatives are peculiar.
    (h) You must love ice-cream; everybody does.
    (i) The hurricane destroyed everything in its path.
    (j) I have never told a lie.

12. Write statements which everyone would accept, beginning with:
    (a) All men
    (b) No adults
    (c) Everybody
    (d) Most girls
    (e) Some air
    (f) A few idiots.

13. Write statements of your own including the following words:
    (a) occasionally
    (b) seldom
    (c) never
    (d) certainly
    (e) probably
    (f) possibly
    (g) may
    (h) might
    (i) often

# Section B
# Descriptive Passages

# Unit 7. The Island

The first rhythm that they became used to was the slow swing from dawn to quick dusk. They accepted the pleasures of morning, the bright sun, the whelming sea and sweet air, as a time when play was good and life so full that hope was not necessary and therefore forgotten. Towards noon, as the floods of light fell more nearly to the perpendicular, the stark colours of the morning were smoothed in pearl and opalescence; and the heat — as though the impending sun's height gave it momentum — became a blow that they ducked, running to the shade and lying there, perhaps even sleeping.

Strange things happened at midday. The glittering sea rose up, moved apart in planes of blatant impossibility; the coral reef and the few, stunted palms that clung to the more elevated parts would float up into the sky, would quiver, be plucked apart, run like rain-drops on a wire or be repeated as in an odd succession of mirrors. Sometimes land loomed where there was no land and flicked out like a bubble as the children watched. Piggy discounted all this learnedly as a 'mirage'; and since no boy could reach even the reef over the stretch of water where the snapping sharks waited, they grew accustomed to these mysteries and ignored them, just as they ignored the miraculous, throbbing stars. At midday the illusions merged into the sky and there the sun gazed down like an angry eye. Then, at the end of the afternoon, the mirage subsided and the horizon became level and blue and clipped as the sun declined. That was another time of comparative coolness but menaced by the coming of the dark. When the sun sank, darkness dropped on the island like an extinguisher and soon the shelters were full of restlessness, under the remote stars.

(Lord of the Flies, William Golding)

1. Find three 'colour' words from the passage, and use each in a sentence of your own.

Unit 7. *The Island* 37

2. Re-state in your own words what appeared to happen to:
   (a) the sea,
   (b) the coral reef,
   (c) the palms,
   (d) the land masses.

3. What effect does the writer achieve by suggesting movement of these things?

4. Look up and copy out from your dictionary the meaning of each of the following:
   (a) whelming
   (b) impending
   (c) momentum
   (d) blatant
   (e) illusions
   (f) subsided
   (g) mirage

5. Write two contrasting sentences in your own words, one for morning and one for afternoon, describing what the island was like. Include the reaction of the boys. ['They' in the passage comprise a group of boys who survive a plane wreck on an island.]

6. Writers use similes to draw attention to the similarity between objects. Usually the word 'like' is a pointer for a simile. Complete, by adding the missing half of each of these similes this writer uses.
   (a) .... (would run) like rain-drops on a wire.
   (b) Land flicked out like ....
   (c) The sun gazed down like ....
   (d) .... like an extinguisher.

7. In using 'menaced', 'restlessness', 'remote' and similar words, what does the writer indicate about the boys' future on the island?

## Similes and Metaphors

8. We often borrow the idea of one thing to help describe another. Sometimes the idea is stated simply:
   - Freshly washed sheets as white as snow
   - A mind as sharp as a needle
   - A dancer light as thistledown.

Sometimes the idea involves more detail.
- The dusty road writhed like a snake.
- The old horse sagged like a couch with broken springs.
- The drivers of the three damaged cars circled each other like dogs about to attack.

Such similarities are called similes.

Complete your own similes, with a second new idea.
(a) The old man's boots were like ....
(b) As the shark attacked the boat, the water was like ....
(c) The women at the bargain counter fought like ....
(d) The town hit by Cyclone Robyn looked like ....
(e) The people battled on like ....
(f) The huge motorbike roared like ....
(g) The horror film was like ....
(h) My father's temper is like ....
(i) Her empty purse was like ....
(j) They panicked like ....

9. Pick out two ideas being likened in these:
    (a) The champion's javelin was a rainbow as it arced in the sunlight.
    (b) The cattle had eaten every blade of grass, so that the ground, parched and cracked by drought, became a giant jig-saw puzzle.
    (c) From a distance the crowds, so tightly packed, were hundreds and thousands jumbled together.
    (d) The walking black toadstool was the stooping minister, with his umbrella pulled down over his shoulders.
    (e) Curled up in the hammock, the little fat man was a parcel in a stringbag.
    (f) The pile of dirty dishes loomed — a mountain to be conquered.
10. Notice that in exercise 9 one thing is claimed *to be* another, not just like it. We call such expressions metaphors. Make up six metaphors of your own. (Remember to leave out the words 'like' or 'as'.)
11. Match the pairs below.
    (a) a twisted piece of driftwood    an unexpected visitor
    (b) a telephone ringing             a cradle
    (c) a rocking chair                 a disused spider web
    (d) lashing hail                    a torture chamber
    (e) dentist's waiting room          a skeleton
    (f) a long lecture                  a round of gunfire
    (g) tangled hair                    a prison sentence
    (h) a snail                         an igloo
12. Write similes or metaphors for these:
    (a) homework
    (b) a lizard
    (c) television
    (d) beetroot

## Unit 8. Nightmare

At last, to my unspeakable relief, something woke me. And what was it that had suggested the tremendous tumult? Merely the branch of a fir-tree that touched my lattice, as the blast wailed by, and rattled its dry cones against the panes! I listened doubtingly an instant; detected the disturber, then turned and dosed, and dreamt again: if possible, still more disagreeably than before.

This time, I remembered I was lying in the oak closet, and I heard distinctly the gusty wind, and the driving of the snow; I heard, also, the fir-bough repeat its teasing sound, and ascribed it to the right cause: but it annoyed me so much, that I resolved to silence it, if possible; and, I thought, I rose and endeavoured to unhasp the casement. The hook was soldered into the staple: a circumstance observed by me when awake, but forgotten. 'I must stop it, nevertheless!' I muttered, knocking my knuckles through the glass, and stretching an arm out to seize the importunate branch; instead of which, my fingers closed on the fingers of a little, ice-cold hand! The intense horror of nightmare came over me: I tried to draw back my arm, but the hand clung to it, and a most melancholy voice sobbed, 'Let me in — let me in!' 'Who are you?' I asked, struggling, meanwhile, to disengage myself. 'Catherine Linton,' it replied shiveringly (why did I think of *Linton*? I had read *Earnshaw* twenty times for Linton). 'I'm come home: I'd lost my way on the moor!' As it spoke, I discerned, obscurely, a child's face looking through the window. Terror made me cruel; and, finding it useless to attempt shaking the creature off, I pulled its wrist on to the broken pane, and rubbed it to and fro till the blood ran down and soaked the bedclothes: still it wailed, 'Let me in!' and maintained its tenacious gripe, almost maddening me with fear. 'How can I!' I said at length. 'Let *me* go, if you want me to let you in!' The fingers relaxed, I snatched mine through the hole, hurriedly piled the books up in a pyramid against it, and stopped my ears to exclude the lamentable prayer. I seemed to keep them closed above a quarter of an hour; yet, the instant I

## Unit 8. Nightmare

listened again, there was the <u>doleful</u> cry moaning on! 'Begone!' I shouted, 'I'll never let you in, not if you beg for twenty years.' 'It is twenty years,' mourned the voice: 'twenty years. I've been a <u>waif</u> for twenty years!' Thereat began a feeble scratching outside, and the pile of books moved as if thrust forward. I tried to jump up; but could not stir a limb; and so yelled aloud, in a <u>frenzy</u> of fright. To my confusion, I discovered the yell was not <u>ideal</u>: hasty footsteps approached my chamber door; somebody pushed it open, with a vigorous hand, and a light glimmered.

(*Wuthering Heights*, Emily Bronte)

1. What woke the writer from his first dream?
2. Quote the exact words that indicate the writer was dreaming for a second time.
3. What 5 separate sounds does he hear in his nightmare?
4. What 3 things does he touch in his nightmare?
5. What 4 things does he see in his nightmare?
6. Use the listed emotions below to match the following moments of his description.

| | | |
|---|---|---|
| fear | desperation | cowardice |
| annoyance | panic | cruelty |

   (a) the teasing sound of the fir-tree
   (b) his breaking the glass
   (c) his fingers closing on the little hand
   (d) his being unable to draw back his arm
   (e) his trying to cut the wrist belonging to the little hand
   (f) his piling the books against the window

7. What 2 reactions followed his crying out and waking?
8. From the words underlined in the passage, find a **synonym** for:
   (a) discovered        (c) sadness
   (b) sorrowful         (d) only
9. From the underlined words, find an **antonym** for:
   (a) factual           (c) engage
   (b) clearly           (d) gladdening
10. Find an underlined word to fit the spaces left in the sentences below. Use each word only once.
    (a) One moment the . . . . storm seemed to be lessening; then the wind began again.
    (b) The youngest refugee was a poorly-dressed . . . . of three or four years.
    (c) The group whose latest record had sold a million copies caused a . . . . among their fans.
    (d) The theft was . . . . to a gang already known to the police.

## Synonyms

11. The English language is rich in words of close or allied meaning. In taking in words from many different languages, it has gained the choice of perhaps half a dozen words, from which to take the exact meaning required.
    Use a thesaurus to build up sets of **synonyms**. For example, how many words can you substitute for 'angry'?
12. Make up a word-chain, when the link gradually changes, e.g. bright . . . light . . . pale . . . wan . . . white . . . etc.
13. Find synonyms (more than one if you can) for these:
    (a) quick             (e) difficult
    (b) friend            (f) arrive
    (c) unhappy           (g) reply
    (d) battle            (h) hesitant
14. Write sentences using these:
    (a) shone             (d) twinkled
    (b) glowed            (e) flickered
    (c) sparkled          (f) beamed
15. Some words, alike in meaning, are commonly used wrongly. Check the following in a dictionary, then write pairs of sentences to show you have understood their differences.

(a) hanged/hung
(b) learn/teach
(c) lend/borrow
(d) imaginary/imaginative
(e) can/ may
(f) between/among
(g) both/each
(h) bath/bathe
(i) breath/ breathe
(j) number/amount

16. Make up a straightforward message, then change all the words you can into synonyms so that the meaning is no longer clear. Give the message to somebody else to decipher.

17. Sometimes you can find synonyms that slide gradually from flattering to unflattering, e.g. I am slim ... You are thin ... He is skinny.

    Try some sets of your own. You might like to begin with 'I am cautious', or end with 'She is conceited.'

## Antonyms

18. Antonyms are words of opposite meaning. One group of antonyms consists of different words, e.g. the antonym of 'common' is 'rare'. Another group of antonyms is formed by adding a prefix to the original word, e.g. 'uncommon'.

    In each example below, use the antonym in a sentence of your own.

    Find 'different word' antonyms for these:
    (a) poor
    (b) dangerous
    (c) work
    (d) succeed
    (e) lend
    (f) arrive
    (g) multiply
    (h) shout
    (i) begin
    (j) receive
    (k) amateur
    (l) optimist.

19. Form antonyms by adding 'un'.
    (a) usual
    (b) intelligent
    (c) successful
    (d) interesting
    (e) necessary
    (f) certain
    (g) Find 5 more of your own.
20. Form antonyms by adding 'in'.
    (a) dependent
    (b) visible
    (c) active
    (d) secure
    (e) sincere
    (f) convenient
    (g) Find 5 more.
21. Form antonyms by adding 'dis'.
    (a) comfort
    (b) order
    (c) courage
    (d) approve
    (e) appoint
    (f) honest
22. Form antonyms by adding 'mis'.
    (a) behave
    (b) direct
    (c) judge
    (d) deed
    (e) fire
    (f) lead
23. Find antonyms for these:
    (a) legal
    (b) mortal
    (c) responsible
    (d) climax
    (e) sense
24. Antonyms can also be formed by adding 'less' to the original, e.g. hope, hopeless. Find as many examples as you can of this pattern.

## Unit 9. The Tower

Out I went into the night. The wind was still moaning in the distance, though never a breath of it came near the house of Shaws. It had fallen blacker than ever; and I was glad to feel along the wall, till I came the length of the stair-tower door at the far end of the unfinished wing. I had got the key into the keyhole and had just turned it, when all upon a sudden, without a sound of wind or thunder, the whole sky lighted up with a wild fire and went black again. I had to put my hand over my eyes to get back to the colour of the darkness; and indeed I was already half blinded when I stepped into the tower.

It was so dark inside, it seemed a body could scarce breathe; but I pushed out with foot and hand, and presently struck the wall with the one, and the lowermost round of the stair with the other. The wall, by the touch, was of fine hewn stone; the steps too, though somewhat steep and narrow, were of polished mason-work, and regular and solid under foot. Minding my uncle's word about the bannisters, I kept close to the tower side, and felt my way in the pitch darkness with a beating heart.

The house of Shaws stood five full storeys high, not counting lofts. Well, as I advanced, it seemed to me the stair grew airier and a thought more lightsome; and I was wondering what might be the cause of this change, when a second blink of the summer lightning came and went. If I did not cry out, it was because fear had me by the throat; and if I did not fall, it was more by Heaven's mercy than my own strength. It was not only that the flash shone in on every side through breaches in the wall, so that I seemed to be clambering aloft upon an open scaffold, but the same passing brightness showed me the steps were of unequal length, and that one of my feet rested that moment within two inches of the well.

This was the grand stair! I thought; and with the thought, a gust of a kind of angry courage came into my heart. My uncle had sent me here, certainly to run great risks, perhaps to die. I swore I would settle that 'perhaps', if I should break my neck for it; got me down upon my

hands and knees; and as slowly as a snail, feeling before me every inch, and testing the solidity of every stone, I continued to ascend the stair. The darkness, by contrast with the flash, appeared to have redoubled; nor was that all, for my ears were now troubled and my mind confounded by a great stir of bats in the top part of the tower, and the foul beasts, flying downward, sometimes beat about my face and body.

The tower, I should have said, was square; and in every corner the step was made of a great stone of a different shape, to join the flights. <u>Well, I had come close to one of these turns, when, feeling forward as usual, my hand slipped upon the edge and found nothing but emptiness beyond it.</u> The stair had been carried no higher: to set a stranger mounting it in darkness was to send him straight to death; and (although, thanks to the lightning and my own precautions, I was safe enough) the mere thought of the peril in which I might have stood, and the dreadful height I might have fallen from, brought out the sweat upon my body and relaxed my joints.

(Kidnapped, Robert Louis Stevenson)

1. In your own words, explain exactly what is happening in each of the underlined passages.
    - (a) ' ... when all upon a sudden, without a sound of wind or thunder, the whole sky lighted up with a wild fire and went black again.
    - (b) ' ... but I pushed out with foot and hand, and presently struck the wall with one, and the lowermost round of the stair with the other.'
    - (c) ' ... it seemed to me the stair grew airier and a thought more lightsome;'
    - (d) ' ... and with the thought, a gust of a kind of angry courage came into my heart.'
    - (e) 'Well, I had come close to one of these turns, when, feeling forward as usual, my hand slipped upon the edge and found nothing but emptiness beyond it.'
2. List all the details that indicate physical symptoms of the fear experienced by the person telling the story.

Section B. Descriptive Passages

3. What details does the writer use to emphasise the effect of the darkness?
4. What is the reason given for his climbing the stairs?
5. What were the two hazards of the stair tower revealed by the lightning?
6. What precautions did he take once he knew the danger?
7. What was a third hazard as he neared the top?
8. From the context, what is the meaning of each of the following?
   (a) a body
   (b) fine hewn stone
   (c) I would settle that 'perhaps'.
   (d) the peril in which I might have stood

## Descriptive Writing

9. Good descriptive writing can make a reader respond so that it seems he sees, hears, touches, tastes, smells or feels what the writer has experienced. One of the skills of comprehension is to share as fully as possible what the writer offers. Sometimes you will need to analyse the writer's choice of words, or choice of details, or his ability to get to the essence of whatever he is describing.

   Which of the following words refer to touch, taste, smell, sound and sight? Arrange them in columns. (You may find words that fit more than one category.)

| dessicated | musky | flimsy | harsh | heavy |
| acrid | moist | slippery | flexible | spicy |
| bitter | sweet | pungent | fresh | crumbly |
| elastic | still | gritty | powdery | murmuring |
| stale | mushy | smooth | garish | cold |
| warm | gravelly | lucid | sticky | shining |
| fizzy | acidic | metallic | rough | sibilant |
| sour | spongy | sticky | glossy | furry |
| musty | fragrant | silky | flaky | knotty |
| squashy | fluffy | turbulent | rubbery | feathery |
| coarse | melodious | tinkling | soft | prickly |

10. Try this experiment with touch. Have each student bring one small object (or segment) which is identifiable by touch, such as lambskin, plastic, prickly seedpods, greasy wool, polystyrene foam, velvet, cuttlefish, plasticine, etc. Arrange desks in a circle and place one object in each desk. Numbers can be chalked on desks and the class can move around, fingering the object inside the desk without looking at it. As well as seeing how many objects can be identified, try writing three words to describe each object's texture.

11. Try these experiments with sight.
    (a) By carefully adding small measured quantities of one colour to another, you can create colour charts to test others' ability to re-arrange them in order, from all one colour to all another, e.g. from red through orange to yellow. You will need to give them numbers to check later.
    (b) Go outside and look at the sky, at the distant view, at whatever there is to see. Count the separate greens; discriminate between shades of colour; look at some details in leaves or bark and try describing them accurately.

12. Try these experiments with sound.
    (a) Get the class to shut their eyes and listen for a minute, counting all the different sounds they hear in that time. Get those who claim the most to name what they heard. (Incidentally, it is not always easy to estimate time. Ask the class to raise their hands after they think one minute has passed.)
    (b) Try some experiments with speed talking and recording. See how many words per minute someone can speak and still be understood. Use a tape recorder to see how rates of speech vary.

13. Find out the basic classifications of taste. Collect samples of materials to taste. (Be prepared to act as official taster of whatever you bring. Ancient kings employed officials to make sure they weren't being quietly got rid of!) Blindfold one of the people in the class. See if he/she can identify substances or classify them as bitter, sweet or sour.

14. Similarly, experiment with substances with distinct odours. Make some pot pourri for yourself (very useful for presents and as a room deodoriser.)

15. Should we add 'intuition' as a sixth sense? Some of the ideas listed below might give some direction to your discussion.
    - experiments such as sensing a near object when blindfolded.
    - the sensory ability of animals such as bats.
    - extrasensory perception — what it means and what is claimed about it.
    - 'bush telegraph' communication among primitive peoples.
    - sensitivity of aborigines, 'pointing the bone'.
    - unspoken messages, including body language.

# Unit 10. To Paint the Portrait of a Bird

First paint a cage
with an open door
then paint
something pretty
something simple
something beautiful
something useful ...
for the bird
then place the canvas against a tree
in a garden
in a wood
or in a forest
hide behind the tree
without speaking
without moving. ...
Sometimes the bird comes quickly
but he can just as well spend long years
before deciding.
Don't get discouraged
wait
wait years if necessary
the swiftness or slowness of the coming
of the bird having no rapport
with the success of the picture.
When the bird comes
if he comes
observe the most profound silence
wait till the bird enters the cage
and when he has entered
gently close the door with a brush
then
paint out all the bars one by one

## 52  Section B. Descriptive Passages

taking care not to touch any of the feathers of the bird.
Then paint the portrait of the tree
choosing the most beautiful of its branches
for the bird
paint also the green foliage and the wind's freshness
the dust of the sun
and the noise of insects in the summer heat
and then wait for the bird to decide to sing.
If the bird doesn't sing
it's a bad sign
a sign that the painting is bad
but if he sings it's a good sign
a sign that you can sign.
So then so very gently you pull out
one of the feathers of the bird
and you write your name in a corner of the picture.

(Jacques Prévert)

1. Explain the poet's use of the symbol of the painted bird, and the care needed to get it onto the canvas. What does he want us to understand by this?
2. Which of the following alternative titles best explains what the poet intended his readers to think about?
   (a) Himself as an Artist
   (b) Creativity
   (c) Art Appreciation
   (d) Problems of the Modern World

3. From the poem, what three things would seem impossible to paint?
4. Re-read the lines beginning with 'Sometimes the bird comes quickly', down to 'with the success of the picture.' Paraphrase (put into your own words) what the poet is saying in these lines.
5. What does the bird's singing symbolize?
6. What personal qualities does an artist need, according to this poet?
7. In what hobby or skill do you show your own creativity? Name it and describe a particular attempt that gave you the greatest satisfaction.
8. Look up the meaning of:
   (a) rapport,
   (b) profound,
   (c) foliage.
   Use each one in a sentence of your own.

Symbols
9. Symbols can be found everywhere: in literature, flags, signs, advertising, etc. If every member of the class draws or describes a well-known symbol, leaving out any identifying words, see how many each of the class can identify.

   Use the suggestions listed below as the basis for some library research.
   (a) Find out the original meaning of 'chaos'. What other interpretations of the beginning of the world can you find?
   (b) In what ways has the wheel been used as a symbol?
   (c) Draw a chimaera. What does the word mean today?
   (d) Find out all you can about angels, cherubs, etc. Research the way they were shown in art.
   (e) How has music been used as symbolism? Find examples (and play them) to illustrate.
   (f) Find out what you can of omens and the way they were once decided.
   (g) Look up the various kinds of cross used as symbols. See if you can find out which countries used them.
   (h) Find out all you can about clowns and jesters. Are they really stupid?
   (i) Find ways in which numbers were thought of as symbols.

(j) What symbolism is associated with a ring or a circle?
(k) What is a cornucopia? Draw one or make one. What does it represent?
(l) Read all you can about the art of Australian aborigines and explain the symbols of their paintings.
(m) What is mandrake? What other plants were supposed to have special properties?
(n) Draw a fleur-de-lis. What organisation uses this as its symbol?
(o) Find out all the alternative names for the devil.
(p) In what ways are toys symbols for children? Discuss your approval or disapproval of weapons as toys.
(q) Find stories that involve humans with natural forces such as lightning.
(r) What did the dolphin signify?
(s) Why do people get tattooed? Find out how the process is done and what symbols are often used.
(t) Make up your own symbolism for the things you care most about.

10. From the following suggestions, investigate the use of symbolism in:
(a) uniforms
(b) art
(c) religion
(d) science.

11. The Japanese have a form of short poem called a haiku, in which some natural plant or phenomenon such as the weather is commented upon, with an implied moral for people.

> Nuts that are sweetest
> Prove difficult to open
> Cased in rock-hard shells.

Notice the fixed pattern of three lines with five syllables (not words) in the first and third lines, and seven in the second. Try writing some haiku of your own.

## Unit 11.  Journey in Time

It was at ten o'clock today that the first of all Time Machines began its career. I gave it a last tap, tried all the screws again, put one more drop of oil on the quartz rod, and sat myself in the saddle. I suppose a suicide who holds a pistol to his skull feels much the same wonder at what will come next as I felt then. I took the starting lever in one hand and the stopping one in the other, pressed the first, and almost immediately the second. I seemed to reel; I felt a nightmare sensation of falling; and, looking round, I saw the laboratory exactly as before. Had anything happened? For a moment I suspected that my intellect had tricked me. Then I noted the clock. A moment before, as it seemed, it had stood at a minute or so past ten; now it was nearly half past three!

I drew a breath, set my teeth, gripped the starting lever with both hands, and went off with a thud. The laboratory got hazy and went dark. Mrs Watchets came in and walked, apparently without seeing me, towards the garden door. I suppose it took her a minute or so to traverse the place, but to me she seemed to shoot across the room like a rocket. I pressed the lever over to its extreme position. The night came like the turning out of a lamp, and in another moment came tomorrow. The laboratory grew faint and hazy, then fainter and even fainter. Tomorrow night came black, then day again, night again, day again, faster and faster still. An eddying murmur filled my ears, and a strange dumb confusedness descended on my mind.

I am afraid I cannot convey the peculiar sensations of time travelling. They are excessively unpleasant. There is a feeling exactly like that one has upon a switchback — of a helpless headlong motion! I felt the same horrible anticipation, too, of an imminent smash. As I put on pace, night followed day like the flapping of a black wing. The dim suggestion of the laboratory seemed presently to fall away from me, and I saw the sun hopping swiftly across the sky, leaping it every minute, and every minute marking a day. I suppose the laboratory had been destroyed and I had come into the open air. I had a dim impression of scaffolding, but I was already going too fast to be conscious of any moving things. The slowest snail that ever crawled dashed by too fast for me. The twinkling succession of darkness and light was excessively painful to the eye. Then, in the intermittent darknesses, I saw the moon spinning swiftly through her quarters from new to full, and had a faint glimpse of the circling stars. Presently, as I went on, still gaining velocity, the palpitation of night and day merged into one continuous greyness: the sky took on a wonderful deepness of blue, a splendid luminous colour like that of early twilight; the jerking sun became a streak of fire, a brilliant arch, in space; the moon a fainter fluctuating band; and I could see nothing of the stars, save now and then a brighter circle flickering in the blue.

The landscape was misty and vague. I was still on the hillside upon which this house now stands, and the shoulder rose above me

Unit 11. Journey in Time 57

grey and dim. I saw trees growing and changing like puffs of vapour, now brown, now green; they grew, spread, shivered, and passed away. I saw huge buildings rise up faint and fair, and pass like dreams. The whole surface of the earth seemed changed — melting and flowing under my eyes. The little hands upon the dials that registered my speed raced round faster and faster. Presently I noted that the sun belt swayed up and down, from solstice to solstice, in a minute or less, and that consequently my pace was over a year a minute; and minute by minute the white snow flashed across the world, and vanished, and was followed by the bright, brief green of spring.

The unpleasant sensations of the start were less poignant now. They merged at last into a kind of hysterical exhilaration. I remarked indeed a clumsy swaying of the machine, for which I was unable to account. But my mind was too confused to attend to it, so with a kind of madness growing upon me. I flung myself into futurity.

(*The Time Machine*, H.G. Wells)

1. Why does the author choose several very ordinary actions to mention before starting the Time Machine?
2. What is his first proof that he has moved forward in time?
3. Quote from the extract a sentence that indicates the apprehension felt by the author.
4. Quote words to indicate his feeling:
    (a) of tension
    (b) of fear.
5. List the succession of images the writer uses to describe the passing of day and night.
6. Does the machine reach maximum speed immediately?
7. What physical sensations did the writer experience during his time flight?
8. What happens to his laboratory as time passes?
9. Which words listed below fit the tone of the passage?
    (a) formal          (e) emotional
    (b) scientific      (f) vague
    (c) humorous        (g) detailed
    (d) disjointed      (h) orderly
10. From words used in the extract, fill in the spaces below. (The first letter is given).
    (a) The term s .... is used for the time of the year when the sun is furthest from the equator.

58  Section B. Descriptive Passages

    (b) The earliest steam trains reached only a low v .... compared with later inventions.
    (c) The pulse of the injured man was irregular and f ....
    (d) The torch light was f .... before it finally went out.
    (e) The film ended with a p .... scene that engaged the sympathy of those watching it.
    (f) They raced to the beach and plunged into the water with e ....
    (g) No one guessed that danger was i .... as the plane left the runway.
    (h) Chess has always been claimed to exercise the i .... of its players.
    (i) Technology intrigues everyone who makes a study of f .... and the job changes that are likely to happen.

11. The novel from which this extract is taken was written in 1895. How close to space exploration of this century was Wells's imagined travel?

12. Every writer has his own style and often readers feel a sense of familiarity with other books by the same author, even though he may have chosen a different theme and set about creating a different tone or atmosphere for each book. A writer will vary the impression he wants to give according to his subject: he may use different words — colloquial language, blunt everyday vocabulary or less-used words that define subtler shades of meaning. He may use dialogue, imagery, similes and metaphors, or not. He may write in very short sentences or more involved prose. He may write very objectively or choose to write as one who is personally involved in an emotional way with his subject. His intention in writing, too, may be quite different: he may want to report an actual event, instruct us, narrate a story, create a believable character or persuade readers to accept a particular viewpoint.
    Read each of the following passages, then decide:
    (a) what the writer intended to do,
    (b) what words best describe the tone of the writing.

    A. A bowl of water will be needed on the right side of the wheel. The soupier the water is with clay slush, the better lubricant it is, and the less likely to cause cracking in the clay. A good plan is to consider a throwing programme some days ahead if special clay is required. Very soft clay can be used to throw wide, flat plates. Firmer clay will be necessary for tall work. Thick ware should be well grogged.

With supreme optimism, the beginner will select clay to use with absolute disregard to its use or condition. Watch an experienced thrower carefully select the clay and then spend time preparing it to a perfect condition by wedging or kneading, after which the clay ball is shaped without flaws and of the correct weight for the size to be thrown.

Wedging not only removes the air from the clay; it also seems to make it more plastic. No lumps, cracks or crusty surfaces are acceptable in the ball of clay about to be thrown. The ball of clay should be circular, with its ends flattened, something like a cheese. A crease left in the clay ball may remain on the pot bottom, creating a flaw which will develop into a crack later. Only sufficient clay balls should be made for immediate use, because the clay condition deteriorates quickly forming a crust on the outer surface. There should be no water or wet clay on either the clay ball or the wheel head as this will prevent adhesion.

Prepare the surface of the wheel to accept the clay ball by smearing some clay on it. The residue left when a pot has been cut and removed from the wheel is ideal to throw on. Under no circumstances throw the clay on a dry, dusty or wet, slushy wheel. In both cases, the surface may reject the clay ball and send it flying.

Adherence to the wheel is best obtained if the clay is thrown on to a moving wheel. If the clay lands off centre, stop the wheel, and try again or simply push the clay into the centre.

(Harry Memmott)

B. The hardest thing is to begin. This morning I set up the typewriter and then I discovered a million things that just had to be done right then in the house, so I spent two hours doing them all, convincing myself that when I had finished I would go straight to the typewriter and write. But when I had finished I thought I might as well have a cup of coffee and a little rest, for of course I was feeling rather tired from all that housework that just had to be done — even got the top of the stove cleaned, the pot plants watered and washed all their leaves down with milk. Someone told me milk made them shine, and it does. Fancy all these years and I've never done that before, but this morning, before I settled down to write, I just had to try it out.

But now I have a very clean house, clean washing, even the mirrors all shiny, not to mention the leaves of the pot-plants, all neatly put back into their respective places. And now I have run out of excuses and I keep passing by the eating bench where my typewriter keeps looking at me. So I have taken the three steps which were needed to seat myself in front of it, and it still keeps looking at me, and I can't think of a thing to write.

(Gwen Wesson)

C. 'My dear boy, no woman is a genius. Women are a decorative sex. They never have anything to say, but they say it charmingly. Women represent the triumph of matter over mind, just as men represent the triumph of mind over morals.'

'Harry, how can you?'

'My dear Dorian, it is quite true. I am analyzing women at present, so I ought to know. The subject is not so abstruse as I thought it was. I find that, ultimately, there are only two kinds of women, the plain and the coloured. The plain women are very useful. If you want to gain a reputation for respectability, you have merely to take them down to supper. The other women are very charming. They commit one mistake, however. They paint in order to try and look young. Our grandmothers painted in order to try and talk brilliantly. Rouge and *esprit* used to go together. That is all over now. As long as a woman can look ten years younger than her own daughter, she is perfectly satisfied. As for conversation, there are only five women in London worth talking to, and two of these can't be admitted into decent society.'

(Oscar Wilde)

D. 'Ah didn't like to put them in on a grand 'ot day like this. We'll drive them up to that little house.' He pointed to a tumble down grey-stone barn at the summit of the long,

steeply sloping pasture and blew out a cloud of choking smoke. 'Won't take many minutes.'

At his last sentence a cold hand clutched at me. I'd heard these dreadful words so many times before. But maybe it would be all right this time. We made our way to the bottom of the field and got behind the heifers.

'Cush, cush!' cried Mr Kay.

'Cush, cush!' I added encouragingly, slapping my hands against my thighs.

The heifers stopped pulling the grass and regarded us with mild interest, their jaws moving lazily, then in response to further cries they began to meander casually up the hill. We managed to coax them up to the door of the barn but there they stopped. The leader put her head inside for a moment then turned suddenly and made a dash down the hill. The others followed suit immediately and though we danced about and waved our arms they ran past us as if we weren't there. I looked thoughtfully at the young beasts thundering down the slope, their tails high, kicking up their heels like mustangs; they were enjoying this new game.

Down the hill once more and again the slow wheedling up to the door and again the sudden breakaway. This time one of them tried it on her own and as I galloped vainly to and fro trying to turn her the others charged with glee through the gap and down the slope again.

(James Herriot)

## 62 Section B. Descriptive Passages

12. Language contains many words that have an inbuilt emotional meaning; others are themselves unemotional, although they can become part of an emotional phrase with other words.
    Divide the words below into those you consider have emotional appeal (we call these emotive words) and those which do not.

    | dowdy | barefaced | expedition | clodhopper |
    |-------|-----------|------------|------------|
    | forest | reply | darling | dynamic |
    | hammock | moment | piano | egoistic |
    | cynical | bully | betray | crabby |
    | sweep | ranch | despot | arrogant |
    | leaf | easel | cadge | degree |
    | mood | indication | brave | comfortable |

13. The emotive content of some words varies with the point of view of the user. For each of the words below, describe two different people for whom the word would have opposite responses.
    (a) conservative   (c) eccentric   (e) criminal
    (b) defiant        (d) aggressive  (f) cousin

14. From your own point of view, what do you:
    (a) dislike   (b) loathe   (c) abhor?
    What do you find:
    (d) absurd   (e) silly   (f) unreasonable?

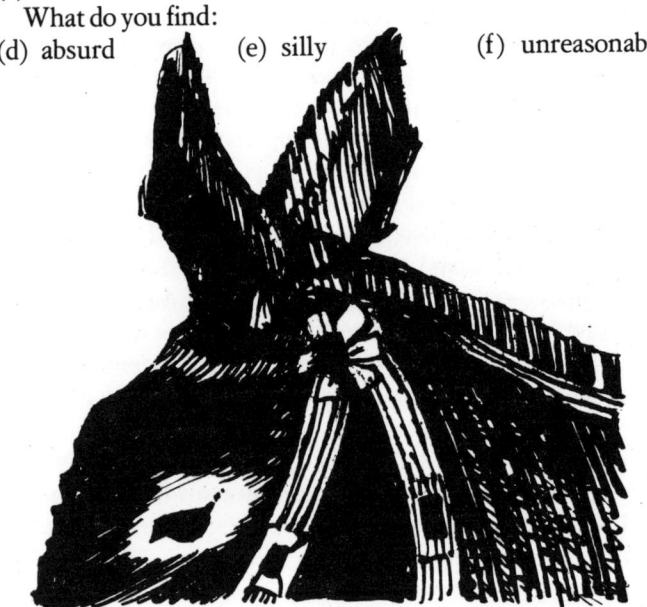

## Unit 11. Journey in Time 63

15. Read the letter below, which was written by scientists who had been involved in nuclear research that led to the possibility of atomic warfare. Discuss the tone of their letter and what they intended to be its effect.

The development of nuclear power not only constitutes an important addition to the technological and military power of the United States, but also creates grave political and economic problems for the future of this country.

Nuclear bombs cannot possibly remain 'a secret weapon' at the exclusive disposal of this country for more than a few years. The scientific facts on which construction is based are well known to scientists of other countries. Unless an effective international control of nuclear explosives is instituted, a race for nuclear armaments is certain to ensue following the first revelation of our possession of nuclear weapons to the world. Within ten years other countries may have nuclear bombs, each of which, weighing less than a ton, could destroy an urban area of more than ten square miles. In the war to which such an armaments race is likely to lead, the United States, with its agglomeration of population and industry in comparatively few metropolitan districts, will be at a disadvantage compared to nations whose populations and industry are scattered over large areas.

We believe that these considerations make the use of nuclear bombs for an early unannounced attack against Japan inadvisable. If the United States were to be the first to release this new means of indiscriminate destruction upon mankind, she would sacrifice public support throughout the world, precipitate the race for armaments and prejudice the possibility of reaching an international agreement on the future control of such weapons.

Much more favourable conditions for the eventual achievement of such an agreement could be created if nuclear bombs were first revealed to the world by a demonstration in an appropriately selected uninhabited area.

In case chances for the establishment of an international control of nuclear weapons should have to be considered slight at the present time, then not only the use of these weapons against Japan, but even their early demonstration, may be contrary to the interests of this country. A postponement of such a demonstration will have in this case the advantage of delaying the beginning of the nuclear armaments race as long as possible.

If the government should decide in favour of an early demonstration of nuclear weapons, it will then have the possibility of taking into account the public opinion of this country and of the other nations before deciding whether these weapons should be used against Japan. In this way, other nations may assume a share of responsibility for such a fateful decision.

Composed and signed by

       J. FRANCK
       D. HUGHES
       L. SLIZARD
       T. HOGNESS
       E. RABINOWITCH
       G. SEABORG
       C.J. NICKSON

# Section C
# Fiction

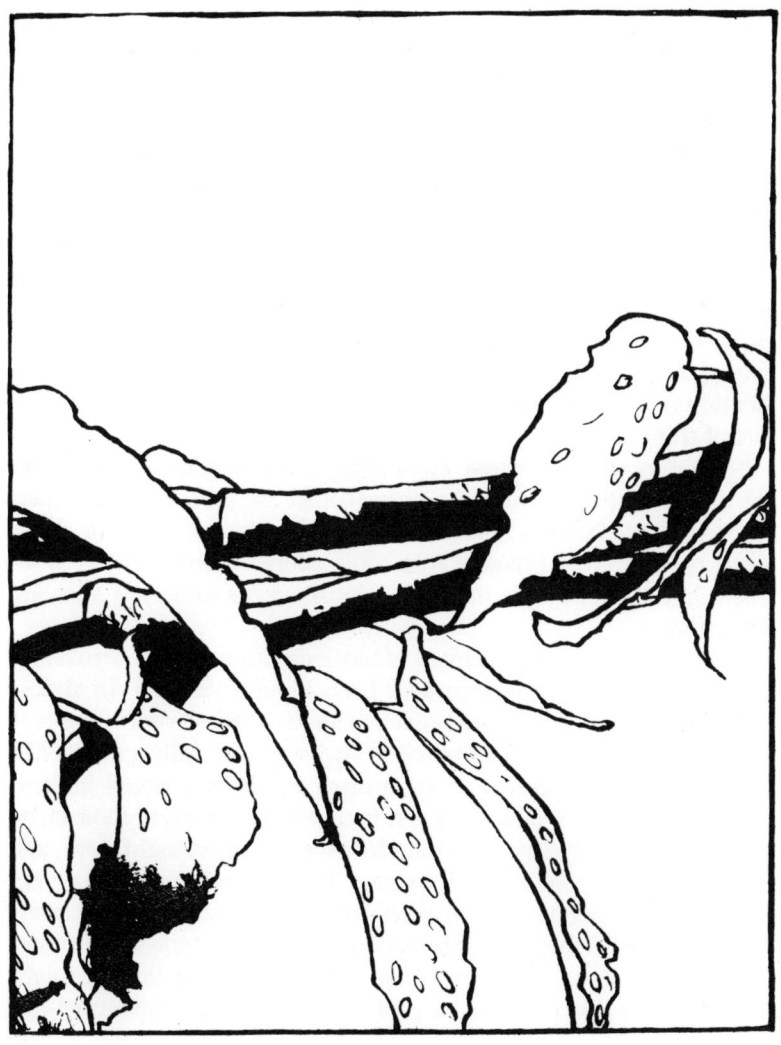

## Unit 12.  The Coming of the Triffids

My introduction to a triffid came early. It so happened that we had one of the first in the locality growing in our own garden. The plant was quite well developed before any of us bothered to notice it, for it had taken root along with a number of other casuals behind the bit of hedge that screened the rubbish heap. It wasn't doing any harm there, and it wasn't in anyone's way. So when we did notice it later on we'd just take a look at it now and then to see how it was getting along, and let it be.

However, a triffid is certainly distinctive, and we couldn't help getting a bit curious about it after a time. Not, perhaps, very actively, for there are always a few unfamiliar things that somehow or other manage to lodge in the neglected corners of a garden, but enough to mention to one another that it was beginning to look a pretty queer sort of thing.

Nowadays when everyone knows only too well what a triffid looks like it is difficult to recall how odd and somehow *foreign* the first ones appeared to us. Nobody, as far as I know, felt any misgiving or alarm about them then. I imagine that most people thought of them — when they thought of them at all — in much the same way that my father did.

I have a picture in my memory of him examining ours and puzzling over it at a time when it must have been about a year old. In almost every detail it was a half-size replica of a fully-grown triffid — only it didn't have a name yet, and no one had seen one fully grown. My father leant over, peering at it through his horn-rimmed glasses, fingering its stalk, and blowing gently through his gingery moustache as was his habit when thoughtful. He inspected the straight stem, and the woody bole from which it sprang. He gave curious, if not very penetrative attention to the three small, bare sticks which grew straight up beside the stem. He smoothed the short sprays of leathery green leaves between his finger and thumb as if their texture might tell him something. Then he peered into the curious, funnel-like

## Unit 12. The Coming of the Triffids

formation at the top of the stem, still puffing reflectively but inconclusively through his moustache. I remember the first time he lifted me up to look inside that conical cup and see the tightly-wrapped whorl within. It looked not unlike the new, close-rolled frond of a fern, emerging a couple of inches from a sticky mess in the base of the cup. I did not touch it, but I knew the stuff must be sticky because there were flies and other small insects struggling in it.

More than once my father ruminated that it was pretty queer, and observed that one of these days he really must try to find out what it was. I don't think he ever made the effort, nor, at that stage, was he likely to have learned much if he had tried.

The thing would be about four feet high then. There must have been plenty of them about, growing up quietly and inoffensively, with nobody taking any particular notice of them — at least, it seemed so, for if the biological or botanical experts were excited over them no news of their interest percolated to the general public. And so the one in our garden continued its growth peacefully, as did thousands like it in neglected spots all over the world.

It was some little time later that the first one picked up its roots, and walked.

(*The Day of the Triffids*, John Wyndham)

1. Quote words which show the triffid is not an ordinary plant.
2. Quote words which show that at first the triffids were not considered frightening.
3. Was the triffid which was seen by the author as a child the only one in existence?
4. Approximately what height could the triffid eventually reach? What is the metric equivalent?
5. How do you know the triffids became a problem?
6. What portion of the plant seems likely to become most dangerous? Why?
7. Make two drawings of a triffid, labelling the parts, as follows:
   (a) the entire plant
   (b) half the formation at the top of the stem, as it would appear if cut through the middle.
8. If you could imagine an ordinary insect enlarged many, many times, which would you choose for a science fiction story to threaten mankind? Draw or explain why it would be frightening.

9. Match up the following words found in the extract with their meanings.
   (a) distinctive           thought over
   (b) lodge                 shaped like a cone
   (c) misgiving             duplicate
   (d) replica               noticeably different
   (e) bole                  stump
   (f) conical               come to rest
   (g) ruminated             uneasy feeling
   (h) percolated            filtered through

**Science Fiction**

10. Science fiction begins with one or more fictional premises. If the story is to be convincing, what follows must be logical and possible, once you accept the original premises (e.g. the level of water in the sea begins to rise dramatically ... capital cities near the shore are engulfed; chaos because these are the centres of communication; exodus of people towards high ground; food shortage, etc.).

    Write a paragraph about any science fiction novel you have read, stating what were the premises that made the story 'possible'. Discuss whether or not you found the rest of the story easy to accept. Lastly, say whether you found the ending satisfactory.

11. Construct your own science fiction plot outline, after you have worked out answers to the questions below. You must give your story a title and describe an Og. Use the fictional premise: Earth has been invaded by creatures (Ogs) from the far planet, Oggaroo.
    (a) Are the Ogs like humans?
    (b) Are any Earth people still alive?
    (c) Do the Ogs know of their survival?
    (d) Who is in control?
    (e) Who is/are the hero/heroine(s)?
    (f) Who is the villain?
    (g) What is the problem?

12. Write the last paragraph of your Og story.

## Unit 13. A Picnic Setting

Manmade improvements on Nature at the Picnic Grounds consisted of several circles of flat stones to serve as fireplaces and a wooden privy in the shape of a Japanese pagoda. The creek at the close of summer ran sluggishly through long dry grass, now and then almost disappearing to re-appear as a shallow pool. Lunch had been set out on large white tablecloths close by, shaded from the heat of the sun by two or three spreading gums. In addition to the chicken pie, angel cake, jellies and the tepid bananas inseparable from an Australian picnic, Cook had provided a handsome iced cake in the shape of a heart, for which Tom had obligingly cut a mould from a piece of tin. Mr Hussey had boiled up two immense billycans of tea on a fire of bark and leaves and was now enjoying a pipe in the shadow of the drag where he could keep a watchful eye on his horses tethered in the shade.

The only other occupants of the Picnic Grounds were a party of three or four people encamped some distance away under some blackwoods on the opposite side of the creek, where a large bay horse and a white Arab pony were lunching from two chaffbags beside an open wagonette. 'How dreadfully quiet it is out here,' observed Edith, helping herself lavishly to cream. 'How anyone can prefer to live in the country I can't imagine. Unless of course they are dreadfully poor.'

'If everyone else in Australia felt like that, you wouldn't be making yourself fat on rich cream,' Marion pointed out.

'Except for those people over there with the wagonette we might be the only living creatures in the whole world,' said Edith, airily dismissing the entire animal kingdom at one stroke.

The sunny slopes and shadowed forest, to Edith so still and silent, were actually teeming with unheard rustlings and twitterings, scufflings, scratchings, the light brush of unseen wings. Leaves, flowers and grasses glowed and trembled under the canopy of light; cloud shadows gave way to golden motes dancing above the pool where water beetles skimmed and darted. On the rocks and grass the diligent ants were crossing miniature Saharas of dry sand, jungles of seeding grass, in the never ending task of collecting and storing food. Here, scattered about amongst the mountainous human shapes were Heavensent crumbs, carroway seeds, a shred of crystallized ginger — strange, exotic but recognizably edible loot. A battalion of sugar ants, almost bent in half with the effort, were laboriously dragging a piece of icing off the cake towards some subterranean larder dangerously situated within inches of Blanche's yellow head, pillowed on a rock. Lizards basked on the hottest stones, a lumbering armour-plated beetle rolled over in the dry leaves and lay helplessly kicking on its back; fat white grubs and flat grey woodlice preferred the dank security of layers of rotting bark. Torpid snakes lay coiled in their secret holes awaiting the twilight hour when they would come sliding from hollow logs to drink at the creek, while in the hidden depths of the scrub the birds waited for the heat of the day to pass. . . .

Insulated from natural contacts with earth, air and sunlight, by corsets pressing on the solar plexus, by voluminous petticoats, cotton stockings and kid boots, the drowsy well-fed girls lounging in the shade were no more a part of their environment than figures in a photograph album, arbitrarily posed against a backcloth of cork rocks and cardboard trees.

(*Picnic at Hanging Rock*, Joan Lindsay)

1. A writer must know (or imagine) in detail the setting of his story; he will use words as cleverly as he can to make sure his readers also 'see' the scenes he sets. After reading the extract carefully, sketch the opening scene, adding only those details the writer mentions. After ten minutes, compare your version with others. (Perhaps a competent artist in the class might like to spend the rest of the period illustrating what others have found hard to draw.)
2. Other than the people and the horses they bring with them, list the other living creatures mentioned.
3. What impression does the writer give of all these creatures?
4. What is Edith's attitude to:
    (a) living in the country,   (b) her surroundings?
5. What is suggested by:
    (a) 'insulated from',   (b) 'part of their environment'?
6. Why don't the girls seem natural in the setting?

7. Why do you think the writer makes this observation?
8. The story takes place many years ago. List all the evidence that suggests this.
9. If you were to plan a picnic for your friends at Hanging Rock, what would you suggest for their transport, food, clothing etc?

## Importance of Details

10. Every writer succeeds only if his story is convincing. The reader must be able to visualise the setting and believe in the characters. Careful use of detail is vital and the choice of detail must be appropriate to what the author intends: to amuse, to frighten, to arouse sympathy, to explain, etc.

    Read each of the following passages. In each case:
    (a) What are the most interesting details?
    (b) What effect does the detail achieve?

    A. I went to the corner of the schoolyard which was surrounded by a bumpy red brick wall and climbed up on the pile of earth covering an air raid shelter. The all-clear had just sounded after the alert and I was watching my friends arrive. A red dragonfly alighted on the wall right before my eyes. I saw it clearly. I realise even then I was hearing the characteristic sound of a B-29 engine, but, lulled by the security and relief of the all-clear, I let the sound go in one ear and out the other. My little brother had just put out his hand when there was a flash and my whole body received a shock as if I had been thrown into a furnace.

    When I opened my eyes after being blown at least eight yards, it was as dark as if I had come up against a black-painted fence. After that, as if thin paper was being peeled off one piece at a time, it gradually began to grow brighter. The first thing that my eyes lighted upon then was the flat stretch of land with only dust clouds rising. Everything had crumbled away in that one moment, and changed into streets of rubble, street after street of ruins.

    (Shintaro)

    B. Stephen was once again seated beside his father in the corner of a railway carriage at Kingsbridge. He was travelling with his father by the night mail to Cork. As the train steamed out of the station he recalled his childish wonder of years before and every event of his first day at Clongowes. But he felt no wonder now. He saw the darkening lands slipping away past him, the silent telegraph-poles passing his window swiftly every four seconds, the little glimmering stations, manned by a few silent sentries, flung by the mail behind her and twinkling for a moment in the darkness like fiery grains flung backwards by a runner.

(James Joyce)

C. I felt that I adapted very rapidly to weightlessness. I had no tendency to over-reach nor did I experience any other sign of lack of coordination, even on the first movements after separation. I found myself unconsciously taking advantage of the weightless condition, as when I would leave a camera or some other object floating in space while I attended to other matters. This was not done as a preplanned manœuvre but as a spur-of-the-moment thing when another system needed my attention. I thought later about how I had done this as naturally as if I were laying the camera on a table in a 1 g field. It pointedly illustrates how rapidly adaptable the human is, even to something as foreign as weightlessness.

We discovered from this flight that some problems are still to be solved in properly determining how to stow and secure equipment that is used in a space vehicle. I had brought along a number of instruments, such as cameras, binoculars, and a photometer, with which to make observations from the spacecraft. All of these were stowed in a ditty bag by my right arm. Each piece of equipment had a 3-foot piece of line attached to it. By the time I had started using items of the equipment, these lines became tangled. Although these lines got in the way, it was still important to have some way of securing the equipment, as I found out when I attempted to change film. The small canisters of film were not tied to the ditty bag by lines. I left one floating in midair while working with the camera, and when I reached for it, I accidentally hit it and it floated out of sight behind the instrument panel.

(John Glenn)

D.  A couple of old tarts from Toorak were sniffing around. Instantly Geoffrey was all charm, showing them the tapestry couch.

'Excuse this young man,' he said. 'He's doing a rubbing of me for the Archibald Prize. I've been suffocating under a sheet of rice paper all morning. Now, the couch, as you can see, is a major piece.'

The church ladies couldn't see, and said so. 'It's very knocked about, Mr Harris.'

'So would you be, madam, if you had been dragged down the steps of the Winter Palace and carried across the steppes of mother Russia in a troika, just moments ahead of the Revolution. Those scratches on the leg? The teeth marks of wolves.'

'The stuffing's a bit far gone,' said her friend.

'That stuffing is the stuff of history. What you're feeling is swan's down. And not the down from your ordinary swans. The down inside this piece came from the swans on the pond of the Petrograd Gardens. The very swans that inspired Tchaikovsky to write *Swan Lake*.'

Geoffrey accepted a cash deposit and promised delivery on Friday. 'Silly old cows,' he stage-whispered through clenched teeth, while smiling and waving as they climbed into their car.

'Ruby,' he called out, 'I've just sold that rotten, borer-ridden couch we got at Richmond auctions. $850. $50 deposit. For the dowager duchess of St George's Road.

(Phillip Adams)

E. One day, there was the long awaited news on the notice board. *0600 11 FEB. 1943. Regiment will prepare to move etc. etc.*

Great excitement, packing, renewing kit, selling kit, buying fruit for the journey, writing 'Farewell for ever' etc. to sweethearts, etc. The day before the move I developed toothache. It started at two in the morning, the pain shot up my head down the back of my neck, disappeared down my spine then reappeared in my chest sideways up the tent pole. How could one tiny hole neutralise a whole man? Will-power! *That* would stop it. I did will-power till three o'clock. It got worse. Old wives' recipe! Stuff tobacco into the cavity. I lit the lamp. Edgington woke, he saw what appeared to be Gunner Milligan splitting open cigarettes and poking the tobacco down his throat. 'Look mate,' he said, 'you're supposed to smoke 'em.'

Next morning, I drove to the Dental Surgery, in a villa on the sea at Cap Matifou. The dentist, a young fair-haired Captain sat me in the chair, and drove his prodder down till it got through to the collar bone.

'OWWWWWWWWWWWWWWWWWWWW Sir,' I said.

'You scream very well.'

'Yes sir, I'm practising for the front line.'

I drove back with the left side of my face frozen dead. You may ask, what use is half a frozen face? Well, it keeps longer. To this day, the left side of my face is two hours younger than the right. We were to fill in our wills in the back of our Army Pay Books. I had no possessions, no money, two cheap fifty shilling suits, a second-hand evening dress, a few Marks and Spencer shirts, and a mess of ragged underwear. My trumpet was my only bounty, so I wrote 'I leave my trumpet to my mother and the H.P. payments to my father.' Others made lavish entries, Gunner White 'I leave my Gas Stove to the Sgt. Major,' etc. To some it wasn't funny. Reg Griffin said 'When millions of perfectly healthy young men have to make their wills out, there's something nasty going on in the world.'

(Spike Milligan)

## Unit 14.  Charles

The day my son Laurie started kindergarten he renounced corduroy overalls with bibs and began wearing blue jeans with a belt; I watched him go off the first morning with the older girl next door, seeing clearly that an era of my life was ended, my sweet-voiced nursery-school tot replaced by a long-trousered, swaggering character who forgot to stop at the corner and wave good-bye to me.

He came home the same way, the front door slamming open, his cap on the floor, and the voice suddenly become raucous shouting, 'Isn't anybody *here?*'

At lunch he spoke insolently to his father, spilled his baby sister's milk, and remarked that his teacher said we were not to take the name of the Lord in vain.

'How *was* school today?' I asked, elaborately casual.

'All right,' he said.

'Did you learn anything?' his father asked.

Laurie regarded his father coldly. 'I didn't learn nothing,' he said.

'Anything,' I said. 'Didn't learn anything.'

'The teacher spanked a boy, though,' Laurie said, addressing his bread and butter. 'For being fresh,' he added, with his mouth full.

'What did he do?' I asked. 'Who was it?'

Laurie thought. 'It was Charles,' he said. 'He was fresh. The teacher spanked him and made him stand in a corner. He was awfully fresh.'

'What did he do?' I asked again, but Laurie slid off his chair, took a cookie, and left, while his father was still saying, 'See here, young man.'

The next day Laurie remarked at lunch, as soon as he sat down, 'Well, Charles was bad again today.' He grinned enormously and said, 'Today Charles hit the teacher.'

'Good heavens,' I said, mindful of the Lord's name, 'I suppose he got spanked again?'

'He sure did,' Laurie said. 'Look up,' he said to his father.

'What?' his father said, looking up.

'Look down,' Laurie said. 'Look at my thumb. Gee, you're dumb.' He began to laugh insanely.

'Why did Charles hit the teacher?' I asked quickly.

'Because she tried to make him colour with red crayons,' Laurie said. 'Charles wanted to colour with green crayons so he hit the teacher and she spanked him and said nobody play with Charles but everybody did.'

The third day — it was Wednesday of the first week — Charles bounced a see-saw on to the head of a little girl and made her bleed, and the teacher made him stay inside all during recess. Thursday Charles had to stand in a corner during story-time because he kept pounding his feet on the floor. Friday Charles was deprived of blackboard privileges because he threw chalk.

On Saturday I remarked to my husband, 'Do you think kindergarten is too unsettling for Laurie? All this toughness, and bad grammar, and this Charles boy sounds like such a bad influence.'

'It'll be all right,' my husband said reassuringly. 'Bound to be people like Charles in the world. Might as well meet them now as later.'

On Monday Laurie came home late, full of news. 'Charles,' he shouted as he came up the hill; I was waiting anxiously on the front steps. 'Charles,' Laurie yelled all the way up the hill, 'Charles was bad again.'

'Come right in,' I said, as soon as he came close enough. 'Lunch is waiting.'

'You know what Charles did?' he demanded, following me through the door. 'Charles yelled so in school they sent a boy in from first grade to tell the teacher she had to make Charles keep quiet, and so Charles had to stay after school. And so all the children stayed to watch him.'

'What did he do?' I asked.

'He just sat there,' Laurie said, climbing into his chair at the table. 'Hi, Pop, y'old dust mop.'

'Charles had to stay after school today,' I told my husband. 'Everyone stayed with him.'

'What does this Charles look like?' my husband asked Laurie. 'What's his other name?'

'He's bigger than me,' Laurie said. 'And he doesn't have any rubbers and he doesn't ever wear a jacket.'

## Unit 14. Charles

Monday night was the first Parent-Teachers meeting, and only the fact that the baby had a cold kept me from going; I wanted passionately to meet Charles's mother. On Tuesday Laurie remarked suddenly, 'Our teacher had a friend come to see her in school today.'

'Charles's mother?' my husband and I asked simultaneously.

'Naaah,' Laurie said scornfully. 'It was a man who came and made us do exercises, we had to touch our toes. Look.' He climbed down from his chair and squatted down and touched his toes. 'Like this,' he said. He got solemnly back into his chair and said, picking up his fork, 'Charles didn't even *do* exercises.'

'That's fine,' I said heartily. 'Didn't Charles want to do exercises?'

'Naaah,' Laurie said. 'Charles was so fresh to the teacher's friend he wasn't *let* do exercises.'

'Fresh again?' I said.

'He kicked the teacher's friend,' Laurie said. 'The teacher's friend told Charles to touch his toes like I just did and Charles kicked him.'

'What are they going to do about Charles, do you suppose?'

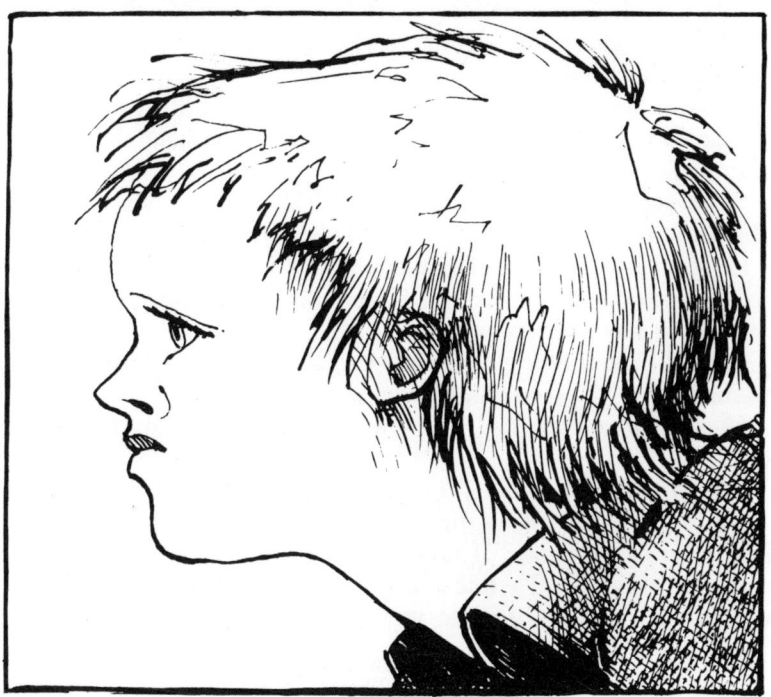

Laurie's father asked him.

Laurie shrugged elaborately. 'Throw him out of school, I guess,' he said.

Wednesday and Thursday were routine; Charles yelled during story hour and hit a boy in the stomach and made him cry. On Friday Charles stayed after school again and so did all the other children.

With the third week of kindergarten Charles was an institution in our family; the baby was being a Charles when she cried all afternoon; Laurie did a Charles when he filled his wagon full of mud and pulled it through the kitchen; even my husband, when he caught his elbow in the telephone cord and pulled telephone, ashtray, and a bowl of flowers off the table, said, after the first minute, 'Looks like Charles.'

During the third and fourth weeks it looked like a reformation in Charles; Laurie reported grimly at lunch on Thursday of the third week, 'Charles was so good today the teacher gave him an apple.'

'What?' I said, and my husband added warily, 'You mean Charles?'

'Charles,' Laurie said. 'He gave the crayons around and he picked up the books afterwards and the teacher said he was her helper.'

'What happened?' I asked incredulously.

'He was her helper, that's all,' Laurie said, and shrugged.

'Can this be true, about Charles?' I asked my husband that night. 'Can something like this happen?'

'Wait and see,' my husband said cynically. 'When you've got a Charles to deal with, this may mean he's only plotting.'

He seemed to be wrong. For over a week Charles was the teacher's helper; each day he handed things out and he picked things up; no one had to stay after school.

'The P.T.A. meeting's next week again,' I told my husband one evening. 'I'm going to find Charles's mother there.'

'Ask her what happened to Charles,' my husband said. 'I'd like to know.'

'I'd like to know myself,' I said.

On Friday of that week things were back to normal. 'You know what Charles did today?' Laurie demanded at the lunch table, in a voice slightly awed. 'He told a little girl to say a word and she said it and the teacher washed her mouth out with soap and Charles laughed.'

'What word?' his father asked unwisely, and Laurie said, 'I'll have to whisper it to you, it's so bad.' He got down off his chair and went around to his father. His father bent his head down and Laurie whispered joyfully. His father's eyes widened.

'Did Charles tell the little girl to say *that?*' he asked respectfully.
'She said it *twice*,' Laurie said. 'Charles told her to say it *twice*.'
'What happened to Charles?' my husband asked.
'Nothing,' Laurie said. 'He was passing out the crayons.'

Monday morning Charles abandoned the little girl and said the evil word himself three or four times, getting his mouth washed out with soap each time. He also threw chalk.

My husband came to the door with me that evening as I set out for the P.T.A. meeting. 'Invite her over for a cup of tea after the meeting,' he said. 'I want to get a look at her.'

'If only she's there,' I said prayerfully.

'She'll be there,' my husband said. 'I don't see how they could hold a P.T.A. meeting without Charles's mother.'

At the meeting I sat restlessly, scanning each comfortable matronly face, trying to determine which one hid the secret of Charles. None of them looked to me haggard enough. No one stood up in the meeting and apologized for the way her son had been acting. No one mentioned Charles.

After the meeting I identified and sought out Laurie's kindergarten teacher. She had a plate with a cup of tea and a piece of chocolate cake; I had a plate with a cup of tea and a piece of marsh-mallow cake. We manoeuvred up to one another cautiously, and smiled.

'I've been so anxious to meet you,' I said. 'I'm Laurie's mother.'
'We're all so interested in Laurie,' she said.
'Well, he certainly likes kindergarten,' I said. 'He talks about it all the time.'
'We had a little trouble adjusting, the first week or so,' she said primly, 'but now he's a fine little helper. With occasional lapses, of course.'
'Laurie usually adjusts quickly,' I said. 'I suppose this time it's Charles's influence.'
'Charles?'
'Yes,' I said, laughing, 'you must have your hands full in that kindergarten, with Charles.'
'Charles?' she said. 'We don't have any Charles in the kindergarten.'

(*Charles*, Shirley Jackson)

1. Who *was* Charles?
2. At what point in the story did you realise who 'Charles' really was?
3. Did 'Charles' behave differently at home and at school?
4. What were four of the things he did that got him into trouble?
5. Do you think everybody stayed after school?
6. In your opinion, was the teacher right in not contacting Laurie's parents? Explain why you think so.
7. Why did 'Charles' turn into a helper?
8. How do you think his parents would react on realising there *was* no Charles?
9. Briefly recount an incident from your own early schooling. What did you do, and what were your reasons for your act?
10. A word for the reason a person acts in a particular way is 'motivation'. What are some likely motivations:
    (a) for vandalism?
    (b) for stealing?

Endings

11. Some writers like to keep their ending a surprise, even although they may drop hints throughout the story. We speak of such a technique as 'sting-in-the-tail' writing. Most detective stories follow this pattern. Read the passages that follow, then try writing some of your own in the same style.

    A. The Least Successful Air Attack
        To celebrate 'Air Force Week' in 1975, thirty Peruvian fighter planes took part in a demonstration attack on fourteen old fishing boats.
        These ramshackle old vessels were sailed out off the coast of Peru and abandoned as targets.
        Then the impressive fighter force flew over the craft, high and low, strafing and bombing for the best part of fifteen minutes. To the amazement of the watching crowd, they failed to sink a single boat.

    B. The Most Unsuccessful Attempt to Propose Marriage
        In the late 1900s a teacher in London was enamoured of a well-to-do young woman called Gwendolin who lived in

Sussex. One weekend he went to the family's ancestral home near Lewes, to ask her to marry him. On his first night he woke at three a.m. wanting a glass of water. Feeling his way to the basin in the dark he knocked something over. Next morning he awoke to find that he had spilt ink over the priceless fourteenth century tapestry which was the pride and joy of Gwendolin's mother. He left immediately without seeing his beloved.

After the fuss had died down he returned to make another attempt. In order to minimize the chances of disaster he decided to call in for just half an hour in the afternoon. He asked Gwendolin's mother if he might speak to her daughter. While she was out of the room he sat down on what he took to be a cushion. It was however the family Pekinese, which did not survive the experience. He left again without seeing her. They both married other people.

C. The Least Successful Bank Robber
Not wishing to attract attention to himself, a bank robber in 1969 at Portland, Oregon, wrote all his instructions on a piece of paper rather than shout.

'This is a hold-up and I've got a gun,' he wrote and then held the paper up for the cashier to read.

The bemused bank official waited while he wrote out, 'Put all the money in a paper bag.'

This message was pushed through the grille. The cashier read it and then wrote on the bottom, 'I don't have a paper bag,' and passed it back.

The robber fled.

(*The Book of Heroic Failures*, Stephen Pile)

## Unit 15. In the Forest

Some writers like to make their readers work out for themselves what a story is about or how it should end. Before you can reach your own conclusion, you must make certain you have extracted all the clues the writer has given. You might find you have to discard several possible conclusions as the story unfolds.

As you read the following story, fill in the answers to the questions. At the end you will still need to draw your own conclusion.

There was a wind. It blew through the topmost branches of the tall trees in a silent, autumnal forest. Dry leaves trembled nervously as the dark tree trunks stirred in a thrust of the wind. A scarlet maple leaf lay unmoving on the inky surface of a cold spring. Behind an interlacing of nakedly-white birches a young deer stood still with wide lacquered eyes fixed on him. Its tarblack nostrils shone in a quivering of fright and then like the wind it rustled momentarily on the forest floor of crackling leaves and disappeared.

He breathed heavily with disappointment. He had transmitted fear, his own apprehensions, again.

He moved from the protection of an overhanging rock. The ease with which he moved delighted him sensuously. This sportive exhilaration had to be curbed; it made him less sensitive to the problem at hand. He had to communicate.

There were obviously lower orders, mainly the winged beings. Some were tiny and fragile. They would approach and light on him with the unwariness of the naïve, trusting to their speed to escape from danger. From them he had no consciousness of intelligence. They buzzed and swarmed and hummed with monotonous idiocy. The larger winged beings were more interesting but they wore the drabness of the forest on their sleek wings. They would not come close but made inquiring sounds and swooped away at his approach.

## Unit 15. In the Forest

He had learned to move silently through the silent forest. He felt almost weightless and infinitely agile and this delight he had to renounce for the time. He could walk erect, or run with incredible rapidity. And when he stood erect his body attained a new vitality and with his head above the lower woody vegetable growths he experienced a new dignity and regality. He was no petitioning refugee from the pitiless vice of unending cold. Here in this autumnal forest was the warmth and promise of spring, for him.

Excitement made him warmer and more jubilant still. He had to communicate. But with whom? With which of these beings could he share his unbelievable adventure? He ran down a sloping floor of the forest and ran and ran, slipping and sliding on the leaves until he was breathless. And came to halt in a marshy spot with the spikes of dried vegetation towering about him. His heart beat with transcendental joy. He ached to babble of his happiness and then to relive his adventure in the telling of it to another intelligence the equal of his.

He breathed more slowly and more slowly yet. Above the trees, caught in the web of branches, a brilliant blue sky gleamed and virgin cloud forms of purest white drifted slowly above the trap of the forest. And there, lower than the clouds, was the magnificence of a burning sun, a brilliance whose golden shadow warmed the tree trunks, the faces of the dry leaves, the soft, sucking black earth of the marsh and — him. In this warmth he luxuriated, with every sensibility in his being. His body had starved for warmth.

And while he stood thus, a long slithering form passed before him, describing in its movement across the moss the rocks and black leaf-moulded earth resilient, graceful curves. It passed him without notice, conveying nothing, an impenetrable life form.

And then, as suddenly, his muscles tightened and he withdrew reluctantly from the warmth of the sun.

He moved closer into the dried, tassel-topped grasses, feeling the scrape of sharp seed-bearing burrs as they clung to him. In a closely woven burrow, hidden from the sun and the reach of the wind, he heard a new sound, a louder, sharper crackle in the forest. A new scent crowded into the burrow and overpowered him with a new sensation, a suffocating awareness of danger.

He was cold again, and taut. The shadow from which he had escaped enclosed him again. This same deadly shadow of fear sapped his new vitality and destroyed his sensuous joy.

There was that sharper sound, a baying shrillness that resounded through the forest quiet and hammered at the tree trunks and unresisting vegetation with an unreasoning insistence. The echo of this new, insane voice of danger stirred him.

He moved cautiously and quickly from the burrow and through the marsh. He was not erect now, but low and rapid-moving. He thought desperately of survival now, not communication. This howling, yapping being had found him out, scented him in the forest and he knew only that he had to escape.

The forest floor rose gradually to greater and greater heights. He recognized the terrain and the character of this part of the forest. There was, at the summit, a sudden drop down a face of irregular outcroppings of stone. And at the base of this lay a vast body of water in which he could hide. He could manage the tall face of stone, hiding and blending into its cold greyness.

The baying and yapping was closer and he moved even more rapidly. The chase seemed directed to him, not purposeless. Behind the baying and shrill crying of this hunter was yet another will. And this chilled him with hopeless horror. He felt instinctively that he could communicate with *this* will, that this was the intelligence he sought. But between it and him was this unleashed agent for his destruction.

He ran more quickly and with a new sensation of weariness as the slope mounted. The vegetation was green here, and somewhat sparser. There were fewer places of refuge. At times he ran without the protection of any covering, only the moss and green ground vines underfoot.

As he reached the summit he heard a new sound, a sharp undecipherable crack and whine overhead. When he had reached the top of the sharp rise, he stood erect for a moment, seeking the surest path for his descent of the sharp rock face. The body of water below gleamed warmly blue. The sun was a glorious almost perfectly round entity, low in the sky. His body straightened involuntarily, rose up in the warmth of the sun, darkly and strangely outlined against the unbroken blue of the sky. And then as the crack and whine of the gun sounded in the evening quiet, not once but twice, and inexpertly a third time, his shape crumbled against the sky and he toppled from the cliff edge into the still blue lake below.

The man breathed heavily as he came up the hill. He was red-faced from exertion and frustration. He was heavy and clumsy in the perfection Abercrombie and Fitch had tailored into his hunting

# Unit 15. In the Forest

clothes. He held his rifle, an expensive and aesthetically beautiful instrument of destruction, like a blunt, ugly club.

He stood at the edge of the cliff and looked down. There was nothing. Only the serenity of the early evening, the unanswering quiet of the lake, the ridge of mountains, the darkening sky.

'Now what in the hell was that?' the man muttered.

The dog, beside him, shivered and sat down suddenly. Its howl was unbidden, undirected, and it filled the forest with unrest.

(*In the Forest*, Leslie Perri)

1. What does the title tell?
2. What season is it?
3. How did the deer react to him?
4. Is 'he' also afraid?
5. What is 'his' problem?
6. Why are the insects of no use to 'him'?
7. Are the birds any better?

STOP! What *might be* the solution? Go on further.

## Section C. Fiction

8. What explanation can you give for 'his' feeling of being almost weightless?
9. What possible explanations are cut out because 'he' can walk erect?
10. Why, in autumn, should 'he' feel warmth?
11. What could 'his' 'unbelievable adventure' be?
12. Where is 'he' now?
13. Why does 'he' not know where to find 'another intelligence the equal of his'?
14. Does a passing snake bother 'him'?
15. Where does 'he' take shelter?
16. If burrs can cling to 'him', what does this suggest about 'his' appearance?
17. What does 'he' hear?
18. What does 'he' smell?
19. What are 'his' reactions?

STOP! What do you think 'he' is now?

20. What does the baying, howling, yapping indicate?
21. Is the burrow above or below the ground?
22. What is now of the greatest importance to 'him'?
23. Back in the forest, 'he' knows of a hiding-place. Where is it?
24. 'He' is being hunted, but what does 'he' feel is behind the hunter?
25. Why does 'he' feel such great disappointment and sorrow?
26. Where is 'he' now?
27. What does 'he' hear?
28. What is it?
29. When 'he' is outlined against the sun, what happens?
30. Where is 'he' now?
31. Why does the dog howl?
32. What was he?

# Unit 16. The Hamatsa

When the huge grave was dug and ready, forty boxes were placed in it, and all the broken bones and bits of ancient grave posts and carvings. The men who had done the work buried also the clothes they had worn. Then on a sunny, clear morning, Mark held a brief service and the grave was covered. When it was over, he saw relief in the eyes of the old, and again T. P. spoke for them.

'At last a man has come to us who has seen to it that our dead can rest in peace.'

When he returned along the little path to the village, Mark stopped at the house of Peter, the carver, and sat a moment on the steps to chat.

'When spring comes, grass will grow over the huge new grave,' Peter said. 'The air will be sweet smelling again from the wild flowers, and the old people will walk there often.'

'Why will they go there, Peter?' Mark asked slowly.

'To be sure that at last our dead are safe from the hamatsa.'

'I do not know the myth of the hamatsa.'

'The myth is a story. There is no harm in the myth, and I will tell it to you.

'A young man was ready to dance and he did not know what dance to do. He stood up in his red cedar bark dress, and he threw off his blankets, and he walked up a mountain until he came to a lake and saw a loon. The loon said, "I know why you have come and I will help you," and he led him to a house from which smoke came and told him to enter. The doorkeeper let him in and asked him to sit, and the second man, who was the cannibal man, asked why he had come, and the young man answered, "Because I want to be as you are."'

'And then?' Mark asked.

'And then the cannibal man went behind a screen and came out with a body, and he gobbled up one, and he gobbled up two, and he gobbled up four, because that is the ceremonial number, and a lady followed him around and put the bones in a basket. Then he danced four times around the house and disappeared up a pole, and he put into the young man the whistle which makes the cannibal cry, and he tied hemlock branches to his wrists and ankles to protect him, and the young man did the dance as he had been shown, and returned to his village.

'And one night his people decided to give a dance. They lighted a pitch pole and sent four of the villagers to bring water, but none came back. They heard the hamatsa cry and recognized the young man, and they knew he had been bewitched by the cannibal man and had eaten the four people.

'They sang their songs and piled food boxes to the ceremonial house roof and the roof opened, and they heard a skull roll down its side, and were afraid.

'The next night his people tried to get the young man into the house to tame him, and he came four times on four nights, and they thought he was safely cured because he had fallen in love with a maiden. On the last night they knew he was not cured, so they killed him with magic, and he returned to the wood and was not seen again. And this is the myth which the old men tell and it is harmless.'

'And the dance was based on the myth?'

'Yes. In the winter ceremonials, the hamatsa dance was the last and it took four nights. The young man who did it disappeared from the village and he lived beyond the old burial ground in a little cedar house hidden in the deep woods. I know, because when I was a young boy, my father's house was the last in the village, and I was the one who took him food.

'My friend, you cannot imagine what it was like — the tribe waiting on the first night of the dance, and the hamatsa coming at last, crying in the woods. In my father's day if anyone laughed, if he made a mistake in the dances, he was killed. In my father's day when the hamatsa entered on the second night of the dance carrying a real body taken from the old burial ground, the women were afraid, and they said, "Is the body from my family's tree? Is it one of ours?" When I was a boy the hamatsa carried no body because the government forbade it, and he only pretended to bite people, holding a piece of seal liver in his mouth. As a boy I saw the scars on the arms of the old men, and I heard the tales.'

Then Peter was silent, and Mark left him and walked along down the path through the woods.

How had it been in the old days when the magic, and supernatural

## 16. The Hamatsa

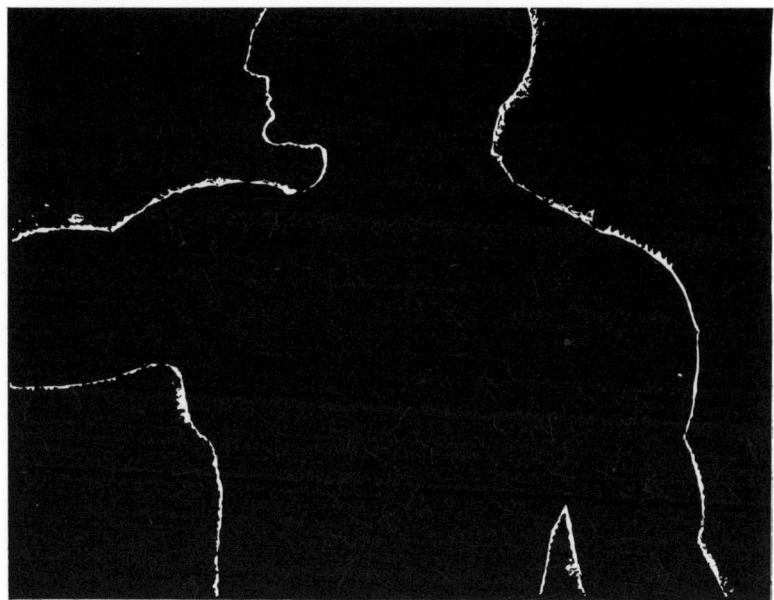

spirits, and the cannibal man who lived at the north end of the world had dominated life here in this village? How had it been when the hamatsa had come in the night through the great trees, crying his soft and terrible call? He would never know. No man would ever know. But Mark had seen the light of the old, old ways reflected on the faces like the glow from a dying campfire, and he knew that it was the hamatsa who had been freed at last from his holy madness, and was at peace in the deep woods.

(*I Heard the Owl Call my Name*, Margaret Craven)

1. What evidence can you find of Indian beliefs?
2. What evidence shows that the ceremonial dances were of great importance to the Indian people?
3. What evidence is there to show that the white man's culture has taken over from the Indian's?
4. If the Indians recognised the Hamatsa as only a myth, why did it have such an impact on the Indian people?

Discussion points:
5. Is it right to impose one set of beliefs on another culture?
6. Are there Australian stories that have become 'myths'?

## Unit 17.  Embroidery

The dark porch air in the late afternoon was full of needle flashes, like a movement of gathered silver insects in the light. The three women's mouths twitched over their work. Their bodies lay back and then imperceptibly forward, so that the rocking chairs tilted and murmured. Each woman looked to her own hands, as if quite suddenly she had found her heart beating there.

'What time is it?'

'Ten minutes to five.'

'Got to get up in a minute and shell those peas for dinner.'

'But —' said one of them.

'Oh yes, I forgot. How foolish of me . . .' The first woman paused, put down her embroidery and needle, and looked through the open porch door, through the warm interior of the quiet house, to the silent kitchen. There upon the table, seeming more like symbols of domesticity than anything she had ever seen in her life, lay the mound of fresh-washed peas in their neat, resilient jackets, waiting for her fingers to bring them into the world.

'Go hull them if it'll make you feel good,' said the second woman.

'No,' said the first. 'I won't. I just won't.'

The third woman sighed. She embroidered a rose, a leaf, a daisy on a green field. The embroidery needle rose and vanished.

The second woman was working on the finest, most delicate piece of embroidery of them all, deftly poking, finding, and returning the quick needle upon innumerable journeys. Her quick black glance was on each motion. A flower, a man, a road, a sun, a house; the scene grew under hand, a miniature beauty, perfect in every threaded detail.

'It seems at times like this that it's always your hands you turn to,' she said, and the others nodded enough to make the rockers rock again.

'I believe,' said the first lady, 'that our souls are in our hands. For we do *everything* to the world with our hands. Sometimes I think we don't use our hands half enough; it's certain we don't use our heads.'

They all peered more intently at what their hands were doing. 'Yes,' said the third lady, 'when you look back on a whole lifetime, it seems you don't remember faces so much as hands and what they did.'

They recounted to themselves the lids they had lifted, the doors they had opened and shut, the flowers they had picked, the dinners they had made, all with slow or quick fingers, as was their manner or custom. Looking back, you saw a flurry of hands, like a magician's dream, doors popping wide, taps turned, brooms wielded, children spanked. The flutter of pink hands was the only sound; the rest was a dream without voices.

'No supper to fix tonight or tomorrow night or the next night after that,' said the third lady.

'No windows to open or shut.'

'No coal to shovel in the basement furnace next winter.'

'No papers to clip cooking articles out of.'

And suddenly they were crying. The tears rolled softly down their faces and fell into the material upon which their fingers twitched.

'This won't help things,' said the first lady at last, putting the back of her thumb to each under-eyelid. She looked at her thumb and it was wet.

'Now look what I've done!' cried the second lady exasperated. The others stopped and peered over. The second lady held out her embroidery. There was the scene, perfect except that while the embroidered yellow sun shone down upon the embroidered green field, and the embroidered brown road curved toward an embroidered pink house, the man standing on the road had something wrong with his face.

'I'll just have to rip out the whole pattern, practically, to fix it right,' said the second lady.

'What a shame!' They all stared intently at the beautiful scene with the flaw in it.

The second lady began to pick away at the thread with her little deft scissors flashing. The pattern came out thread by thread. She pulled and yanked, almost viciously. The man's face was gone. She continued to seize at the threads.

'What are you *doing?*' asked the other woman.

They leaned and saw what she had done.

The man was gone from the road. She had taken him out entirely.

They said nothing but returned to their own tasks.
'What time is it?' asked someone.
'Five minutes to five.'
'Is it supposed to happen at five o'clock?'
'Yes.'
'And they're not sure what it'll do to anything, really, when it happens?'
'No, not sure.'
'Why didn't we stop them before it got this far and this big?'
'It's twice as big as ever before. No, ten times, maybe a thousand.'
'This isn't like the first one or the dozen later ones. This is different. Nobody knows what it might do when it comes.'

They waited on the porch in the smell of roses and cut grass. 'What time is it now?'
'One minute to five.'
The needles flashed silver fire. They swam like a tiny school of metal fish in the darkening summer air.

Far away a mosquito sound. Then something like a tremor of drums. The three women cocked their heads, listening.
'We won't hear anything, will we?'
'They say not.'
'Perhaps we're foolish. Perhaps we'll go right on, after five o'clock, shelling peas, opening doors, stirring soups, washing dishes, making lunches, peeling oranges ...'
'My, how we'll laugh to think we were frightened by an old experiment!' They smiled a moment at each other.
'It's five o'clock.'

At these words, hushed, they all busied themselves. Their fingers darted. Their faces were turned down to the motions they made. They made frantic patterns. They made lilacs and grass and trees and houses and rivers in the embroidered cloth. They said nothing, but you could hear their breath in the silent porch air.

Thirty seconds passed.

The second woman sighed finally and began to relax.
'I think I just *will* go shell those peas for supper,' she said. 'I —'
But she hadn't time even to lift her head. Somewhere, at the side of her vision, she saw the world brighten and catch fire. She kept her head down, for she knew what it was. She didn't look up, nor did the others, and in the last instant their fingers were flying; they didn't glance about to see what was happening to the country, the town,

this house, or even this porch. They were only staring down at the design in their flickering hands.

The second woman watched an embroidered flower go. She tried to embroider it back in, but it went, and then the road vanished, and the blades of grass. She watched a fire, in slow motion almost, catch upon the embroidered house and unshingle it, and pull each threaded leaf from the small green tree in the hoop, and she saw the sun itself pulled apart in the design. Then the fire caught upon the moving point of the needle while still it flashed; she watched the fire come along her fingers and arms and body, untwisting the yarn of her being so painstakingly that she could see it in all its devilish beauty, yanking out the pattern from the material at hand. What it was doing to the other women or the furniture or the elm tree in the yard, she never knew. For now, yes, now! it was plucking at the white embroidery of her flesh, the pink thread of her cheeks, and at last it found her heart, a soft red rose sewn with fire, and it burned the fresh, embroidered petals away, one by delicate one ...

(From *Golden Apples of the Sun*, Ray Bradbury)

1. What details does the author use to create an atmosphere of waiting?
2. Why are the women embroidering?
3. Why do their memories concern their hands?
4. Is there evidence to show they are afraid?
5. When the first lady says, 'Sometimes I think we don't use our hands enough; it's certain we don't use our heads,' do you think she means the women or everybody by 'we'? Give your reason.
6. Why does the second lady embroider something wrong with the man's face?
7. Why does she remove him completely from the embroidery?
8. At five minutes to five, what is 'it' that is about to happen?
9. How do they try to reassure each other?
10. What are the sounds they hear? What do they sound like?
11. Read the last paragraph again. Apart from ending his story, what added message is the author implying?
12. It is impossible to embroider as quickly as the story suggests. Does this spoil the story? Give a reason for your answer.
13. A good storyteller chooses detail very carefully. What effect do the details have in this story?
14. What methods do you use to control panic, excitement or fear

while you are waiting — for an exam, for a race, for an interview, for example?

15. Although we use words such as 'kind', 'cruel', 'generous', 'malicious', 'vague' and so on to describe people, competent writers seldom label their characters in this way. Instead, they imply qualities through their characters' actions, comments, responses, conduct, and attitudes. A clever writer chooses this subtler approach. A responsive reader is perceptive, that is, he is attuned to the writer in such a way that he can pick up the author's unstated messages.

What are the unstated qualities or faults of the characters in the extracts below?

A. Biff: I've had twenty or thirty different kinds of jobs since I left home before the war, and it always turns out the same. I just realised it lately. In Nebraska when I herded cattle and the Dakotas, and Arizona and now in Texas. (Arthur Miller)

B. 'If the worst comes to the worst,' he said, 'there's things I could do where I come from. I might do a bit of wool-sorting, for instance. I'm a pretty fair expert. I'd just have to sit down and they'd bring the sheep to me, and I'd feel the wool and tell them what it was — being blind improves the feeling, you know.' (Henry Lawson)

C. And when a girl walks around and reads all the signs with all of the famous historical names it really makes you hold your breath. Because when Dorothy and I went on a walk, we only walked a few blocks but in only a few blocks we read all the historical names like Coty and Cartier and I knew we were seeing something educational at last and our whole trip was not a failure. I mean I really try to make Dorothy get educated and have reverence. (Anita Loos)

D. We are expected to give charity to this man's wife and children, who, you tell us, were dependent upon him. They may have been; I do not care whether they were or not. I object to the whole thing on principle. It is high time a stand was made against this sentimental humanitarianism. The country is eaten up with it. I object to my money being paid to these people of whom I know nothing, who have done nothing to earn it. (John Galsworthy)

E. Cokey was a good housekeeper and what they call a good mother. She kept her kid clean and fed it like a prize for the show. In fact she was mad about the kid. She used to smile sometimes, when the kid brought up his wind or hit himself on the nose. But she wasn't happy because she was not that sort. A million a year and a kind husband out of the films wouldn't have made Cokey happy. She took life too seriously. (Joyce Cary)

F. You were born where you were born and faced the future that you faced because you were black and for no other reason. The limits of your ambition were, thus, expected to be set forever. You were born into a society which spelled out with brutal clarity and in as many ways as possible, that you were a worthless human being. You were not expected to aspire to excellence: you were expected to make peace with mediocrity. (James Baldwin)

G. Deserted, debt-ridden, flurried, doomed by ambitions that never came off, yet our mother possessed indestructible gaiety which welled up like a thermal spring. Her laughing, like her weeping, was instantaneous and child-like and switched without warning — or memory. Her emotions were entirely without reserve; she clouted you one moment and hugged you the next — to the ruin of one's ragged nerves. (Laurie Lee)

# Section D
# Character and Values

## Unit 18. The Old Grandfather and the Child

Folk tales distil the wisdom of ordinary people's experience, and show the values they admire. Greed, laziness, dishonesty, etc. are *always* punished, whereas concern for others, honesty, fairness, etc. *always* win. Often animals are used to represent these virtues and vices at work. The 'hero' or 'heroine' is often a humble, poor person, who 'earns' success or riches (and usually marries the prince/princess)!

When a story has a secondary or figurative meaning, beyond the incident it relates, we say that a message or *moral* is being implied.

Being able to see beyond the immediate facts, or reading-between-the-lines is an important comprehension skill. The next exercises ask you to do this, as well as give the facts of the extracts, which we call the literal meanings.

Once there was a very old man; his eyes were dim, his ears deaf, and his knees trembled. When he sat at the table and tried to eat, his hand shook so that he could not guide the spoon to his mouth, and whatever it held spilled on the table-cloth or on his clothes. His son and daughter-in-law were so annoyed over his conduct at the table that finally they made him sit in the corner behind the stove and eat out of an earthen dish. Often the poor old man had not enough to eat, and would look sadly at the table with tears in his eyes.

One day his trembling hands could not hold even the dish, and it fell to the floor and broke. The young wife scolded him loudly, but he said nothing, only sighed. Then they bought him a wooden dish for a few pennies, and gave him his meals in that.

As they were sitting at the table one day, their little four-year-old boy brought in some little pieces of board, and tried to fasten them together.

'What are you making?' asked the father.

'A little trough for you and mother to eat out of when I become big,' replied the child.

The parents looked at each other in astonishment, and then began to cry. The little child had taught them a lesson.

After this the old man came to the table, and not a word was said when he spilt anything.

(*Fables*, Aesop)

First, some questions on the *literal* meaning of the story.

1. In your own words, what particular action of the old man annoyed his son and daughter-in-law?
2. What did they insist the old man must do?
3. What further incident made the young wife scold the old man?
4. What was the little boy trying to make?

Now, some questions to test if you can find the *implied* meaning.

5. Why was the old man given a cheap wooden dish?
6. Re-read the last sentence. What does this suggest about the son and his wife?
7. Re-read the words spoken by the child. How does he believe he should act towards his parents when he is grown-up?
8. How had the child learned about adults' behaviour?
9. What is implied by the words 'in astonishment'?
10. Of the following values, which does the story stress? (You may choose any number.)
    (a) tolerance
    (b) being practical
    (c) need for compassion
    (d) importance of being strong and able to cope
    (e) respect for the aged
    (f) children should always follow the examples set by adults.

Proverbs

11. Proverbs also summarise wisdom. Each language has its own. Although the proverb expresses an idea in real things (such as animals, fire, buildings, etc.) there is always a secondary or implied wider meaning that makes it suitable to apply to many more incidents and people.

    Choose one of the proverbs that follow, and first describe what

actually happens (i.e. its literal meaning). Then explain what message or moral you think it implies and lastly write a modern incident that illustrates the same message.
(a) You can't use paper to wrap up a fire.
(b) Best to be off with the old love before you are on with the new.
(c) Content lodges oftener in cottages than in palaces.
(d) Better a bare foot than none.
(e) The hen knows when the dawn has come but she nevertheless looks to the cock to announce it.
(f) The fish who once escapes the hook will not easily bite another.
(g) Dead dogs bark not.
(h) How can you view the plain if you don't climb the high mountain?
(i) The thread breaks where it is weakest.
(j) You cannot lose what you never had.
(k) No lock will hold against the power of gold.
(l) If two men feed a horse it will be thin; if two men mend a boat it will leak.
(m) He that lies down with dogs must rise up with fleas.
(n) No one knows how fast he can run until the bear is close behind him.
(o) A leopard cannot change his spots.
(p) When a witch's child dies, it makes her sad.
(q) Swallow it and your mother dies; spit it out and your father dies.
12. Look up some folk tales or proverbs of other countries and be prepared to act them out for the class.
13. • Penny wise; pound foolish.
   • Take care of the pennies and the pounds will take care of themselves.

These two proverbs seem to contradict each other. Can you find other pairs that also contradict?

## Unit 19. Boarding School

I was sent to boarding school when I was ten, and hated every minute of it. The worst of it was being imprisoned, in corridors and classrooms and <u>bleak</u> dormitories and concrete yards, when no one was allowed to <u>step</u> outside the school gates on pain of <u>expulsion</u>. I learnt fear and hate for the first time towards what seemed an alien and <u>malevolent</u> authority. But I found <u>allies</u> among the other girls, many of whom were in much the same situation as I was, coming as they did from properties in northern New South Wales and Queensland that were even larger and more isolated than Ilparran. 'Bush heifers' my father used to call us, for we were wild, <u>uncouth</u> and shy, and resented being cooped up and herded together in a few <u>dreary</u> acres.

The school had one long winter and one long summer holiday every year, as well as a week in spring and autumn. Home was only eighty miles away, but getting there was such a complicated <u>undertaking</u> that the two worlds seemed very far apart. In midwinter the journey home was particularly dramatic for we travelled at night in the bitter cold. We left our beds at midnight to catch the 'Midnight Horror', the inevitable nickname for the rickety old Brisbane Express, which left at 2.30 a.m. and arrived at my home town at 5 a.m., if it was on time, which it seldom was. We often had more than an hour's wait on the icy platform, unheated and blacked out because of the war. We did not mind: it all added to the drama. The longer we waited, the colder we got, the more exciting was the appearance of the two pinpricks of light on the railway track that heralded the arrival of the train. We slept fitfully in the carriages, our limbs <u>intertwined</u> in affectionate heaps in the tiny, tight, dog-boxes, as excitement gave way to <u>drowsiness</u>. I had to <u>disentangle</u> myself from the Queenslanders and get off alone at our unlit station, <u>groggy</u> with sleep and half sick with excitement, and board the Inverell mail bus. I was always the only schoolgirl on it and the only passenger not going all the way to Inverell, which was enough to make me feel self-conscious.

Our bus driver, called Happy because he never smiled, had to put my suitcases in a special place by themselves, because I was let down before all the others, and I felt I was being a nuisance. He let me off at the Ilparran turn-off, five miles from home and about half way to Inverell, and this must have been on Father's instructions because I would much rather have been put down at the small wooden bungalow that was the Matheson Post Office, only half a mile further from home up the road. In midwinter the temperature was below freezing, with a heavy frost on the ground or sometimes light snow, and unless the bus was very late, it would still be dark.

Father was never there. I would not have minded if Happy had been more casual about it, if he had dropped me and my suitcases by the side of the road and just driven off. But he always kept the whole busload of people waiting while he gazed anxiously up the road for the headlights of Father's car. He asked me was I warm enough and even gave my ice-cold, gloveless hands a good rub between his huge ones. On one terrible occasion he offered to build and light a fire for me. In front of all those people! Fortunately he must have heard the anguish in my voice as I assured him I did not need it, because he did not insist. As soon as the bus went I left my cases by the side of the road and set off for the Post Office, where even at 6 a.m. I got a

sympathetic and tactfully casual welcome. I telephoned Father, and then sat waiting for him on the edge of a battered old plush armchair in a room exactly like the living room of the MacDonalds' house. I began to feel on home territory at last.

I always intended to be cross with Father, but when he arrived all my anger vanished and all I could think of was how good it was to see him, and how wonderful was the ride back through the valley to our house, where breakfast would be ready with hot porridge and cold thick cream on the table and the kitchen warm from the wood stove and smiles and hugs and kisses from Mum and Gill and Bet. And, anyway, he always arrived just as the warm winter sunshine started to pour down the hill-side and the magpies started to sing and the whole valley seemed to glow with happiness.

(*Memories of a Country Childhood*, Judith Wallace)

1. What did the author resent about being at boarding school?
2. What did the school see as important?
3. Why was the term 'bush heifer' appropriate?
4. What evidence is there that the author was self-reliant?
5. In your own words, describe her journey home each school holiday.
6. How did Happy show his concern for her wellbeing?
7. How can you tell that her father intended to be on time although he never made it?
8. What impression do you gain of the author's family?
9. Choose and quote any two details that bring her experience to life.
10. What suggests that many years have passed since the author was a child?
11. Use the underlined words to answer the following. Do not use any word more than once.
    (a) Two synonyms meaning lacking warmth
    (b) A stronger word than discomfort
    (c) Two antonyms meaning tied and untied
    (d) An antonym of enemies
    (e) An antonym of benevolent
    (f) Two nouns formed from expel and drowsy
    (g) A synonym for task
    (h) An adjective suggesting a lack of sleep
    (i) A word meaning lacking in social graces
12. Discussion: Would you have liked to go to boarding school?

## Unit 20. Request to a Year

If the year is meditating a suitable gift,
I should like it to be the attitude
of my great-great-grandmother,
legendary devotee of the arts;

who having had eight children
and little opportunity for painting pictures
sat one day on a high rock
beside a river in Switzerland,

and from a difficult distance viewed
her second son, balanced on a small ice-floe,
drift down the current towards a waterfall
that struck rock-bottom eighty feet below,

while her second daughter, impeded,
no doubt, by the petticoats of the day,
stretched out a last-hope alpenstock*
(which luckily later caught him on his way).

Nothing, it was evident, could be done;
and with the artist's isolating eye
my great-great-grandmother hastily sketched the scene.
The sketch survives to prove the story by.

Year, if you have no Mother's Day present planned,
reach back and bring me the firmness of her hand.

(Judith Wright)

---

*a sturdy stick used in Alpine country, as an aid in climbing.

1. Give three words of your own (not from the poem) that indicate the character of the poet's great-great-grandmother.

2. Use your dictionary to check which of the following words apply to her.
   (a) excitable
   (b) hysterical
   (c) imperturbable
   (d) strong-willed
   (e) masterful
   (f) vapid
   (g) artistic
   (h) intrepid
   (i) nervous
   (j) matriarch

3. Sketch the incident described. Be sure to put in all three characters.

4. Quote lines which indicate:
   (a) that stories about her have been handed down for generations,
   (b) evidence which suggests this is a true story,
   (c) the danger the boy faced,
   (d) the busy life of the great-great-grandmother.

5. What do you think is meant by 'the artist's isolating eye'?

6. Why does the poet mention Mother's Day gifts?

7. What does the great-great-grandmother's 'firmness of hand' symbolize?

8. In comparison with the number of children in your own family, what advantages and disadvantages would you see in being one of eight children?

9. Discussion: Take a quick survey of the numbers of brothers and sisters (siblings) of each member of the class. Then discuss the advantages/disadvantages of being the eldest, the youngest, one of twins, etc.

## Unit 21. Suicide Attempt

Among the incidents which took place during the breaking up, was one which it is necessary to chronicle. Near Philip's Island, on the north side of the harbour, is situated Coal Head, where a party had been lately at work. This party, hastily withdrawn by Vickers to assist in the business of devastation, had left behind it some tools and timber, and at the eleventh hour a boat's crew was sent to bring away the *débris*. The tools were duly collected, and the pine logs — worth twenty-five shillings apiece in Hobart Town — duly rafted and chained. The timber was secured, and the convicts, towing it after them, pulled for the ship just as the sun sank. In the general relaxation of discipline and haste, the raft had not been made with as much care as usual, and the strong current against which the boat was labouring assisted the negligence of the convicts. The logs began to loosen, and though the onward motion of the boat kept the chain taut, when the rowers slackened their exertions the mass parted, and Mr Troke, hooking himself on to the side of the *Ladybird*, saw a huge log slip out from its fellows and disappear into the darkness. Gazing after it with an indignant and disgusted stare, as though it had been a refractory prisoner who merited two days 'solitary', he thought he heard a cry from the direction in which it had been borne. He would have paused to listen, but all his attention was needed to save the timber, and to prevent the boat from being swamped by the struggling mass at her stern.

The cry had proceeded from Rufus Dawes. From his solitary rock he had watched the boat pass him and make for the *Ladybird* in channel, and he had decided — with that curious childishness into which the mind relapses on such supreme occasions — that the moment when the gathering gloom swallowed her up, should be the moment when he would plunge into the surge below him. The heavily-labouring boat grew dimmer and dimmer, as each tug of the oars took her farther from him. Presently, only the figure of Mr Troke in the stern sheets was visible; then that also disappeared, and as the

## Unit 21. Suicide Attempt

nose of the timber raft rose on the swell of the next wave, Rufus Dawes flung himself into the sea.

He was heavily ironed, and he sank like a stone. He had resolved not to attempt to swim, and for the first moment kept his arms raised above his head, in order to sink the quicker. But, as the short, sharp agony of suffocation caught him, and the shock of the icy water dispelled the mental intoxication under which he was labouring, he desperately struck out, and, despite the weight of his irons, gained the surface for an instant. As he did so, all bewildered, and with the one savage instinct of self-preservation predominant over all other thoughts, he became conscious of a huge black mass surging upon him out of the darkness. An instant's buffet with the current, an ineffectual attempt to dive beneath it, a horrible sense that the weight at his feet was dragging him down, — and the huge log, loosened from the raft, was upon him, crushing him beneath its rough and ragged sides. All thoughts of self-murder vanished with the presence of actual peril, and uttering that despairing cry which had been faintly heard by Troke, he flung up his arms to clutch the monster that was pushing him down to death. The log passed completely over him, thrusting him beneath the water, but his hand, scraping along the splintered side, came in contact with the loop of hide rope that yet hung round the mass, and clutched it with the tenacity of a death grip. In another instant he got his head above water, and making good his hold, twisted himself, by a violent effort, across the log.

For a moment he saw the lights from the stern windows of the anchored vessels low in the distance, Grummet Rock disappeared on his left, then, exhausted, breathless, and bruised, he closed his eyes, and the drifting log bore him swiftly and silently away into the darkness.

(*For the Term of his Natural Life*, Marcus Clarke)

1. Did Rufus Dawes expect to survive?
2. What details indicate his intention?
3. What caused him to change his mind?
4. Re-state in your own words exactly how he managed to survive.
5. Write out any three examples of language that suggest the passage was written a long time ago.
6. What details indicate the severity of punishment of early Australian convicts such as Rufus Dawes?
7. What coincidence was responsible for his survival?
8. What was the purpose behind the convicts' trip to Coal Head?
9. Why did one of the logs come adrift?
10. What actions show that he was:
    (a) courageous?
    (b) strong?
11. Discussion:
    (a) Is a person who commits suicide weak or strong?
    (b) When does coincidence become unacceptable in stories or films?

## Dilemma

12. In the following cases, you may wish to discuss the possibilities, or have one of the class act out his/her answers in the role of the person concerned.
    (a) X is a girl, aged sixteen, whose parents are from a different country and who have very strict rules for her behaviour. Should she leave home and get a job or stay at school, as her parents want her to do, for another two years?
    (b) Y is a boy aged fourteen, an only child of very religious parents. He is accepted into a gang whose company he enjoys, but he knows that some of their activities are illegal. Should he leave the gang?
    (c) Z is aged thirteen and wants to see a film rated 'R'. He/she looks old enough to get past the ticket office. Should he/she go?

## Unit 22. Niño's Last Bullfight

After all, bullfighting wasn't some kind of an esoteric act, taking place behind temple veils in an aura of mysticism, but a hard, plain thing that involved guts and blood and valour; a physical test, in which the advantage lay with the enemy, because the enemy was hampered by no rules, and had not to satisfy twenty thousand people who insisted on having their money's worth.

The hysteria of the crowd had barely died down when the fourth bull, Peleador, slid into the ring, and Gusano and Camillo ran out, trailing their capes. Chano moved up beside him.

'It's an uncle; it's hooking both ways. Take it wide, and save up the fancywork till Curro's been at it.'

He had them shouting 'No, no!' before he tied the bull up with a rebolera. There were two loops of gold hanging down from the taleguilla, and twice, as the shoulder caught him, he had nearly lost his balance. An old trick — that of holding his breath — which he thought he had mastered, had revived, and as he walked away, his ribs were heaving, but he managed to pin the smile on his face. He'd got them at last; broken down their antagonism and their apathy.

During the next eight minutes, Niño de Maderas defeated the traditionalists by an exhibition which, for skill and valour, was not to be matched by any of his contemporaries. For the first time, Madrid settled down seriously to contemplate one who, so far, had never made much impression upon the most selective audience in the world. It was altogether another school of thought and of technique. It was cold, it was athletic, but it had its moments of pure artistry, and for suicidal daring, it had not been matched for years. Those who had feared, on the strength of his previous adorno, that the Niño would produce a succession of circus antics, were reassured by his gravity.

It seemed like a mile, back to the callejon. He drank more water. And this, Jesus and Mary, wasn't the end. For at least another hour he must go on, offering his flesh and blood up to twenty-three thousand people whose insistence had given Ildefonso the ear; who must be made to award him the same. There was three-quarters of a metre of bull's blood from his chest down on to the upper thigh.

He had not heard the trumpet, but Tonio was handing him the stick and sword. Now. Now.

The space between himself and the President's box seemed to prolong itself like elastic, but he was there at last. The tiers dazzled as he looked up at them, to receive the nod. As he turned away, emptiness and solitude folded round him like a wet cloth. Slowly he raised the montera. and, as he pivoted, the whole plaza became like pink snowflakes, dancing around him. Without looking, he tossed the montera backwards. Now.

As he shook out the muleta gently, and spread it with the sword, he saw Chano had the bull well placed. He moved up four short steps, chopped his heels down into the sand and called the bull. As it came thundering down on him like an express, he opened up his first pass.

The silence was unnatural. Flagging the bull from horn to horn, his mind was very clear; as soon as he had it in control, he would go slowly into the redondo, pulling it round to the right and then changing to the left; then some slow, two-handed passes, finishing with the pase por bajo — and then start on his adornos: the stunts for which Niño de Maderas was famous, some of which he had copied and improved, and others he had invented. Time was the thing to be remembered. He was facing towards the big clock, and in the split second after the horn ploughed past his chest he glanced up to reassure himself.

He felt the bump, but did not realise until he took the slam behind him of the barrera that he was being carried on the horn. It was so simple, so sudden, there was no time for fear, until he heard the screams and, in a flash like lightning, saw the bull's head in front of his eyes: the muzzle going down, the great weapon of bone and hair between the horns — hardly less formidable than they, the hot gust from the nostrils — and something falling on the top of him and yellow and red and trampling and more yellow and red — and lying doubled up between the sand and the estribo, and a pair of human eyes staring into his. . . .

(*Bulls of Parral*, Marguerite Steen)

1. Who was 'the enemy'?
2. What two reasons are given for the enemy having 'the advantage?'

## Unit 22. Nino's Last Bullfight

3. What is meant by the comment that the bull, Peleador, is an 'uncle'?
4. What do the spectators expect 'for their money's worth'?
5. What was the name of Niño's rival who was also a bullfighter?
6. Who were the others involved in the ring with Niño and what did they have to do?
7. To whom must Niño bow?
8. What is the permission he is given by a nod?
9. What made Niño anxious in his first few minutes in the ring?
10. Which of the words below would you apply to describe Niño's style of bullfighting?
    (a) controlled        (e) energetic
    (b) serious           (f) artistic
    (c) showy             (g) dangerous
    (d) slow              (h) hilarious
11. Choose 'agree' or 'disagree' for each of the statements below, giving a reason for your answer.
    (a) Success or failure in the bullfight depends upon some mysterious rite.
    (b) Bullfighting needs courage but not physical strength.
    (c) There is a ritual involved in bullfighting.
    (d) The crowd was not on Niño's side before he began his fight with Peleador.
    (e) Niño both looked and felt calm in the ring.
    (f) The fight was being held in a small country town bullfighting ring.
    (g) Niño's display outclassed all the other bullfighters of his day.
12. In your own words, tell what had happened by the end of the passage, listing the separate details of Niño's experience.

## Experts

13. It is interesting to read of the skills of other specialists. Who is the expert and in what way does he use his expertise in each of following?

    A. During the war there was created at the behest of Washington, the most astonishing propaganda agency which met and sat in New York, called the Writers' War Board. Its chairman was Mr Rex Stout the mystery writer, and its committee embraced some fifteen or twenty American writers of every stamp. I was a member of this board; its purpose and function was simple and easy to understand. When the psychological warfare boffins in Washington needed a writing job of any kind, the problem was dumped into the lap of the War Board in New York which found the right author in the shortest possible time and got the job done. This would be in the guise of short stories, novelettes, magazine and newspaper articles or even circulars and pamphlets. It worked.

I remember that one time the problem handed us was the fact that there were not sufficient young men opting for the job of bombardier in the airforce. They all wanted to be pilots. The shortage of bombardiers was making itself felt in the airforce.

Ways and means of propagandizing to make the bombardier's job romantic and attractive were discussed and I was assigned to write a short story in the *Saturday Evening Post* about an heroic bombardier. This I did, the story was duly sold and published and to my astonishment, shortly after its appearance, the airforce reported a satisfactory rise in the candidates for the bombardier's job.

(Paul Gallico)

B. Little skill is needed to make a comfortable, thatched, weatherproof hut using only material locally available.

Such huts can be expected to have a useful service life of 4 to 6 years without maintenance. With maintenance, such as renewing lashings, and repairs to ridge thatch, the life is anything up to 20 years.

Where rammed earth is used for walls, the life of the structure is indeterminate. Many earth wall buildings have stood undamaged for hundreds of years.

The building of a thatched hut from local materials is a creative exercise. Design must provide for the anticipated weather conditions. Finding suitable materials almost anywhere presents no problem, but considerable organisation may be required to collect the material. For the actual structure and thatching, good teamwork is required.

The final hut, with its promise of long periods of protection and shelter, is the result of a combination of head work and hands. With this comes the inward reward of having created a weather-proof hut out of nothing except the natural materials garnered from the surrounding area.

(Richard Graves)

C. Siegfried rose from the table and stretched luxuriously. 'You're probably right. Anyway, I'm sending you to see a really big man this morning. John Skipton of Dennaby Close — he's got some tooth rasping to do. Couple of old horses losing condition. You'd better take all the instruments, it might be anything.'

I went through to the little room down the passage and surveyed the tooth instruments. I always felt at my most mediaeval when I was caught up in large animal dentistry and in the days of the draught horse it was a regular task. One of the commonest jobs was knocking the wolf teeth out of young horses. I have no idea how it got its name but you found the little wolf tooth just in front of the molars and if a young horse was doing badly it always got the blame.

It was no good the vets protesting that such a minute, vestigial object couldn't possibly have any effect on the horse's health and that the trouble was probably due to worms. The farmers were adamant; the tooth had to be removed.

We did this by having the horse backed into a corner, placing the forked end of a metal rod against the tooth and giving a sharp tap with an absurdly large wooden mallet. Since the tooth had no proper root the operation was not particularly painful, but the horse still didn't like it. We usually had a couple of fore-feet waving around our ears at each tap.

And the annoying part was that after we had done the job and pointed out to the farmer that we had only performed this bit of black magic to humour him, the horse would take an immediate turn for the better and thrive consistently from then on. Farmers are normally reticent about our successful efforts for fear we might put a bit more on the bill but in these cases they cast aside all caution. They would shout at us across the market place: 'Hey, remember that 'oss you knocked wolf teeth out of? Well, he never looked back. It capped him.'

(James Herriot)

# Section E
# Humour

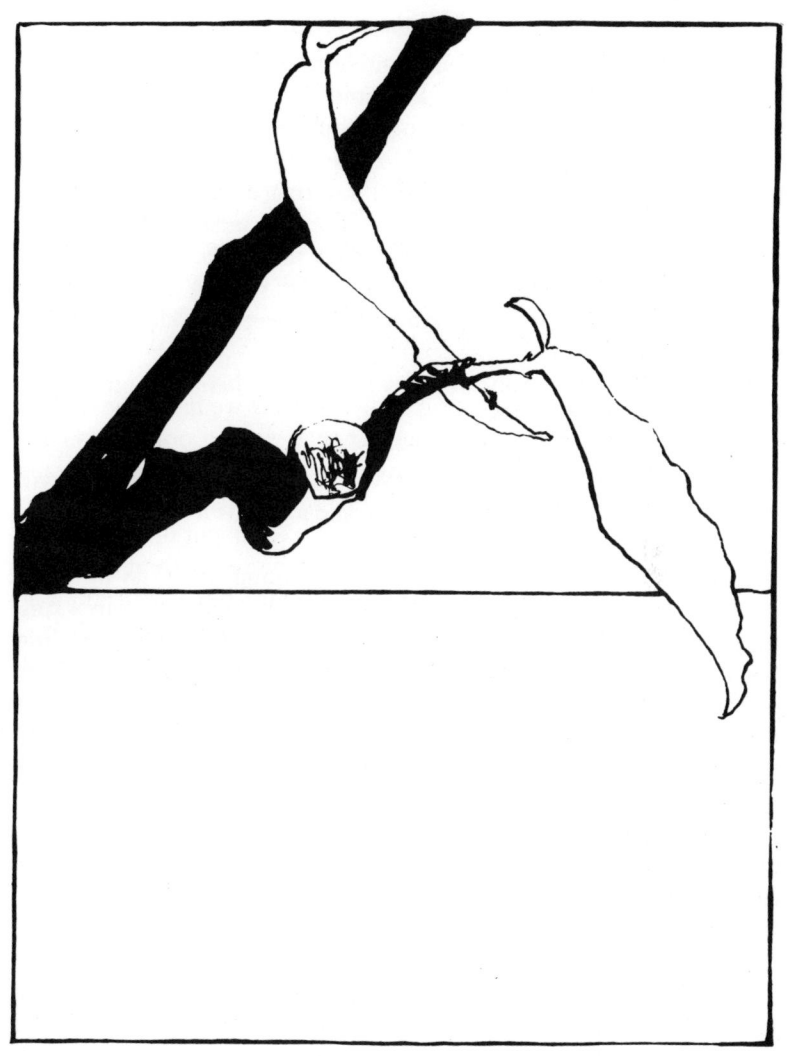

## Unit 23. The Merino Sheep

People have the impression that the merino is a gentle, bleating animal that gets its living without trouble to anybody, and comes up every year to be shorn with a pleased smile upon its amiable face. It is my purpose here to exhibit the merino sheep in its true light.

First let us give him his due. No one can accuse him of being a ferocious animal. No one could ever say that a sheep attacked him without provocation; although there is an old bush story of a man who was discovered in the act of killing a neighbour's wether.

'Hello!' said the neighbour, 'what's this? Killing my sheep!'

'Yes,' said the man, 'I *am* killing your sheep. I'll kill *any* man's sheep that bites *me!*'

But as a rule the merino refrains from using his teeth on people. He goes to work in another way.

The truth is that he is a dangerous monomaniac, and his one idea is to ruin the man who owns him. With this object in view he will display a talent for getting into trouble and a genius for dying that are almost incredible.

If a mob of sheep see a bush fire closing round them, do they run away out of danger? Not at all; they rush round and round in a ring till the fire burns them up. If they are in a river-bed, with a howling flood coming down, they will stubbornly refuse to cross three inches of water to save themselves. Dogs may bark and men may shriek, but the sheep won't move. They will wait there till the flood comes and drowns them all, and then their corpses go down the river on their backs with their feet in the air.

A mob will crawl along a road slowly enough to exasperate a snail, but let a lamb get away in a bit of rough country, and a racehorse can't head him back again. If sheep are put into a big paddock with water in three corners of it, they will resolutely crowd into the fourth, and die of thirst.

When being counted out at a gate, if a scrap of bark be left on the ground in the gateway, they will refuse to step over it until dogs and men have sweated and toiled and sworn. At last one will gather courage, rush at the fancied obstacle, spring over it about six feet in the air and dart away. The next does exactly the same, but jumps a bit higher. Then comes a rush of them following one another in wild bounds like antelopes, until one overjumps himself and alights on his head. This frightens those still in the yard, and they stop running out.

There is a well-authenticated story of a ship-load of sheep that was lost because an old ram jumped overboard, and all the rest followed him. No doubt they did, and were proud to do it. A sheep won't go through an open gate on his own responsibility, but he would gladly and proudly 'follow the leader' through the red-hot portals of Hades: and it makes no difference whether the lead goes voluntarily, or is hauled struggling and kicking and fighting every inch of the way.

For pure, sodden stupidity there is no animal like the merino. A lamb will follow a bullock-dray, drawn by sixteen bullocks and driven by a profane person with a whip, under the impression that the aggregate monstrosity is his mother. A ewe never knows her own lamb by sight, and apparently has no sense of colour. She can recognize its voice half a mile off among a 1000 other voices apparently exactly similar; but when she gets within five yards of it, she starts to smell all the other lambs within reach, including the black ones — though her own may be white.

There is another kind of sheep in Australia, as great a curse in his own way as the merino — namely, the cross-bred, or half-merino-half-Leicester animal. The cross-bred will get through, under or over any fence you like to put in front of him. He is never satisfied with his owner's run, but always thinks other people's runs must be better, so he sets off to explore. He will strike a course, say, south-east, and so long as the fit takes him he will keep going south-east through all obstacles — rivers, fences, growing crops, anything. The merino relies on passive resistance for his success; the cross-bred carries the war into the enemy's camp, and becomes a living curse to his owner day and night.

Once there was a man who was induced in a weak moment to buy twenty cross-bred rams. From that hour the hand of Fate was upon him. They got into all the paddocks they shouldn't have been in. They scattered themselves over the run promiscuously. They visited the cultivation paddock and the vegetable-garden at their own sweet will. And then they took to roving. In a body they visited the neighbouring stations, and played havoc with the sheep all over the district.

The wretched owner was constantly getting fiery letters from his neighbours. He tried shutting them up in the sheep-yard. They got out and went back to the garden. Then he jailed them in the calf-pen. Out again and into a growing crop. Then he set a boy to watch them; but the boy went to sleep, and they were four miles away across country before he got on to their tracks.

At length, when they happened accidentally to be at home on their owner's run, there came a big flood. His sheep, mostly merinos, had plenty of time to get on to high ground and save their lives; but, of course, they didn't, and were almost all drowned. The owner sat on a rise above the waste of waters and watched the dead animals go by. He was a ruined man. But he said, 'Thank God, those cross-bred rams are drowned, anyhow'. Just as he spoke there was a splashing in the water, and the twenty rams solemnly swam ashore and ranged themselves in front of him. They were the only survivors of his 20,000 sheep. He broke down, and was taken to an asylum for insane paupers. The cross-breds had fulfilled their destiny.

The cross-bred drives his owner out of his mind, but the merino ruins his man with greater celerity. Nothing on earth will kill cross-breds; nothing will keep merinos alive. If they are put on dry salt-bush country they die of drought. If they are put on damp, well-watered country they die of worms, fluke and foot-rot. They die in the wet seasons and they die in the dry ones.

The hard, resentful look on the faces of all bushmen comes from a long course of dealing with merino sheep. The merino dominates the bush, and gives to Australian literature its melancholy tinge, its despairing <u>pathos</u>. The poems about dying boundary-riders, and lonely graves under mournful she-oaks, are the direct <u>outcome</u> of the poet's too close association with that soul-destroying animal. A man who could write anything cheerful after a day in the drafting-yards would be a freak of nature.

(*The Merino Sheep*, A.B. Paterson)

## Unit 23. The Merino Sheep

Choose the best of the possible alternatives. Sometimes more than one answer might be reasonably close, but there is one that is best and you should choose that one.

1. Merinos are best described as:
    (a) slow-moving and helpful,
    (b) ferocious and clever,
    (c) gentle and silent,
    (d) stupid and bleating.
2. Cross-bred sheep are:
    (a) fun-loving and black,
    (b) intelligent and delicate,
    (c) strong-willed and tough,
    (d) stupid and timid,
3. Merinos:
    (a) can jump over ten-foot fences,
    (b) enjoy swimming,
    (c) both (a) and (b),
    (d) neither (a) nor (b).
4. Merinos:
    (a) always act independently,
    (b) are generally co-operative,
    (c) follow their own leader,
    (d) are good at rounding up dogs.
5. This author tells several stories about particular sheep. Do you believe:
    (a) all his stories,
    (b) some of his stories,
    (c) any of the stories,
    (d) none of his stories?
6. Write 'A' for advantage or D for disadvantage to sheep owners against each of the following facts he claims about sheep.
    (a) easily frightened
    (b) are devoted mothers
    (c) can be shorn regularly
    (d) will escape and roam for miles
    (e) look very similar
    (f) can be 'heeled' by dogs
    (g) seldom bite
    (h) suffer from many diseases

## Section E. Humour

7. In a bushfire, sheep will:
   (a) travel at speed for great distances,
   (b) go towards the fire,
   (c) lie on their backs with their feet in the air,
   (d) none of these.

8. In a flood, sheep will:
   (a) always travel south-east,
   (b) go visit the neighbours,
   (c) follow a bullock-dray,
   (d) practise swimming,
   (e) none of these.

9. The writer claims a sheep's one idea is to ruin the man who owns him. After reading the 'evidence' given, do you consider the author:
   (a) is exaggerating a little,
   (b) is telling the exact truth,
   (c) has proved scientifically everything he claims,
   (d) is exaggerating a great deal.

10. From the context, decide which of the given meanings best suits the word given. (These are in order, as they appear in the extract.)
    (a) amiable
        (i) turned inside-out
        (ii) sweet-tempered
        (iii) slow-walking
        (iv) French
    (b) provocation
        (i) teeth
        (ii) cause for angry act
        (iii) spell
        (iv) speech of welcome
    (c) wether
        (i) alternative
        (ii) climate
        (iii) male sheep
        (iv) second wife
    (d) monomaniac
        (i) politician
        (ii) single man

## Unit 23. The Merino Sheep  121

      (iii) madness about one subject
      (iv) mountain-climber
 (e) exasperate
      (i)   whistle
      (ii) outdistance
      (iii) irritate
      (iv) squash
 (f) portals
      (i)   gateways
      (ii) alcoholic drink
      (iii) foliage
      (iv) fat people
 (g) obstacles
      (i)   part of an octopus
      (ii)  instructions
      (iii) objects blocking the way
      (iv) leg-irons
 (h) celerity
      (i)   vegetable
      (ii)  over-eating
      (iii) musical ability
      (iv) speed
 (i) pathos
      (i)   silly songs
      (ii)  friendships
      (iii) outdoor entertainment areas
      (iv) deep feeling
 (j) outcome
      (i)   exit
      (ii)  input
      (iii) result
      (iv) annual earnings

11. What reason do you think this author had for writing this story?
   (a) to complain
   (b) to amuse readers
   (c) to teach how to look after sheep
   (d) to write a typically Australian story.

12. Draw a scene that amused or interested you.

## Exaggeration

13. Sometimes a writer chooses to exaggerate what he is saying. We call this exaggeration (hyperbole). Used cleverly, hyperbole can make your writing lively and amusing. Used in the wrong place, that is, when you want to be believed or taken seriously, it weakens what you are saying.
    Cut out the exaggeration in these:
    (a) You are the slowest hockey-player in the world.
    (b) I could eat a mountain of fish and chips.
    (c) Everybody gets more pocket money than I do.
    (d) In a fraction of a second all the plans were decided.
    (e) Your feet are the same size as tennis racquets.
    (f) I held my breath for five minutes while he was prowling around.
    (g) He was given a week's work to do in one period.
    (h) My mother thinks I should starve after school.
    (i) You're a pig and a worm and not worth wasting time on.
    (j) Her cakes were as flat as pancakes.
    (k) The smell of freshly baked bread spread for miles around.
    (l) The toffee was like tar.
    (m) Everything went wrong today.
    (n) He never wanted to face anybody again as long as he lived.
14. Use exaggeration deliberately to mislead your reader, to see how effective exaggeration can be. Imagine someone is trying to spray a fly with insecticide. Write about it as if the person was armed with a terrible weapon and the fly was a dangerous enemy. Can you keep your reader misled about what is happening until the end?

## Understatement

15. The opposite to hyperbole or exaggeration is understatement (litotes). When a writer (or a debater) wishes to emphasise the point he thinks is important, he often tries to undervalue whatever his opponent might claim.
    How effective do you find the use of understatement in the following?

A year ago, a rather secret flight took place in a new super aircraft. Many VIPs were aboard. The flight had started and a few minutes passed when the pilot, an American, came on the intercom:

'It is my pleasure to be your pilot and captain on this memorable first flight. My report is — all going well and according to plan, that is plan B. I'm afraid I must tell you all of one small thing that has cropped up. Those of you may care to look at it who are sitting on the starboard side. Look along the wing and you will see that the nearest engine to you is vibrating a little, in fact quite a lot, really. This is nothing to worry about as we have four engines so there is plenty of safety margin and we are still at the incredible height of 62,000 feet and flying right on schedule at 1,950 mph.

'Looking at this engine you may also have noticed that the other engine on that wing is sparking. In fact, flames are pouring out of it. Don't worry. We have the other wing and still our height and speed are 100 per cent O.K.

'If you happen to be sitting on the port side, don't worry if you can't see one of the engines that should be on your wing — it dropped off three miles back.

'I must now tell you one fault I do consider a little serious. There is a widening crack appearing in the central gangway towards the rear of the plane. Many of you who are now, I'm sure, looking through this crack will be able to see the Atlantic rollers down below you. Some with good sight, will be able to see a small rubber dinghy on those rollers.

'Ladies and Gentlemen, your pilot is speaking from that rubber dinghy!'

16. Sometimes understatement can be used to add humour to your own writing. Read the examples below and make up some of your own.
    (a) Breaking both legs was a slight setback to the high jump champion's training program.
    (b) She had a snack consisting of three hamburgers and a couple of thick shakes, knowing breakfast would be later than usual.
    (c) On his way to the station, Mr Heroic stopped a runaway train, cleared the track of the debris of the truck it had hit at the crossing, resuscitated the driver and went on his way, still wondering how he could make some contribution to others.

## Unit 24.  A Romance of the Peerage Unburked

I am four-and-twenty years of age, tall, well-looking, and a duke! I have not gone very deeply into the family history, because I have always been afraid of what I should find out, and I remember the old proverb, 'Where ignorance is bliss, 'tis folly to be wise.' I have no doubt that my ancestors came over with the Conqueror, but I don't think they did much good.

I don't trouble now very much about my ancestors, but I am rather concerned about myself. To tell you the honest truth, I am in what my mamma, the duchess, would call a 'bit of a mess.'

My mamma, the duchess, has never quite forgotten the language of her youth, and her youth was passed in the land of comic songs.

My mamma, the duchess, was a celebrated serio-comic in her day, and my papa fell in love with her and married her when he was very young. There is a portrait of her in an old volume of the *Entr' acte* which I found in a library, and from this I should think that she was very charming and very 'chic' in those days. Some of the old boys I meet sometimes tell me she was quite the rage of the music-halls once, and that her song 'Sarah's up to Snuff' took the town by storm, and got three encores nightly.

My papa, the marquis, died at the North Pole after five years of happy married life — he was sent to the North Pole by my grandpapa, the duke, who thought it was the best place for him. My mamma remained at home, and still, I believe, continued to do 'three turns nightly' at the principal halls of the Metropolis.

Being a marchioness, she got magnificent terms. I even heard that one manager paid her as much as £100 a week, on condition that she would come on in her coronet to sing 'Sarah's up to Snuff' — and she did. My papa became a duke while he was at the North Pole, owing to the death of my grandpapa; and then, of course, my mamma became a duchess — and I was a marquis. I was a tiny baby at that time and knew nothing about it. All I know I have learned since.

After my papa, the duke, died there was a lot of trouble. My

## Unit 24. A Romance

grandpapa had, it seems, gambled very nearly all the estates away, and my papa had finished the rest, so that there was very little left for us — only enough to bring us in a very modest income, all our property, which was not much, having been parted with before we came into it.

I have taken my seat in the House of Lords because mamma wishes me to do so, but that is all the benefit I have derived from the position.

My mamma, the duchess, married again two years after my papa died. She married Mr Tom Lingham, a lion-comique, and they made a good deal of money by appearing together as 'The Duchess of Shadwell and Mr Tom Lingham,' in an entertainment, with a dog who was very clever.

The dog was Mr Tom Lingham's. We had a house in the Wandsworth Road, I remember, and there I was brought up, with my younger brothers and sisters, the young Linghams, and the dog.

They thought a lot of me, and so did the servants, because I was a duke, and so did Mr Lingham's and Mamma's relations, who used to come to tea on Sunday, and call me 'your grace'; but my papa's relations never came to tea on Sunday or any other day, and we never saw anything of them at all.

Mamma said they were a stuck-up lot, and I suppose they must have been; but she said she didn't care, for she was a duchess, and if they didn't like her using the coronet on the stage at the music-halls, they could lump it. It was her coronet, and she should do as she liked with it. Mamma was very fond of her coronet; she had it on everything.

It was awfully big on the <u>brougham</u> that used to take her and Mr Lingham to the Halls of an evening, and there was a very big gilt one on our front door in the Wandsworth Road; and when we went to Margate I had a coronet on my spade and bucket when I went on the sands.

I was a great success in the House of Lords. I didn't say anything, but everybody stared at me; and in the smoking-room a lot of the other lords came and talked to me, and asked me questions, and they got me on to sing a comic song I had learned of my mamma, the duchess.

At the time I took my seat in the House of Lords, Mamma had become very stout, and had retired from the profession; and Mr Lingham, who had lost his voice, had made a ready-money book in the little ring at race-meetings and I don't think we were quite as well off as we used to be.

When I had been to the House of Lords once or twice, and found out how other dukes enjoyed themselves, I began to feel dissatisfied with my position, and I went home and had a long talk with Mr Lingham and the duchess. It was then I learnt that my papa had left me nothing but the title, and that all the family property had gone to the money-lenders.

Mr Lingham says he has quite enough to do to support his own family, and my mamma, the duchess, has given me to understand that it is time I looked out for myself, and earned my own living.

That is where the difficulty comes in. There are so few things a duke can do, especially a duke who is not particularly clever at anything. Mamma says I had better go to America and advertise that

I am open to offers from millionaires with a daughter to spare. But how am I to go to America? I won't go <u>steerage</u>; and how am I to live when I get there? The one pound a week that Mamma allows me won't go far in America. Besides, I am in love!

Oh! if you could see her you would understand all I feel as I write these words —

She is the charmingest, prettiest girl in all the world, and she serves behind the counter at Messrs Jones and Co.'s, the drapers in the Wandsworth Road, and her name is Daisy.

Daisy Smith!

I like to write it. I write it everywhere. I write it with the soap on my looking-glass. I write it on my cuffs with a lead-pencil. I write it with my fingers in the dust on the mantelshelf in our front parlour. I write it in chalk on our front door. If I were a prisoner, I should write it with my blood on my dungeon walls!

My darling Daisy is eighteen; her father is a four-wheel cabman, and her mother is pew-opener at St Mary's Church, Shoreditch. They idolize her — and so do I.

I am always going into Jones and Co.'s on some excuse — if it is only to buy a penny packet of pins — and then I take a chair and gaze at Daisy till the <u>shopwalker</u> comes along and starts me off.

And of an evening I wait outside till the shop shuts, and then I walk with Daisy as far as her home. She would like to ask me to tea on Sunday, but there are difficulties in the way. She has found out that I am a duke, and she says that if it were known that she had a duke to tea her character would be gone.

I cannot see why, but I suppose there is plenty of gossip if a shop-girl takes a duke home to tea with a four-wheel cabman and a pew-opener.

But though I have not yet been home to tea with Daisy, we are engaged — we have plighted our troth and broken a sixpence, and both sworn never to marry anyone else.

I see more of Daisy, too, than I used to, because the shopwalker doesn't interfere, and Jones and Co., understanding that we are an engaged couple, allow me to sit on the big chair at the counter for an hour a day. They have recognised my position by putting a big card in the window, on which is printed 'By appointment to the Duke of Shadwell.' That's because I sometimes buy a pennyworth of pins there!

(*Tinkletop's Crime*, George R. Sims)

## Section E. Humour

1. Briefly re-state the writer's family history.
2. What opinion of the British aristocracy do you form from this account? Is it fair to generalize about a group of people? Why? Why not?
3. What were the social distinctions between the writer's parents?
4. Why was the coronet used so widely by the writer's mother?
5. Is the writer being naive when he says 'I was a great success in the House of Lords'?
6. What impression of the writer do you gain from his statements beginning 'I like to write'?
7. What was the symbol used by the writer and Daisy for becoming engaged? Can you suggest an explanation for it?
8. From the context in which each is used, what do you think is the meaning of these?
   (a) serio-comic
   (b) the rage
   (c) brougham
   (d) steerage
   (e) shopwalker
9. A euphemism restates an unpleasant fact in a milder, less upsetting way. Quote the euphemistic descriptions that match the following:
   (a) The duke is unqualified to earn a living.
   (b) We had become poor.
   (c) He should marry an heiress to get some money.
   (d) The duke wanted to send his son as far away as possible.
10. Choose the best answer from the following:
    (a) Why hasn't the writer 'gone very deeply into the family history'?
        (i) He isn't interested.
        (ii) He doesn't know who his ancestors were.
        (iii) He suspects his ancestors were not very honorable.
        (iv) He can't read or write.
    (b) Why did the duchess dislike her husband's relatives?
        (i) They weren't musically talented.
        (ii) They were gamblers.
        (iii) They belonged to the aristocracy.
        (iv) They regarded her as inferior to her husband.
    (c) Why was Daisy reluctant to ask the writer to tea?
        (i) She was too shy.

(ii) She worked on Sundays at Jones and Co.
(iii) She feared what the neighbours might think if they knew he was a duke.
(iv) Her boyfriend wouldn't approve.

11. Discussion: Do social distinctions still exist today?

## Archaisms

12. Because language is continually changing, some words become out of date and are found only in literature of an earlier time. We call such words **archaisms**.

    Find the archaisms in the following sentences. Having guessed their meanings by their context, check with a dictionary to see if you guessed correctly.
    (a) The subject of face-painting may be considered in two points of view. First there is room for dispute with respect to the consistency of the practice with good morals; and secondly, whether it be on the whole convenient or not, may be a matter worthy of agitation.
    (b) Threescore and ten I can remember well
    Within the volume of which time I have seen
    Hours dreadful and things strange, but this sore night
    Hath trifled former knowings.
    (c) At last the Dodger trod upon his toes or ran upon his boot accidentally, while Charley Bates stumbled up against him behind; and in that one moment, they took from him, with the most extraordinary rapidity, snuff-box, note-case, watch-guard, chain, shirt-pin, pocket handkerchief, even the spectacle-case. If the old gentleman felt a hand in any one of his pockets, he cried out where it was; and then the game began all over again. (Charles Dickens)

## Euphemisms

13. Sometimes writers (and debaters) substitute a more pleasant word or phrase to make an idea more acceptable to others, or to make it appear less drastic, perhaps so that its importance seems less. For example, what are some of the substitute words people use for death? We call such 'softer' substitutes **euphemisms**.

    In the case of some professions, language, euphemistic or not, can be understood only by those sharing the profession. After reading the article below, collect some special language for occupations such as computer technology, a special sport, photography, music.

'The term buffed up the gomer, who had the dwindles and figured he would have a bounceback,' said a doctor to a nurse. 'But the player flatlined from fascinoma and we all hit the fluids and electrolytes.'

In the inside lingo of the medical profession, a 'term' is an intern; to 'buff up' means to prepare a patient for discharge.

'The Sultan of Frogmore needs that bed. Buff this guy up and send him home'; a 'gomer' is a patient (often called a player) who is whining and otherwise undesirable.

The term is said to be an acronym for 'Get Out of My Emergency Room' but may originate in 'gomeral,' Scottish dialect for simpleton, influenced by the television hillbilly Gomer Pyle.

Paul Horvits, a *Times* colleague who has a friend in medical school, passed along many of these terms.

He adds that the 'dwindles' is medical jargon for advancing years leading to death from old age; a 'bounceback' is a recidivist patient, or one who keeps coming back to the hospital; to 'flatline' is to expire, a verb taken from the lack of activity on the scope measuring vital signs; 'fascinoma' is any interesting disease, and 'fluids and electrolytes' is the beer, wine and other booze that interns and nurses head for after too many players are boxed or lost.

Other students of hospital language have noticed how doctors have become addicted to initialese and arcane symbols.

In *The England Journal of Medicine*, Dr Nicholas Christy chastised interns who say 'Zero Delta' when asked about patients' progress; such talk scares patients, who do not know the symbol means merely 'no change'.

He added that 'oids' has become a word in itself: 'What are you giving this lady?' 'Oids.' This is meditalk for 'steroids', which in turn is a shortened version of corticosteroids. Patients have been known to turn gomeroid.

14. In the style of the article below, write your own school report and reference, treating your own weaknesses as euphemistically as possible.

## Unit 24. A Romance

A Glossary of Common Words and Phrases used in Scientific Literature and their meanings

### Introduction
It has long been known that ... *I haven't bothered to look up the original reference* ... of great theoretical and practical importance ... *interesting to me.*

While it has not been possible to provide definite answers to these questions ... *the experiment didn't work out, but I figured I could at least get a publication out of it.*

### Experimental Procedure
The W-Pb system was chosen as especially suitable to show the predicted behaviour ... *the fellow in the next lab already had some made up.*

High purity ... Very high purity ... Extremely high purity ... Super purity ... Spectroscopically pure ... *Composition unknown except for the exaggerated claims of the supplier.*

Three of the samples were chosen for special study ... *the results on the others didn't make sense and were ignored.*

... handled with extreme care throughout the experiments ... *not dropped on the floor.*

... given a homogenizing anneal ... *oxidized.*

### Results
Typical results are shown ... *the best results are shown.*

Although some detail has been lost in reproduction, it is clear from the original micrograph that ... *it is impossible to tell from the micrograph.* ... Presumably at longer times ... *I didn't take time to find out.*

The agreement with the predicted curve is:
good ............................................. *poor*
satisfactory .................................. *doubtful*
fair ............................................ *imaginary*

... as good as could be expected considering the approximations made in the analysis ... *non existent.*

The result will be reported at a later date ... *I might possibly get around to it sometime.*

The most reliable values are those of Jones ... *he was a student of mine* ... accuracy $+ 0.001\%$ ... *nobody can say their work is any better.*

### Discussion
It is suggested that ... It is believed that ... It may be that ... *I think*.

It is generally believed that ... *A couple of other guys think so too*. It might be argued that ... *I have such a good answer to this objection that I shall now raise it*.

It is clear that much additional work will be required before a complete understanding ... *I don't understand it*.
Unfortunately, a quantitative theory to account for these effects has not been formulated ... *Neither does anybody else*. Correct within an order of magnitude ... *wrong*.
It is hoped that this work will stimulate further work in the field.
... *This paper isn't good but neither are any of the others on this miserable subject*.

### Acknowledgements
Thanks are due to Joe Bloggs for assistance with the experiments, and to John Doe for valuable discussions ... *Bloggs did the work and Doe explained what it meant*.

(*Panacea*, March '77)

# Unit 25. Flax

The humour of some writers is very subtle. They might use sarcasm or pretend to have one point of view but make fun of it so that their readers are persuaded to support the opposite.

Flax is what school is all about. In my own old-fashioned geography books I went to various countries in the company of Bedouin and Greek and Turkish kids and the thing that most remains in my mind now about those imaginary kids is that they always grew flax. I myself put flax on my maps alongside corn and wheat and coal; I wrote down flax to answer questions about the products of countries. I never knew what flax was, but I knew that if I kept it in mind and wrote it down a lot and raised my hand and said it a lot, I would be making it.

Flax is actually a slender erect plant with a blue flower, the seeds of which are used to make linseed oil. Linen is made from the fibre of the stalk. I know this now because I've just looked it up in the dictionary. It is quite possible that it does grow in all those countries like the book and my test papers said. But beyond that, a thing like flax has an important place in a school. Unlike corn, say, which in L.A. we could drive out and see in fields and buy from roadside stands and take home and eat, unlike wheat or cotton or potatoes, I think you could live your entire life in America and never see or even hear of flax, never know about it or need to know about it. Only in the school, only from the geography book, only from the teacher, could you learn about flax.

It showed you how smart the school was, for one thing. For another, it showed you what Learning was; corn, for example, wasn't Learning precisely because you *could* go out and see it in the fields and buy it from roadside stands and take it home and shuck it and eat it and your mother and father could tell you about how they used to grow corn and how to tell fresh corn and about names of corn like Country Gentleman, which my father preferred. You could do all

## 134 Section E. Humour

that without ever going to school and so it didn't count. Finally, it showed the school who among the students was willing and able to keep flax in mind, to raise his hand and say it aloud, to write it down, and put its name on maps. So that in the cumulative records of each child the teacher could write down for the next teacher the information that

| | |
|---|---|
| • Child reads flax, writes down flax and says flax. | *Leader.* |
| • Child sometimes remembers flax. | *Nice kid.* |
| • Child can't remember flax. | *Child is black and/or deprived.* |
| • Child digs flax, but inadvertently says 'chili-dog' instead. | *Brain-damaged?* |
| • Child don't dig flax at all. | *Reluctant learner.* |

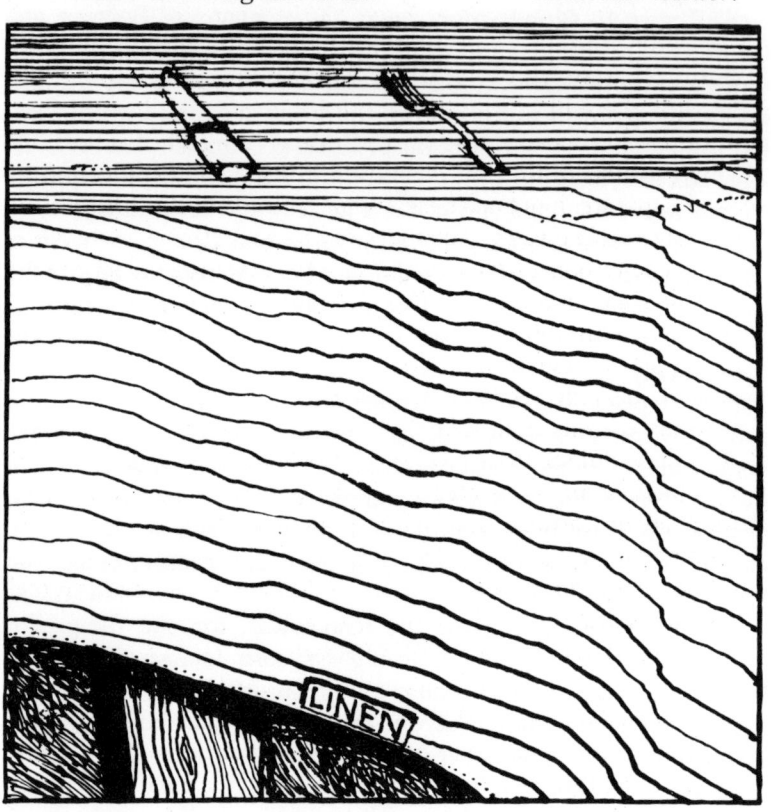

# Unit 25. Flax

I think you could make up an entirely new Achievement Test, doing away with expensive and tedious vocabulary and graphs and reading comprehension, doing away with special pencils for IBM scoring and doing away with filling in all those rows. Just pass out a sheet with the word *flax* printed on it in big letters and count the seconds it took for a kid to raise his hand. That would tell you everything that an Achievement Test is designed to tell you.

Even in the Victory Gardens of 1942 America (where such an outlandish name as *Swiss Chard* became part of my experience, growing non-stop in the back yard), no one was ever known to grow flax, no one saw flax sprouting under the eucalyptus trees, no newspaper articles were written about anyone raising flax in the vacant lots, no war hero mentioned flax as contributing to the war effort. It remained, like Learning, a monopoly of the schools.

(*How to Survive in Your Native Land*, James Herndon)

1. Apart from studying flax, what else is this article about?
2. What is the subject this author is criticising?
3. What reason does he have for contrasting flax and corn?
4. Quote sentences from the extract that suggest the following:
   (a) People are impressed by learning about topics they themselves have no knowledge about.
   (b) Students don't have to understand something in order to give the right answer.
   (c) Experience gained outside school is often not valued as highly as what is taught officially.
   (d) Schools judge people by marks and behaviour in class.
   (e) Flax is really quite useful.
   (f) Successful students have to answer a lot in class.
5. How successful is this author's method of getting his readers to think about learning? Explain your answer fully.
6. Discussion.
   (a) Are there any school subjects you feel are as remote from real life as flax?
   (b) What should be taught in schools?

136   Section E. Humour

## Unit 26.   Cinderella and Other Tales of Subversion

My dear Prime Minister,
  I have, as you requested, investigated the various nursery rhymes and fairy stories being told in Australia's kindergartens and schools. As a result, it is my duty to inform you that ASIO's allegations are substantially correct, that many of the stories are of foreign origin and express quite unacceptable political or moral views.
  Let us consider the case of *Cinderella*, which tells of a working-class girl who aspires to marry a handsome prince. Clearly this is capable of a number of differing interpretations.
  On the one hand, Cinderella has a strong ambition to improve her social standing, something that we much admire in Liberal circles. Unfortunately, her means of achieving this ambition is through intervention of a more powerful force, viz., a fairy godmother. And as you are aware, during the brief and catastrophic Labor Government, there was a tendency to use various Ministers as fairy godmothers who distributed largesse from the Treasury.
  So it seems to me that Cinderella's dreams are fulfilled, as it were, by a sort of Federal grant which is inconsistent with the political realities at this point in time whilst being in direct conflict with your own philosophies. After all, working people are being asked to lower their expectancies. So either we'll have to rewrite the story so that Cinderella obtains her coach and gold slippers through (a) an increase in productivity and (b) frugal living, or we'll need to delete it from the approved text.
  Or you might prefer us to provide schools with a revised version in which Cinderella stays happily in her hearth, knowing her place. She could be reminded that, at her salary level, she'll enjoy the full rate of indexation and that public ward care will be available under Medibank should her consumption of soot and dust cause health problems.
  In contrast, *The Little Red Hen*, is an excellent piece of propaganda for the rural industry. The splendid fowl sets about

planting, raising and harvesting grain without any help from the uncaring populace. Indeed, they deride her efforts. Yet when the grain has been made into wheat and hence into life-sustaining loaves of bread, everyone rushes to eat it. What a perfect expression of the situation in this country where the urban populations are totally disinterested in the problems of the farmer. Moreover, the moral of the story, which has the hen (not red, I submit) eating bread alone, should bring home to the city electorates a sense of their ultimate dependency on their country cousins.

There are a number of stories which deal effectively with the dole-bludger. Take *The Grasshopper and the Ant*. In this account the ants represent the stable, well-behaved work-force striving constantly for the ultimate good of the entire community. No go-slows or stop-work meetings. No one works to regulations or goes on strike.

In contrast, there's a large grasshopper who exhibits drop-out tendencies, clearly preferring singing and dancing to working. Unfortunately the ants take pity on this worthless creature and, unlike the more conservative hen, evince socialist tendencies by allowing him to share their food.

I'm in favour of the story remaining in the repertoire, as it were, provided the grasshopper freezes to death in the snow. Incidentally, one committee member has suggested that we update the story by having the grasshopper a member of a rock group or at very least electrifying his fiddle.

*Jack and the Beanstalk* presents a number of problems. On the one hand, it emphasises the plight of the rural sector which your coalition partners will enthusiastically endorse. In particular, the sale of a cow for a few worthless beans emphasises the plight of the beef industry. However, this may tend to intensify the political protest from both the beef and dairy people. Worse still, the beanstalk could be seen as thriving on the superphosphate bounty while the giant could be viewed as big government. As you know, many ill-informed critics suggest that the farmers are stealing a great many golden eggs from Treasury. All in all, on balance, all things considered, we favour the tale's elimination.

Next story on our list is *The Emperor's New Clothes*. Unfortunately, the rather fatuous central character in his imaginary regalia reminds radical elements of Sir John Kerr. Clearly we've enough demonstrations against the monarchy's representative already.

138  *Section E. Humour*

For years mothers have been telling children the story of *The Ugly Duckling* without realising that it is a seditious Bolshevik fable. Once again, as in *Cinderella*, the downtrodden in society are told to expect a miraculous reversion of their fortunes. Clearly this hints at the urgent need for revolution, so that *all* the ugly ducklings can become swans. We believe that this story should be banned immediately and charges laid against any subversive who attempts to tell it.

In contrast, the committee found *The Three Little Pigs* to be a solid bourgeois morality tale with special appeal to middle-class home owners and to the small shopkeeper. As well, the major companies involved in brickbuilding can only applaud its general tenor.

In essence, the story tells how two decent, solid citizens build their own homes only to have them blown down by the dark, wolf-like forces of radicalism. Whereupon these completely respectable tax-payers are devoured. However, the third pig prepares for the worst by building in brick and is able to both ward off and ultimately destroy the enemy of society. Clearly here is a parable about the individual in society, about self-help and about ideological purity.

This brings us to the nursery rhymes which, as you know, almost invariably began their lives as political tracts. Therefore it is proper to view them in political terms today.

Thus we view the sad story of *Humpty Dumpty* as a warning to those who would oppose orderly egg marketing. The various egg boards around Australia are constantly faced with the problems of farmers who sell their goods outside the system, sometimes smuggling them interstate. This could lead to the fragile balance in

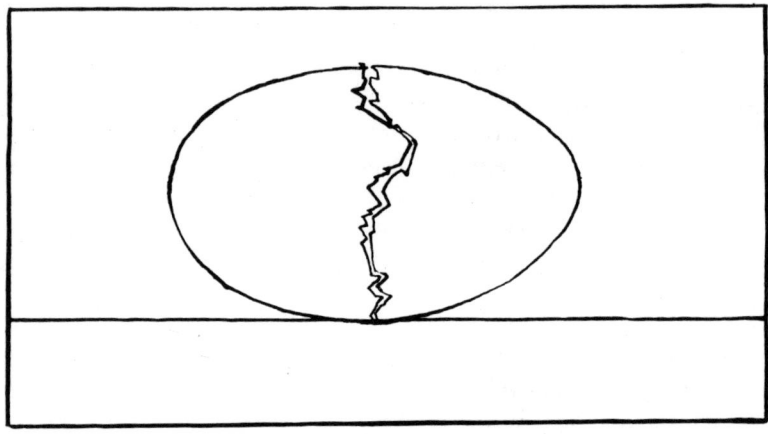

the industry being disturbed, with the result that all the 'king's men' in the marketing bureaucracies would be unable to remedy the situation.

More positive imagery is provided by the rhyme which has a cow jumping over the Moon: given the dispirited state of the dairy industry, this exhilarating image might have a very therapeutic effect.

It's much the same with *Baa Baa Black Sheep* and *This Little Pig Went to Market* which, respectively, suggest a rosy future for our woolgrowers and our pig men.

We disapprove of *Wee Willie Winkie* on moral grounds as anyone who rushes around the city in his nightgown is suspect. Furthermore Mr Winkie seems to spread his favours both upstairs and downstairs, showing a lamentable lack of class consciousness.

Nor should *Ten Little Nigger Boys* be encouraged as its ever-diminishing number of blacks reminded some of our respondents of certain unfortunate occurrences in Tasmania, not to mention the infant mortality rate among Aborigines on mission stations.

Yours sincerely,
Professor Basil Goodbody
(University of Queensland)
(*The Unspeakable Adams*, Phillip Adams)

1. What does the author pretend is the reason for his investigation?
2. What political party does he claim to be supporting?
3. What individuals or groups of people does he really support or favour?
4. If this is not just nonsense, what ideas do you think he has suggested to his readers?
5. Write accounts of the following nursery rhymes as they might be seen by the characters given. Can you imply a serious message as well as humour?
   (a) 'Little Miss Muffet' by a well known TV nature expert
   (b) 'Mary, Mary' by a garden expert
   (c) 'Jack Sprat' by a dietician
   (d) 'Old Mother Hubbard' by a poverty reporter
   (e) 'There was an Old Woman' by a social worker
   (f) 'Twinkle, Twinkle Little Star' by a science fiction writer
   (g) 'Mirror, Mirror on the Wall' by a door-to-door saleslady

## Unit 27.  Alice's Adventures

(i)

'When we were little,' the Mock Turtle went on at last, more calmly, though still sobbing a little now and then, 'we went to school in the sea. The master was an old Turtle — we used to call him Tortoise —'

'Why did you call him Tortoise, if he wasn't one?' Alice asked.

'We called him Tortoise because he taught us,' said the Mock Turtle angrily; 'really you are very dull!'

'You ought to be ashamed of yourself for asking such a simple question,' added the Gryphon; and then they both sat silent and looked at poor Alice, who felt ready to sink into the earth. At last the Gryphon said to the Mock Turtle, 'Drive on old fellow! Don't be all day about it!' and he went on in these words:

'Yes, we went to school in the sea, though you mayn't believe it —'

'I never said I didn't!' interrupted Alice.

'You did,' said the Mock Turtle.

'Hold your tongue!' added the Gryphon, before Alice would speak again. The Mock Turtle went on.

'We had the best of educations — in fact, we went to school every day —'

'*I've* been to a day-school, too,' said Alice, 'you needn't be so proud as all that.'

'With extras?' asked the Mock Turtle a little anxiously.

'Yes,' said Alice, 'we learned French and music.'

'And washing?' said the Mock Turtle.

'Certainly not!' said Alice indignantly.

'Ah! then yours wasn't a really good school,' said the Mock Turtle in a tone of great relief. 'Now at *ours* they had at the end of the bill, ''French, music, *and washing* — extra.'''

'You couldn't have wanted it much,' said Alice, 'living at the bottom of the sea.'

'I couldn't afford to learn it,' said the Mock Turtle with a sigh. 'I only took the regular course.'

'What was that?' inquired Alice.

'Reeling and Writhing, of course, to begin with,' the Mock Turtle replied: 'and then the different branches of Arithmetic — Ambition, Distraction, Uglification and Derision.'

'I never heard of "Uglification,"' Alice ventured to say. 'What is it?'

The Gryphon lifted up both its paws in surprise. 'Never heard of uglifying!' it exclaimed. 'You know what to beautify is, I suppose?'

'Yes,' said Alice, doubtfully: 'it means — to —make — anything — prettier.'

'Well then,' the Gryphon went on, 'if you don't know what to uglify is, you *are* a simpleton.'

Alice did not feel encouraged to ask any more questions about it, so she turned to the Mock Turtle, and said, 'What else had you to learn?'

'Well, there was Mystery,' the Mock Turtle replied, counting off the subjects on his flappers — 'Mystery, ancient and modern, with Seaography: then Drawling — the Drawling-master was an old conger-eel that used to come once a week: *he* taught us Drawling,

Stretching and Fainting in Coils.'

'What was *that* like?' said Alice.

'Well, I can't show it you myself,' the Mock Turtle said: 'I'm too stiff. And the Gryphon never learned it.'

'Hadn't time,' said the Gryphon: 'I went to the Classical master, though. He was an old crab, *he* was.'

'I never went to him,' the Mock Turtle said with a sigh: 'he taught Laughing and Grief, they used to say.'

'So he did, so he did,' said the Gryphon, sighing in his turn, and both creatures hid their faces in their paws.

'And how many hours a day did you do lessons?' said Alice, in a hurry to change the subject.

'Ten hours the first day,' said the Mock Turtle: 'nine the next, and so on.'

'What a curious plan!' exclaimed Alice.

'That's the reason they're called lessons,' the Gryphon remarked: 'because they lessen from day to day.'

This was quite a new idea to Alice, and she thought it over a little before she made her next remark. 'Then the eleventh day must have been a holiday?'

'Of course it was,' said the Mock Turtle.

'And how did you manage on the twelfth?' Alice went on eagerly.

'That's enough about lessons,' the Gryphon interrupted in a very decided tone: 'tell her something about the games now.'

(ii)

'Thank you,' said Alice, 'it's very interesting. I never knew so much about a whiting before.'

'I can tell you more then, if you like,' said the Gryphon. 'Do you know why it's called a whiting?'

'I never thought about it,' said Alice. 'Why?'

'*It does the boots and shoes*,' the Gryphon replied very solemnly.

Alice was thoroughly puzzled. 'Does the boots and shoes!' she repeated in a wondering tone.

'Why, what are *your* shoes done with?' said the Gryphon. 'I mean, what makes them so shiny?'

Alice looked down at them, and considered a little before she gave her answer. 'They're done with blacking, I believe.'

'Boots and shoes under the sea,' the Gryphon went on in a deep voice, 'are done with whiting. Now you know.'

'And what are they made of?' Alice asked in a tone of great curiosity.

'Soles and eels, of course,' the Gryphon replied rather impatiently: 'any shrimp could have told you that.'

'If I'd been the whiting,' said Alice, whose thoughts were still running on the song, 'I'd have said to the porpoise, "Keep back, please: we don't want *you* with us!"'

'They were obliged to have him with them,' the Mock Turtle said: 'no wise fish would go anywhere without a porpoise.'

'Wouldn't it really?' said Alice in a tone of surprise.

'Of course not,' said the Mock Turtle; 'why, if a fish came to *me*, and told me he was going on a journey, I should say "With what porpoise?"'

'Don't you mean "purpose"?' said Alice.

'I mean what I say,' the Mock Turtle replied in an offended tone.

(*Alice's Adventures in Wonderland*, Lewis Carroll)

1. A pun is a play on words that are similar in sound but different in meaning. List the puns in both extracts, and explain each pun.
2. The opposite to sense is **nonsense**. This isn't the same as a jumble of words that means nothing. Nonsense means a reversal of sense. Because we find it amusing or intriguing, we pay attention. For example, cartoons often use nonsense situations to say something very important. Collect some from the newspapers and bring them to class for discussion.
3. Make up your own cartoons about an umbrella. What might be under it? Who might be using it? What might be over the top of it?
4. Think of some everyday objects and some unusual uses for them:
   (a) fertiliser
   (b) chewing gum
   (c) wheelbarrow
   (d) dog collar
   (e) wet cement
5. Try some nonsense ideas linking people and things and their uses. Example: I know a man (person, grandfather, etc.) who uses spaghetti (or anything else you like) for shoelaces (or any purpose you can imagine).
6. Read the following poem, and, in your own words, explain what the poet suggests we should do.

Your Poem, Man . . .
>unless there's one thing seen
suddenly against another — a parsnip
sprouting for a President, or
hailstones melting in an ashtray —
nothing really happens. It takes
surprise and wild connections,
doesn't it? A walrus chewing
on a ballpoint pen. Two blue tail-
lights on Tyrannosaurus Rex. Green
cheese teeth. May be what we wanted
least. Or most. Some unexpected
pleats. Words that never knew
each other till right now. Plug us
into the wrong socket and see
what blows — or what lights up.
Try
>>untried
>>>circuitry,
>>>>new
>>>>>fuses.
Tell it like it never really was,
>>>>man,
and may be we can see it
>>>>like it is.

>>(Edward Lueders)

## Ambiguity

7. When several meanings are possible for the same statement, we say it is ambiguous. Often the words of the sentence need re-arranging; sometimes an important word has been left out; sometimes the wrong punctuation or a lack of punctuation can cause ambiguity.

   Re-write the following so that they are no longer ambiguous.
   (a) Urgent nurses needed.
   (b) Don't let house repairs kill you; let us do it for you.
   (c) If the milk does not agree with the baby, boil it.

# Unit 27. Alice's Adventures

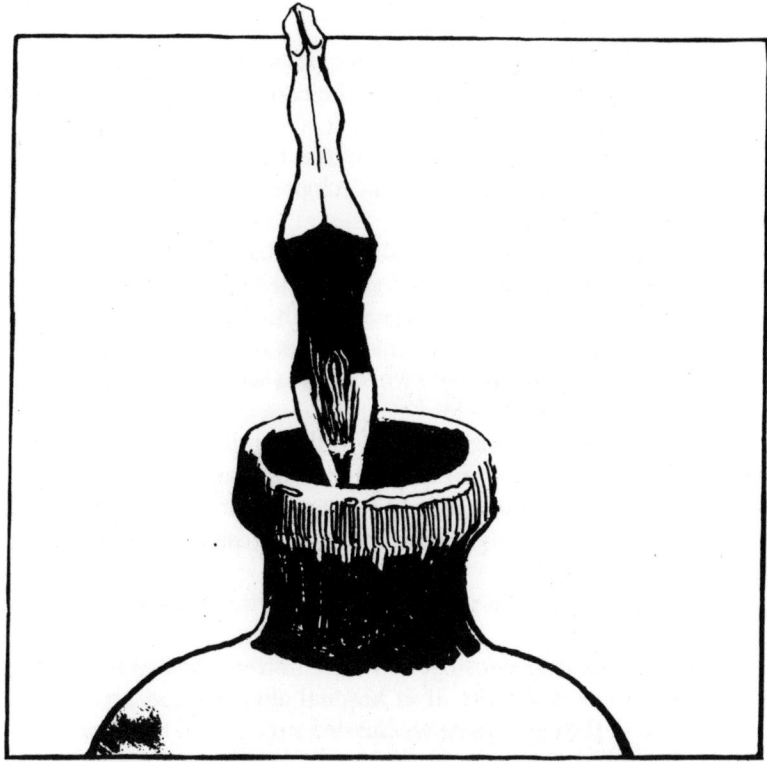

(d) The lady carrying the baby and her husband entered.
(e) Wanted; capable girls for bottling.
(f) Crossing the bridge a magnificent view met our gaze.
(g) Being deaf the candidate's speech was inaudible to the man in the third row.
(h) Secondhand bicycle wanted for young man with several gears.
(i) Urgently required: translators who can speak French for three months.
(j) I am interested in gardening and next week I intend digging for the old lady next door.
(k) Walking on the beach a wave wet my shoes.
(l) Her hair needs cutting badly.
(m) For sale: unbreakable hostess's plates.
(n) The mud stuck to my feet which smelt disgusting.

8. How many different meanings are there for the following sentence?

   I did not take one of the cakes on the plate.

9. Explain why each of these is ambiguous.
   (a) He threw it into the bin after he had taken the sandwich out of its wrapping.
   (b) He took the toast out of the toaster then slapped butter on it.
   (c) He looked up a fact in the encyclopaedia then learned it off by heart.
   (d) The mother told the child that her face was dirty.
   (e) There was plastic around the pie so he quickly ate some.
   (f) People who care about their dogs have proper kennels.
   (g) Whistling the latest hit the car was filled with petrol.
   (h) Racing back to the sand where it was safe the shark appeared.
   (i) Wanted: salesgirls for petfood.
   (j) The new child was the fifth in the family called Debra.
   (k) She ran for the train in pink fluffy slippers.
   (l) The people shouted Long live the President for five minutes.
   (m) We placed the luggage when we went camping on top of the campervan.
   (n) The fire burnt down the tree which was racing towards us out of control.
   (o) The famous opera singer sent the flowers she had been given to people who were ill in hospital after her concert.
   (p) Out of the dark house we hurried surrounded by a green picket fence.
   (q) A dead whale was seen walking along the beach.
   (r) He saw the sun set playing football.
   (s) Away from the police ran a man blowing their whistles.
   (t) The wealthy man wore no clothes that showed how wealthy he was.

# Section F
# Summary

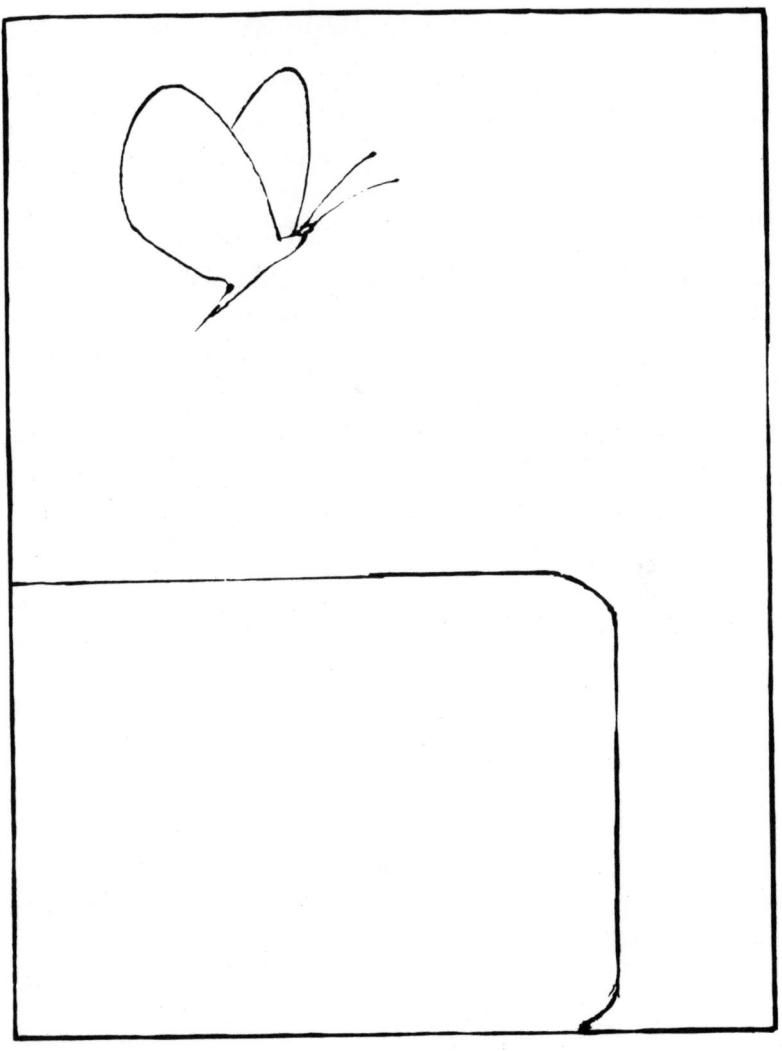

## Summary Method

Making a summary of a longer piece of writing is a very useful skill. Practice in summarising will increase both speed in notetaking and identification of the most important points. To ensure that you have fully understood the material, express your summary in *your own words*. Do NOT merely copy fragments of the original. Keep your summary in the *simplest style* of English possible. Never use words in your summary that you do not understand.

Sometimes a list of main points is a satisfactory summary; sometimes you will be asked to reconstruct the points into a fluent passage. In either case, recognition of the relative importance of information is needed — you must be able to cut out whatever is irrelevant, or repetitive, or merely added to make an account more interesting to the reader.

First extract all the points made. Write the information they give in short sentences, taking a separate line for each point. Keep the points grouped according to their original paragraphs. From each paragraph, choose and underline the one that is central or most important. Place brackets around those that merely give examples. Each underlined main fact should have been the *key* (sometimes called the *topic*) sentence of that paragraph. Your summary should always stress these topic sentences.

# Unit 28. The Sun

Five thousand stars are visible to the unaided eye; a four-inch lens reveals over two million; and over a billion are accessible with the 200-inch mirror. The fainter we go, the more rapidly do the numbers increase. The story is told that Edward C. Pickering of Harvard, was describing a formula that expressed the number of stars brighter than any given magnitude. One of his hearers remarked that the formula required *two* stars brighter than apparent magnitude $-1$, whereas there is only one such star — Sirius. 'Ah!' said Pickering, '*You've forgotten the sun*'. Perhaps familiarity breeds contempt; it is easy to forget that the sun is the nearest of the stars, the most readily studied, the only one that can be kept under continuous surveillance.

The sun is a typical star, a common kind of star. A quarter-million stars have been analyzed in some detail, and 10 percent of them resemble the sun; it merely happens that most of them are far away, and our luminary is near by. A typical specimen of the cosmic population is, so to speak, on our doorstep — giving us a superb opportunity to study the construction and habits of stars in general.

The sun is a gigantic globe of glowing gas, and so is every star that shines, though not one other is near enough to appear as a disc, even to the most powerful telescope. With over a hundred times the diameter of our planet, more than a million times its bulk, three hundred thousand times its mass, the sun is yet a small star and a lightweight. (270 words approx)

(C. Payne-Gaposchin)

1. Read the passage carefully, several times if necessary.
2. List all the important facts given, in your own words as far as possible.
3. Check that these facts are grouped in paragraphs.
4. Cross out any information that seems inessential.
5. Put brackets around examples, or additional facts that merely restate what has been already covered.

6. Underline the most important fact (occasionally facts) in each paragraph.
7. Write your summary, including all the underlined ideas and as much as possible of the rest. Try to keep your summary no longer than about one-third of the original.

## Unit 29. Juvenile Merchandising

One aspect of juvenile merchandising that intrigued the depth manipulators was the craze or fad. To a casual observer the juvenile craze for cowboys or knights or Davy Crockett may seem like a cute bit of froth on the surface of American life. To fad-wise merchandisers such manifestations are largely the result of careful manipulation. They can be enormously profitable or disastrously unprofitable, depending on the merchandiser's cunning.

An evidence of how big the business can be is that the Davy Crockett craze of 1955, which gave birth to 300 Davy Crockett products, lured $300,000,000 from American pockets. Big persuasion indeed!

American merchandisers felt a need for a deeper understanding of these craze phenomena so that they could not only share in the profits, but know when to unload. Research was needed to help the manufacturers avoid overestimating the length of the craze. Many were caught with warehouses full of 'raccoon' tails and buckskin fringe when, almost without warning, the Crockett craze lost its lure. One manufacturer said: 'When they die, they die a horrible death.'

This problem of comprehending the craze drew the attention of such motivation experts as Dr Dichter and Alfred Politz. And *Tide* magazine, journal of merchandisers, devoted a major analysis to the craze.

The experts studied the Crockett extravaganza as a case in point and concluded that its success was due to the fact that it had in good measure all of the three essential ingredients of a profitable fad: symbols, carrying device, and fulfilment of a subconscious need. The carrying device, and the experts agreed it was a superb one, was the song 'Ballad of Davy Crockett', which was repeated in some form in every Disney show. Also it was richer in symbols than many of the fads: coonskin cap, fringed buckskin, flintlock rifle. *Tide* explained: 'All popular movements from Christianity's cross to the Nazi's swastika have their distinctive symbols.'

152  *Section F. Summary*

As for filling a subconscious need, Dr Dichter had this to say of Crockett: 'Children are reaching for an opportunity to explain themselves in terms of the traditions of the country. Crockett gave them that opportunity. On a very imaginative level the kids really felt they were Davy Crockett. . . .' (360 words approx.)

(Vance Packard)

Use the same steps as before:
- Read carefully.
- List facts.
- Group in paragraphs.
- Cross out inessentials.
- Enclose examples in brackets.
- Underline most important facts.
- Write your summary.

# Unit 30. Gale

*Tuesday, March 21.* — The wind returned to the south at 8 last night. It gradually increased in force until 2 a.m., when it was blowing from the S.S.W., force 9 to 10. The sea was breaking constantly and heavily on the ice foot. The spray carried right over the Point — covering all things and raining on the roof of the hut. Poor Vince's cross, some 30 feet above the water, was enveloped in it.

Of course the dogs had a very poor time, and we went and released two or three, getting covered in spray during the operation — our wind clothes very wet.

This is the third gale from the south since our arrival here. Any one of these would have rendered the Bay impossible for a ship, and therefore it is extraordinary that we should have entirely escaped such a blow when the *Discovery* was in it in 1902.

The effects of this gale are evident and show that it is a most unusual occurrence. The rippled snow surface of the ice foot is furrowed in all directions and covered with briny deposit — a condition we have never seen before. The ice foot at the S.W. corner of the bay is broken down, bare rock appearing for the first time.

The sledges, magnetic huts, and in fact every exposed object on the Point are thickly covered with brine. Our seal floe has gone, so it is good-bye to seals on this side for some time.

The dogs are the main sufferers by this continuance of phenomenally terrible weather. At least four are in a bad state; some six or seven others are by no means fit and well, but oddly enough some ten or a dozen animals are as fit as they can be. Whether constitutionally harder or whether better fitted by nature or chance to protect themselves it is impossible to say — Osman, Czigane, Krisravitsa, Hohol, and some others are in first-rate condition, whilst Lappa is better than he has ever been before. (340 words approx.)

(Sir R.F. Scott)

## Section F. Summary

Whenever an article is written in the present tense, as is this article written by Scott when he was snowbound in the Antarctic, in summary, change to the past tense.

Again, use the same procedure as before.

# Unit 31. Applause

First the blue bus drove to Easton, Pennsylvania, up the steep hill of Lafayette College for our first concert. Mr Wagner and all his office staff had come. All of a sudden we became conscious of the fact that this was not just another country — this time we had crossed an ocean; this was now a new continent, and to-night was the first concert. Would it be a success or a failure? These reflections made us more and more solemn, and when finally the great moment came and we had to step out into the footlights, we felt again as miserable and self-conscious as we had been in Salzburg. But there was no Lotte Lehmann sitting in the first row. A thinnish applause greeted the bashful new-comers.

Applause! A whole book could be written about it. The innocent reader might think that applause is applause. How wrong he is! If he only knew how many shades of applause exist, and how finely the ear of the artist is tuned to it. There is the thunderous applause of the later years, when you come back to a hall which is packed with people who are looking forward to your return. How heart-warming and inspiring! There is the polite, thin, applause lasting not long enough to let you get to the middle of the stage to make your bow — the mild applause for the new-comer or beginner — not very helpful. There is the hardly audible applause delivered by society ladies in gloves at morning musicales, and sustained by politely covered yawns. You don't care much because if you have advanced to morning musicales, you don't mind any more. There is the warm, lengthy, enthusiastic applause after a good concert from a sincere audience, demanding encores. That makes you forget your tiredness and makes your encores the best numbers of your programme. There is the routine applause of well-educated people, the concert public, whose ancestors had always attended concerts; who, while they applaud, mildly and steadily, gaze with raised eyebrows into their programmes, questioning: 'Who was that fellow Palestrina, or Vittoria, or Thomas Morley? We have never heard of them before, but it was quite nice.'

These are the staunch supporters of musical life, the ones who give a new-comer a chance.

Later you learn to accept applause as a challenge, and to work up a concert from the 'thinnish' to the 'enthusiastic' response. (400 words approx.)     (Maria Von Trapp)

If an article is written in the first person, either as 'I' or 'we', change to the third person ('he', 'she' or 'they') using the name of the person or persons if it is given.

Write a summary in about one-third of the number of words in the original.

## Unit 32. The Prisons

Before she had got to know as much as a tenth part of Moscow, Nadya was well versed in that sad geography — the location of the city's prisons. They were, she discovered, evenly distributed round the city as a matter of policy so that in any part of Moscow you were never far from jail. What with taking parcels, making enquiries or visiting, Nadya learned the difference between the Greater Lubyanka (which took prisoners from everywhere) and the Lesser Lubyanka (which served the Moscow region only); she learned that there are detention cells at every railway station; she had several times been to the Butyrki and Taganka jails, and, although it was not shown on their destination boards, she knew which trams went to Lefort and which to Krasnaya Presnya.

After Gleb had been brought back from a remote prison camp to Moscow, this time to an extraordinary special prison where they were well fed and employed on scientific work, Nadya again saw her husband at rare intervals. But the wives were not allowed to know where it was that their husbands were being kept, and for these infrequent visits the men were driven into various Moscow prisons. The most cheerful place for visits was the Taganka, where there were no 'politicals', only criminals, and conditions were quite lax. The meetings took place in the warders' recreation room where the warders amused themselves by playing the accordion; the prisoners were driven there along a quiet street in an open bus, so that even before the official beginning of the visit the wives waiting on the pavement could embrace their husbands. They could linger there, talk about subjects forbidden by regulations and even pass things from hand to hand. The meeting itself was very informal, as they were allowed to sit side by side and there was only one warder to listen in to four couples.

Butyrki was also a relatively free-and-easy prison, although the wives found it more depressing. After the Lubyanka, it was a great relief for prisoners coming to Butyrki to discover how much easier

## Section F. Summary

the discipline was there: you were not blinded by the electric light in the transfer cells, you could walk along the corridors without holding your hands behind your back, you could talk aloud in the cells, peep under the window-screens, lie on your plank bed and even sleep under it in the daytime. And there were other little comforts at Butyrki — you could put your hands under the bedclothes, they let you keep your spectacles at night, they allowed matches in the cells, they did not empty the tobacco out of every cigarette and when you got a loaf of bread in a parcel they only cut it into four instead of slicing it into little pieces. But the wives were unaware of all these indulgences. All they saw was a castellated wall as high as four men, stretching the whole length of a block, the iron gates set between massive concrete pillars — gates that were not like ordinary gates, but which slowly opened and closed by mechanical means to swallow or regurgitate a Black Maria. When the women were admitted for a visit they were led through openings in six-foot-thick masonry and between twenty-foot-high walls that skirted the sinister Pugachov Tower. For ordinary prisoners the visit was conducted through a double set of bars, with a warder walking up and down between them as though he were in a cage himself. Prisoners of a higher category, such as those from special prisons, could speak to their visitors across a wide table divided underneath by a solid partition which prevented any contact or signalling with the legs, while a warder sat at the end of the table like an unsleeping statue and listened to every word that was said. But the most depressing thing about Butyrki was that their husbands seemed to emerge straight from the very depths of the prison; they would come up from behind those thick, damp walls for half an hour, smiling wanly and assuring their wives that they were fine and needed nothing; then vanish again. (659 words approx.)
(Alexander Solzhenitsyn)

As the character Nadya is involved in this account, include her briefly, even although most of your account will stress the prison system.

Summarise the passage in about one-third of the original.

# Unit 33. The Migrants

The cars of the migrant people crawled out of the side roads on to the great cross-country highway, and they took the migrant way to the West. In the daylight they scuttled like bugs to the westward; and as the dark caught them, they clustered like bugs near to shelter and to water. And because they were lonely and perplexed, because they had all come from a place of sadness and worry and defeat, and because they were all going to a new mysterious place, they huddled together; they talked together; they shared their lives, their food, and the things they hoped for in the new country. Thus it might be that one family camped near a spring, and another camped for the spring and for company, and a third because two families had pioneered the place and found it good. And when the sun went down, perhaps twenty families and twenty cars were there.

In the evening a strange thing happened: the twenty families became one family, the children were the children of all. The loss of home became one loss, and the golden time in the West was one dream. And it might be that a sick child threw despair into the hearts of twenty families, of a hundred people; that a birth there in a tent kept a hundred people quiet and awestruck through the night and filled a hundred people with the birth-joy in the morning. A family which the night before had been lost and fearful might search its goods to find a present for a new baby. In the evening, sitting about the fires, the twenty were one. They grew to the units of the camps, units of the evenings and the nights. A guitar unwrapped from a blanket and tuned — and the songs, which were all of the people, were sung in the nights. Men sang the words, and women hummed the tunes.

Every night a world created, complete with furniture — friends made and enemies established; a world complete with braggarts and with cowards, with quiet men, with humble men, with kindly men. Every night relationships that make a world, established; and every morning the world torn down like a circus.

## 160  Section F. Summary

At first the families were timid in the building and tumbling worlds, but gradually the technique of building worlds became their technique. Then leaders emerged, then laws were made, then codes came into being. And as the worlds moved westward they were more complete and better furnished, for their builders were more experienced in building them.

The families learned what rights must be observed — the right of privacy in the tent; the right to keep the past black hidden in the heart; the right to talk and to listen; the right to refuse help or to accept, to offer or to decline it; the right of son to court and daughter to be courted; the right of the hungry to be fed; the rights of the pregnant and the sick to transcend all other rights.

And the families learned, although no one told them, what rights are monstrous and must be destroyed; the right to intrude upon privacy, the right to be noisy while the camp slept, the right of seduction or rape, the right of adultery and theft and murder. These rights were crushed, because the little worlds could not exist for even a night with such rights alive. (520 words approx.)

(John Steinbeck)

The impact of Steinbeck's description here of poor people migrating to California, hoping to start a new life there, lies, in part, in his ability to choose details that are interesting and memorable. In your summary, keep a brief mention of some of these.

# Unit 34. Quasimodo

Two men dressed in yellow, the excutioner's assistants, approached the gipsy girl to tie her hands again.
   The unfortunate girl, at the moment of reascending the fatal cart, and moving on towards her final scene, was seized, perhaps, by some last overwhelming clinging to life. She lifted her dry reddened eyes to heaven — to the sky — to the sun — to the silvery clouds, intermingled with patches of brilliant blue; then she cast them around her upon the ground, the people, the houses. All at once, while the man in yellow was pinioning her, she uttered a terrible cry. She fell senseless upon the ground.
   'Come,' said Charmolue, 'carry her into the cart, and let us finish.'
   No one had yet remarked, in the gallery of royal statues carved immediately above the arches of the portal, a strange-looking spectator, who until then had been observing all that passed with such absolute passiveness — a neck so intently stretched — a visage so deformed — that but for his habiliments, half red and half white, he might have been taken for one of the stone monsters through whose mouths the long gutters of the cathedral have disgorged themselves for six hundred years. No visible circumstance of all that had been transacted before the entrance of Notre-Dame since the hour of twelve had escaped this spectator. And at the very commencement, without any one's noticing the action, he had fastened firmly to one of the small columns of the gallery a strong knotted rope, the other end of which fell down below upon the top of the steps of entrance. This being done, he had set himself to look quietly on, only whistling from time to time when some blackbird flew by him. All at once, at the moment that the chief executioner's two assistants were preparing to execute Charmolue's phlegmatic order, he strided over the balustrade of the gallery, gripped the cord with his feet, his knees, and his hands; then he was seen to slide down over that part of the façade like a drop of rain gliding down a pane of

glass — run up to the two sub-executioners with the speed of a cat just dropped from a housetop — knock them both down with a pair of enormous fists — carry off the gipsy girl with one hand, as a child does a doll — and leap at one bound into the church, lifting the girl above his head, and crying out with a formidable voice, 'Sanctuary!'

This was done with such rapidity that had it been night the whole might have been seen by the glare of a single flash of lightning.

'Sanctuary! sanctuary!' repeated the crowd; and the clapping of ten thousand hands made Quasimodo's only eye sparkle with joy and pride.

This shock brought the condemned to her senses. She lifted her eyelids, looked at Quasimodo, then suddenly dropped them again, as if terrified at her deliverer.

Charmolue, the executioners, and the whole escort were confounded. The fact was that within the walls of Notre-Dame the condemned was inviolable. The cathedral was a recognised place of refuge; all temporal jurisdiction expired upon its threshold.

Quasimodo had suddenly plunged with his burden into the darksome interior of the church. The people, fond of any display of prowess, sought him with their eyes under the gloomy nave, regretting that he had so quickly withdrawn himself from their acclamations. All at once he was seen to reappear at one extremity of the gallery of the royal statues. He passed along it, running like a madman, lifting his conquest in his arms, and shouting 'Sanctuary!' Fresh plaudits burst from the multitude. Having traversed the gallery, he plunged again into the interior of the church. A minute afterwards he appeared upon the upper platform, still bearing the gipsy in his arms, still running wildly along, still shouting 'Sanctuary!' and the crowd still applauding. At last he made a third appearance on the summit of the tower of the great bell. From thence he seemed to show exultingly to the whole city the fair creature he had saved. (660 words approx.) (Victor Hugo)

In later study of novels, you might need to summarise chapter content for later revision. Instead of trying to keep the quality of the author's style, merely list as briefly as possible the facts given in the account above.

# Unit 35. Fossils

The earliest animal forms are concealed in the hazy and indistinct records of the very ancient rocks. At first all animals, like plants, were sea dwellers and were long in developing hard parts, such as shells or bones, that would not be easily destroyed and 'sunk without trace.'

In rocks of the Cambrian Period, which began more than five hundred million years ago, we find our first well-preserved evidence of an abundance of animal life. In older rocks, fossils are few in numbers not because living beings were scarce but because few of them had discovered how to utilize the lime in the water to build themselves stony protective armour. When this discovery was made, the rocks at once began to preserve the remains of an abundance of different forms of life, many of them quite complex in their organization. We find in these Cambrian rocks the remains of many hundreds of species of animals. Some are shellfish somewhat like our modern clams and oysters, others are similar to modern snails in having coiled shells, and still others are like corals in structure.

The largest and most complex animal of those times was a trilobite about twenty inches long. It possessed most of the organs found in the animals of the present day. It had a well-developed digestive tract, feeling organs, a coordinated muscular system, an external protective shell like the crab and lobster of today, eyes, and a well-developed nervous system with a central brain of minute size. It had all of our senses with the possible exception of hearing and smelling.

The next step in the evolution of animal life, the conquest of the land, required what to us seems a long period of time — perhaps one hundred and fifty million years. It could not be completed until plants had become land dwellers. The earliest land animals found in the rocks are insects, spiders and scorpions, which appeared about three hundred and sixty million years ago in the Silurian Period, and reached a high development in the Mesozoic Era, which covered the period of time from one hundred and eighty million to one hundred million years ago.

The first vertebrate skeleton was owned by an ancestral fish that lived perhaps four hundred million years ago in the Ordovician Period. He had found that he needed something to keep his head from being driven back into his body as he swam about in search of his prey, and so he grew a bony skeleton and discovered that life was easier. His predecessors all had 'external skeletons,' or shells, that were good armour against his enemies but were cumbersome and cut down the speed with which they could navigate and catch the other organisms upon which they lived. This development of a backbone was an improvement of such great usefulness that all higher types of animals since that time have an internal jointed skeleton, the main feature of which is a flexible, jointed backbone. Nothing has been invented by Nature thus far that is better for its purpose than this great device. It has been the prime factor that has enabled animals to attain to great size.

Since the first animals with a vertebrate skeleton appeared four hundred million years ago, there has been progress in size, until today we now have the largest animal that ever lived: the great blue whale, which is known to have attained a length of one hundred and six feet. Progress was not rapid. One hundred million years had to pass after the invention of the backbone before animals ten feet long developed. It was not until the vertebrates took to living on the land that development to great size occurred. In the Age of Reptiles — the Mesozoic Era — when the dinosaurs and their kin were lords of creation, they so 'quickly' added to their size that no more than thirty or forty million years of this era elapsed before they had attained to maximum lengths of seventy feet. This experiment of increasing the bulk of flesh inside one skin — or, to look at it from the inside out, the bulk of flesh surrounding a single backbone — was successful for about seventy-five million years, and the great animals of the period prospered for a time lasting from one hundred and fifty million years ago to seventy-five million years ago.

The development of these animals to greater size was not accompanied by corresponding brain development. The largest brain of those days was less than a quarter the size of yours or mine.

In the meantime Nature was making a different kind of experiment. The great reptiles did not have any marked maternal instincts. Most of them continued the practice which characterized the poor fish and lower animals that had been left behind in the race. They laid eggs and left their young to hatch out and care for themselves. About one hundred and fifty million years ago there appeared some small animals that hatched their eggs inside their bodies and produced living young, which they nursed and cared for through a period of helpless infancy. From this habit of nursing their young they have been given the name of mammals. With them the great quality of mother love first began to be an important factor in the life of the earth. Through at least eight hundred and fifty million long years of the billion year story living beings got along with little or none of the mother love that is so powerful an influence in the lives of all of the higher animals today.

Mammals also gave up an old practice followed by all other living things, that of being cold-blooded. They found that to elevate the blood temperature gave them advantages over their cold-blooded associates. Warm blood and the habit of nursing their young were the most important new elements in life that distinguished the mammals. They had the same organs; muscles, nervous system and brain as their cold-blooded, egg-laying neighbours, but they had in the two new improvements qualities that were to make them, after a hundred millions of years had elapsed, the dominant type of animals on the face of the globe. For the last sixty million years they have prospered more extensively than any other kind of animal life. (110 words approx.) (W.O. Hotchkiss)

Instead of writing a summary, use the following headings to record the information contained in the passage

| Name of period/era | Approx. dates | Fossils | Specific example |
|---|---|---|---|
|  |  |  |  |

# Acknowledgements

The author and publishers are grateful to the following for permission to reproduce extracts from copyright material:

Granada Publishing Limited for *My Family and Other Animals* by Gerald Durrell; A.D. Peters for *Golden Apples of the Sun* by Ray Bradbury; Pelican Books for *The Hidden Persuaders* by Vance Packard and for *Only One Earth* by Barbara Ward and Rene Dubois; Hughes Massie Ltd for *Confessions of a Story-teller* by Paul Gallico; Collins Publishers for *The First Circle* by Alexander Solzhenitsyn; Garnstone Press Ltd for *The Trapp Family Singers* by Maria Von Trapp; Hughes Massie Ltd for *Autobiography* by Agatha Christie; Johns Hopkins University Press for *The Earth Beneath the Sea* by Francis P. Shephard; Rigby Publishers for *Early Australian Crafts and Tools* by L. Ollif and W. Crossthwaite; Elsevier Dutton Publishing Co. for *Bound For Glory* by Woody Guthrie; Pan Books Ltd for *The Grapes of Wrath* by John Steinbeck; Faber and Faber Limited for *The Lord of the Flies* by William Golding; City Lights Books for the poem 'To Paint a Portrait of a Bird' from *Paroles* by Jacques Prévert; A.P. Watt Ltd for *The Time Machine* by H.G. Wells; Dove Communications for *Brian's Wife, Jenny's Mum* by Gwen Wesson; Paul Hamlyn Australia Ltd for *Discovering Pottery* by Harry Memmott; Michael Joseph Ltd for *Gunner Who* by Spike Milligan, *The Day of the Triffids* by John Wyndham; David Higham Associates Ltd for the two extracts from *It Shouldn't Happen to a Vet* by James Herriot; Penguin Books Australia Limited for *Picnic at Hanging Rock* by Joan Lindsay; Phillip Adams for the two extracts from *The Unspeakable Adams*; Routledge and Kegan Paul Ltd for three extracts from *The Book of Heroic Failures* by Stephen Pile; George G. Harrap and Company Limited for *I Heard the Owl Call my Name* by Margaret Craven; University of Queensland Press for *Memories of a Country Childhood* by Judith Wallace; Angus & Robertson for the poem 'Request to a Year' from *Collected Poems 1942-1970* by Judith Wright and for 'The Merino Sheep' by A.B. Paterson; International Publications Service for *The Bulls of Parrall* by Marguerite Steen, Barthold Fles for *How to Survive in Your Native Land* by James Herndon; Harvard University Press for *Stars in the Making* by C. Payne-Gaposchin; Scott, Foresman & Company for the poem 'Your Poem, Man' by Edward Leuders from *Some Haystacks Don't Have Any Needles* ed. Dunning, Ineders and Smith; John Murray (Publishers) Ltd for *The Diary of Sir R.F. Scott* by Sir R.F. Scott; The Williams and Wilkins Company for *The Story of a Billion Years* by W.O. Hotchkiss; Edward Arnold (Publishers) London Ltd for 'In the Forest' by Leslie Perri from *40 Short Short Stories*; Farrar, Straus and Giroux Inc. for 'Charles' from *The Lottery* by Shirley Jackson.

While every care has been taken to trace and acknowledge copyright, the publishers tender their apologies for any accidental infringement where copyright has proved untraceable. They would be pleased to come to a suitable arrangement with the rightful owner in each case.